Anthropologies of Value

Anthropology, Culture and Society

Series Editors:
Professor Vered Amit, Concordia University
Doctor Jamie Cross, University of Edinburgh
and
Professor Christina Garsten, Stockholm University

Recent titles:

The Limits to Citizen Power: Participatory Democracy and the Entanglements of the State
Victor Albert

Becoming Arab in London: Performativity and the Undoing of Identity
Ramy M. K. Aly

Community, Cosmopolitanism and the Problem of Human Commonality
Vered Amit and Nigel Rapport

In Foreign Fields: The Politics and Experiences of Transnational Sport Migration
Thomas F. Carter

Dream Zones: Anticipating Capitalism and Development in India
Jamie Cross

A History of Anthropology Second Edition
Thomas Hylland Eriksen and Finn Sivert Nielsen

Ethnicity and Nationalism: Anthropological Perspectives Third Edition
Thomas Hylland Eriksen

Fredrik Barth: An Intellectual Biography
Thomas Hylland Eriksen

Small Places, Large Issues: An Introduction to Social and Cultural Anthropology Fourth Edition
Thomas Hylland Eriksen

At the Heart of the State: The Moral World of Institutions
Didier Fassin et al.

Discordant Development: Global Capitalism and the Struggle for Connection in Bangladesh
Katy Gardner

Anthropology and Development: Challenges for the Twenty-first Century
Katy Gardner and David Lewis

Organisational Anthropology: Doing Ethnography in and Among Complex Organisations
Edited by Christina Garsten and Anette Nyqvist

Border Watch: Cultures of Immigration, Detention and Control
Alexandra Hall

Anthropology's World: Life in a Twenty-First Century Discipline
Ulf Hannerz

Humans and Other Animals: Cross-cultural Perspectives on Human–Animal Interactions
Samantha Hurn

Flip-Flop: A Journey Through Globalisation's Backroads
Caroline Knowles

The Anthropology of Security: Perspectives from the Frontline of Policing, Counter-Terrorism and Border Control
Edited by Mark Maguire, Catarina Frois and Nils Zurawski

The Gloss of Harmony: The Politics of Policy Making in Multilateral Organisations
Edited by Birgit Müller

Contesting Publics: Feminism, Activism, Ethnography
Lynne Phillips and Sally Cole

Food For Change: The Politics and Values of Social Movements
Jeff Pratt and Peter Luetchford

Base Encounters: The US Armed Forces in South Korea
Elisabeth Schober

Checkpoint, Temple, Church and Mosque: A Collaborative Ethnography of War and Peace
Jonathan Spencer, Jonathan Goodhand, Shahul Hasbullah, Bart Klem, Benedikt Korf and Kalinga Tudor Silva

Race and Ethnicity in Latin America Second Edition
Peter Wade

The Capability of Places: Methods for Modelling Community Response to Intrusion and Change
Sandra Wallman

The Making of an African Working Class: Politics, Law and Cultural Protest in the Manual Workers' Union of Botswana
Pnina Werbner

Anthropologies of Value

Edited by
Luis Fernando Angosto-Ferrández
and Geir Henning Presterudstuen

PlutoPress
www.plutobooks.com

First published 2016 by Pluto Press
345 Archway Road, London N6 5AA

www.plutobooks.com

British Library Cataloguing in Publication Data
A catalogue record for this book is available from the British Library

ISBN 978 0 7453 3663 3 Hardback
ISBN 978 1 7837 1978 5 PDF eBook

This book is printed on paper suitable for recycling and made from fully managed and sustained forest sources. Logging, pulping and manufacturing processes are expected to conform to the environmental standards of the country of origin.

Typeset by Stanford DTP Services, Northampton, England

Simultaneously printed in the European Union and United States of America

Contents

List of Figures

Series Preface

Anthropology is a discipline based upon in-depth ethnographic works that deal with wider theoretical issues in the context of particular, local conditions – to paraphrase an important volume from the series: *large issues* explored in *small places*. This series has a particular mission: to publish work that moves away from an old-style descriptive ethnography that is strongly area-studies oriented, and offer genuine theoretical arguments that are of interest to a much wider readership, but which are nevertheless located and grounded in solid ethnographic research. If anthropology is to argue itself a place in the contemporary intellectual world, then it must surely be through such research.

We start from the question: 'What can this ethnographic material tell us about the bigger theoretical issues that concern the social sciences?' rather than 'What can these theoretical ideas tell us about the ethnographic context?' Put this way round, such work becomes *about* large issues, *set in* a (relatively) small place, rather than detailed description of a small place for its own sake. As Clifford Geertz once said, 'Anthropologists don't study villages; they study *in* villages.'

By place, we mean not only geographical locale, but also other types of 'place' – within political, economic, religious or other social systems. We therefore publish work based on ethnography within political and religious movements, occupational or class groups, among youth, development agencies, and nationalist movements; but also work that is more thematically based – on kinship, landscape, the state, violence, corruption, the self. The series publishes four kinds of volume: ethnographic monographs; comparative texts; edited collections; and shorter, polemical essays.

We publish work from all traditions of anthropology, and all parts of the world, which combines theoretical debate with empirical evidence to demonstrate anthropology's unique position in contemporary scholarship and the contemporary world.

Professor Vered Amit
Dr Jamie Cross
Professor Christina Garsten

Acknowledgements

This project started to take shape in 2014 in two conference panels, and we are grateful to the organisers of the stimulating academic events that hosted them: the Knowledge/Culture/Economy Conference, held at Western Sydney University, and the Association of Social Anthropologists of Aotearoa and New Zealand/Australian Anthropological Society Conference, organised by colleagues of the University of Otago held in Queenstown.

We also want to very specially acknowledge the work of the contributors to this volume, all of whom showed an impressive commitment to the project from the outset. This has been an enormously enjoyable and enriching collaboration, and for us an example of what scholarly exchange should be.

A special mention of acknowledgement to our home institutions, the University of Sydney and Western Sydney University, which make our work possible. Funding for attending the aforementioned conferences was provided for Luis Fernando by the Schools of Social and Political Sciences and by the School of Languages and Cultures at the University of Sydney, for which he is also grateful. He also acknowledges the support of colleagues of the Center for Intercultural and Indigenous Research (CIIR – Grant: CONICYT/FONDAP/ 15110006). Geir Henning wants in turn to express his gratitude for ongoing support from the School of Social Sciences and Psychology at Western Sydney University, which made possible the development of research plans and their realisation. Many colleagues have provided valuable feedback and encouragement on the project, and chief among them are Mary Hawkins, Neil Maclean and Rob Stones. In our individual chapters we make special mention of other people who have also made much appreciated contributions.

Finally, a note of sincere gratitude for David Castle, the editors of the Anthropology, Culture and Society series (Vered Amit, Jamie Cross and Christina Garsten), and the rest of the team at Pluto Press. For all the volume contributors including ourselves this has been a pleasant and very constructive editorial process. Indeed, people from Pluto made us feel we were on our home planet.

Luis Fernando Angosto-Ferrández
Geir Henning Presterudstuen

The Value of Everything and the Price of Nothingness

Luis Fernando Angosto-Ferrández

Romantic poets and socialist revolutionaries were abundant in nineteenth-century Europe. They had different ways to undertake social critique, needless to say, and generally pursued different political horizons. Yet in some respects their kinds were in spiritual communion, united by strong if invisible ties. The creative forces of those poets and revolutionaries had been moulded in times of unrest and social dislocation, and they all were dissatisfied with the society they had to live in. Indeed, both groups longed for a different world: romantic poets for one already gone, socialist revolutionaries for one still to come. In the meantime, they rebelled against societies that they denounced as fatuous and (more so the socialists than the romantics) as unjust. Many of those poets and revolutionaries could have subscribed one of Oscar Wilde's epigrams as an apt diagnostic of their epoch: more and more people were living as if they knew 'the price of everything and the value of nothing'.

Today, romantic poets are rare and *démodé*, and socialist revolutionaries scarce. If you ask, for instance, a cynic, a pessimist or a neoliberal pundit, why such people have vanished, they will most likely present the fact as a demonstration that there is no possible return to paradises lost, nor any plausible directionality in human affairs other than an evolution towards more perfected and free-of-obstacles market societies. From that point of view, it is only logical that those poets and revolutionaries have been in retreat: no one in her senses would pursue utopias that are unrealisable and, furthermore, go against the inclinations contained in human nature. However, if you ask a believer, an optimist or an anthropologist, you may hear a different tune. Not that neoliberal inclinations are non-existent among these latter types, of course. Yet, regardless of political preferences, these are people who live their lives with the latent certitude that the script of human affairs is never closed, for better or worse. Even though they might readily acknowledge that our times are unpropitious for revolutionaries and poets, they would never present this situation as resulting from a natural law – not even those who might privately celebrate, whether for political or for aesthetic reasons, the dwindled presence of socialists and romantics in the social scene.[1] Because for believers, optimists, and for some anthropologists, things are as they are, but they can always be substantially different. And for the anthropologists in particular that is precisely *the* law that can be considered to rest in nature: if there is something they understand by human nature it is precisely the potential for social and cultural creation, and that is always connected with potential for political transformation – as it can be with political conservatism.

If you share this outlook, you are more likely to enjoy this volume than if you do not. This discussion brings together the efforts of a bunch of anthropologists – we will leave it to you to judge if optimists and believers are among us too. So when going through our essays you might hear this common underlying whisper: 'the script of human affairs is never closed, and human potentials have been and continue to be diversely deployed, shaped and made meaningful in social aggregates across an ever changing world'. Even if you take these whisperings with a pinch of salt, you might find these essays worth a thorough read. The contributions to this volume provide grounding and ideas to discuss both anthropological knowledge and big issues about the state of affairs across the world. How do they do such a thing? By situating the concept of value at the centre of analyses of human sociality in different permutations within, against and (potentially) beyond capitalism. As you will see, while this is not an uncomplicated task, it is a most fruitful one: interrogating capitalism and human sociality through such concept makes both suspects sing out quite a lot.

Poets and Revolutionaries – Apropos of Value

Given the central credit that we are granting to the concept of value, some initial clarifications about it are due. I hope that you do not mind the company of poets and revolutionaries for a bit longer, for the clarifying effort will start with a few comments on Oscar Wilde and Karl Marx.

I already made reference to an epigram authored by Wilde, specifically one extracted from his play *Lady Windermere's Fan* (published in 1892). In the play, a central character (Lord Darlington, one of those quintessentially Wildean dandies) throws it out as the definition of a cynic. However, I recovered that epigram for the way in which, under a different light, it can be read as capturing something central about the social transformations taking place in nineteenth-century Europe. In a period in which, as the authors of the 1848 Communist Manifesto had it, all that had been solid was melting into air, Wilde's epigram could probably have been subscribed to by many as an inspired representation of the *Zeitgeist* of the epoch. Money was apparently becoming the primary drive and the ultimate measure of everything, while in parallel, in the terms that the epigram posed it, people seemed to be forgetting the real 'value' of things – closing down forms of appreciation not subjected to market logics. Wilde, a literary man with a genial mastery of language, captured in one sentence so much about the tendencies of his society (and made his point brilliantly salient, in a literary way) by counterpoising two ambiguously related terms: 'price' and 'value'. Price, conventionally taken as a quantitative expression of value when not directly as synonymous with it, was thus presented as something absolutely detachable from that latter term. Wilde's character suggested that people in his time (or at least cynics) were, in practice, confusing such terms.

Perhaps only coincidentally, a few years before Wilde wrote that remark, Marx, another creative figure with a brilliant mastery of language, had made that very point. In fact, Marx situated those same terms ('value' and 'price') at the core of his most ambitious work, which would eventually be known as *Capital: A Critique of Political Economy*.[2] In that work he not only captured, but also explained quite a lot about the logics and drives of that social system that, in the nineteenth century, was consolidating before everyone's eyes – though he remarked that people could be perfectly blind to its inner logics. However, unlike the poet, always keen to creatively squeeze to the maximum the polysemic character of certain words, Marx, a scientist, embarked on a systematic disambiguation of the key terms he used for his critique. He actually dedicated a few hundred pages to that task, aiming to turn 'value' and 'price' into scientific concepts with demarcated meanings. Marx presented the distinction between those concepts as essential for studying the 'laws of motion' of that systemic force he denominated capital and which traversed the society he was living in. Moreover, he considered that an abstracted theory of value was the necessary starting point for such scrutiny of social life: instead of commencing with a positivist approach to experience, Marx thought that, since such an approach could never be unmediated by preconceptions, it was indispensable to create a theoretical platform from which reality could be coherently interrogated. That theory was to become the (Marxian) labour theory of value,[3] and it contended that, in order to understand those laws of motion of capitalism, it was crucial to unveil that in the generation of wealth in general, and in the production of commodities in particular, there were two independent sources: Nature and Labour. In the particular type of society Marx wanted to discuss (capitalist), commodities are those unit forms of wealth that do not only have a value resting on their usefulness to people (that is, a use-value), but also an exchange-value as a constitutive characteristic – they are produced and conceived to be exchanged. Marx sought to identify what was the substance common to any commodity in order to understand what takes place in market exchanges – in principle. Identifying labour as such common substance permitted him to theoretically explain and compare the relative values of commodities,[4] and therefore to shed light on basic mechanisms of market exchange. The proportion in which people exchange their commodities would *in principle* relate to the proportions of (socially necessary) labour invested in them. Leaving other considerations aside, and notwithstanding the complementary discussion of commodity fetishism, this proposition firmly rooted the configuration of exchange-values within a sphere of social factors – rather than, say, of psychological ones.

That emphasis on social factors was crucial, for Marx's theoretical approach was not ultimately intended to explain concrete mechanisms of price fixing and exchange: it sought to demarcate the grounds for the discussion of broader and deeper questions about so-called modern society. What are the processes that constitute the structures giving shape to this society? How do those structures condition social relations? What are the causes and the effects of the transformation of labour power (that is, people's capacity to work) into a commodity? Who can have property rights and what can be owned in societies in which most people have lost independent means of subsistence? What is being paid for when one receives a wage? Why can some people accumulate wealth whereas some other people work basically to reproduce their labour power? And so forth.

From this perspective, the fact that Marx's theory of value does not work, for instance, to explain the determination of commodity prices in a capitalist market (which has repeatedly been presented by critics, from the impetuous emergence of marginalism in economics onwards, as a demonstration that the theory was flawed, or at least that it was useless) is no reason to discard it. Marx, following in this respect a Socratic and Galilean method, aimed to establish the parameters within which one could scrutinise reality after knowing with precision what one wants to ask of it (Fernández Liria and Alegre Zahonero 2011). He thus delimited an object of study and inaugurated political economy as a modern critical science, recasting and overcoming the classical paradigm nowadays mostly identified with Adam Smith's *Wealth of Nations* (2012).[5] That theoretical grounding made it possible to critically contrast the way in which a capitalist society works overall (subjected to certain 'laws of motion' and 'silent compulsions') with the way in which, as it were, it pretends to work (allegedly resting on natural and universal human economic impulses, and on the political project of the Enlightenment). In other words: by scrutinising society with the newly created analytical tools, one could not only discuss basic mechanisms of capitalist markets, but also reconsider the relation between capital and those concepts of citizenship and law that the Enlightenment had tried to advance and which, allegedly, were the pillars of liberal society. In the light of Marx's analysis, that relation appeared to be quite strained, to say the least: under the forces of capital, citizenship and law, at least as they had been envisaged originally by the Enlightenment tradition, seemed to have vanished in face of farcical replacements.

At this point we can bring Wilde and Marx back together and resume the introduction of this volume's aims. In their own ways, both the poet and the scientist were aware that 'value' and 'price' played crucial roles in the definition of capitalism, and also that those terms could not be taken as synonymous. Yet for Marx it was crucial to explicitly disambiguate them, turn them into concepts, and explore the relation that, in principle, connected them, whereas for Wilde it was enough to bring such words into close proximity so that they could silently project their contrasting meanings – no matter if they did so indeterminately. In this volume we owe more to Marx's efforts, which provided still irreplaceable tools for understanding what a commodity is; the utility of conceptualising value precisely in relation to commodities and the creation of wealth; and why that coupling can contribute to analysing the functioning of capital and to discussing its politics. In fact, the title of this introductory chapter, despite its Wildean flavour, draws from the diverse traditions springing from Marx's scientific efforts. Although Wilde's epigram stimulated my initial comments about the logics of nineteenth-century capitalism, it has aged poorly, and only by breathing some Marxian air into it could one aspire to rejuvenate it. By what nowadays one sees around, Wilde's epigram does not work so well when it comes to capturing the logics of twenty-first-century capitalism, for in these times, unlike a century ago, more and more people live as if they knew *the value of everything and the price of nothingness*. It is around this suggestion that I want to situate this volume as a whole. Let me explain.

At present, commodification processes, the establishment of new forms of property and the search for new avenues for the creation and appropriation of value are global– if culturally mediated – phenomena. The social creations of people across the world seem to be conditioned by the realisation that exchange-value can (potentially) be found in everything and everywhere. It is just a matter of finding the ways to uncover that potential – no longer a matter of producing value with the intervention of labour. The apparent omnipresent immanence of (exchange-)value has become as central a drive of capitalism as spatial/territorial expansion was since its inception.[6] But of course there is more, because the 'everything' in our entitling epigram is all embracing: in a sleight of hand, it can include its total opposite – nothingness.

After the last financial crisis, some tradable products were said to have been sustained by thin air, and many commentators pitched this as a surprise. But should one really be surprised, when the 'laws of motion' of modern society have been inviting the most expert minds to search the way to put a price on nothingness? If people in general, everywhere, can be said to have learnt that there is (exchange-)value in everything, experts everywhere have also known for a long time that nothingness must have it too. Unveil it, objectify it, propertise it; and put a price on it. There might be business in it, and some people will call that benefit obtained out of nothingness 'value'.

Yet while all over the world and in virtually every social aggregate people seem to be aware of these drives, not everyone gives in to them with equal enthusiasm. Exploring differences in their reception and interpretation becomes a source of inspiration when discussing the politics of value and, more generally, contemporary politics. As a whole, the chapters in this book can be read against that background.

We aim to shed light on the intersections of two interrelated social currents: one underpins the ways in which (exchange-)value is continuously being projected onto things and incorporated as a factor into realms that previously lay outside capital (as a social production relation); the other underlines the way in which human groups in different parts of the planet promote, contest or try to reorient that systemic force. Both currents appear as culturally encoded because, while indeed constituting a global process and a common world system, they do so revealing the existence of distinct shared practices and ideas among people in different social aggregates (and classes of people within such aggregates).

For instance, Cook Islands women are currently moving towards a systematic commodification of *tivaivai*, a type of quilt previously circulated only as a gift. But in doing so they try to reproduce traditional notions of personhood, family and ceremonial obligation for whose shaping the *tivaivai*-as-gift was and remains pivotal (see chapter 1 by Jane Horan). In Cuba, the partial liberalisation of a housing market has recently opened new opportunities for small business and self-employment, but the viability of such businesses is strongly dependent on pre-existing non-marketised relations pervaded by the cultural ethos of the socialist revolution. Those relations become a source of indispensable practical support for the new entrepreneurs, who often rely on family favours, friendly suppliers or contacts in government bureaucracies for a successful development of their business. But at the same time, those relations and the ethos that pervades them become counterbalancing forces against the potential of free-of-social-obligations economic behaviour among people embarking on new economic ventures (see chapter 6 by Marina Gold). In turn, contestation of the systemic force that stimulates or imposes the commodification of things can be found in the 'free university' projects emerging in places like Brisbane (Australia), New York (USA) or Halifax (Canada). These projects, always culturally encoded, explicitly seek to reverse the marketisation of university education and the so-called 'enclosure of knowledge', and in doing so participants try to recover basic forms of their sociality that they find endangered by the dynamics they associate with all-pervading marketisation: meeting personally, conversing face to face.

Marxian contributions to the conceptualisation of terms such as commodity, use- and exchange-value or surplus remain indispensable to the examination of the aforementioned interrelated currents on which we aim to shed light.[7] So, apropos of value and the approach that we propose in this volume for the understanding of human sociality in the contemporary world, the scientist deserves more credit than the poet. His contributions, and the avenues they opened to facilitate potential engagements with those big issues about the state of affairs across the world that we set as one of the volume's goals, fertilise the common ground out of which this volume grows – taken as sources of positive or antagonistic inspiration in our essays.

Let me further clarify what is distinctive in this volume's approach to the vast and shape-shifting domain of anthropological takes on theories of value.

Apropos of Value, Anthropologists

We do not present these essays as foundations for *a* theory of value. The possibility of such a theory as an epistemologically distinct object is in fact quite problematic, and particularly so when it becomes (tacitly or explicitly) pitched as a transhistorical theory of self-regulating human aggregates. Whether such aggregates end up being denominated 'cultures', 'societies' or anything else, as soon as they start to be theorised or analytically treated as clearly demarcated, insular units of meaning-creation (or values-creation, for that matter) they become misleading units for the analysis of social life. In contrast to such approach, the essays in this volume have been brought together because, converging upon the common grounds outlined in the previous section, as a whole they provide new insights for the discussion of important contemporary issues: the continuing expansion of capitalism, how cultural forms and political reactions emerge in order to adapt to, facilitate or potentially oppose it, and the prospects of non-capitalist forms of social organisation.

We do not pursue an anthropological theory of value as an end in itself – one that could only demonstrate the existence of self-regulating bounded sets of social aggregates. We rather seek to critically approach Marxian and other contributions to understanding capitalism (through direct and indirect engagements with the former's theory of value), and anthropological theory in general, as a means of exploring and explaining aspects of what Eric Wolf (1990 [1982]) denominated 'the world of humankind' – a whole whose parts are inextricably interrelated and engaged in continuing processes of change and mutual (re)constitution. The aim is to reopen avenues to understand the bases of the interconnections, continuities and transformations of social aggregates within a world partly organised by a globalised capitalism.

One does not have to dig too deeply in the already long track of anthropological work around 'value' to realise that this concept is not used by everyone to refer to the same type of substance or phenomena. In fact, the diversity of approaches to conceptualising this term is the tonic chord within the field (Eiss and Pedersen 2002). These varied approaches do not always facilitate an understanding of humankind as an interconnected whole in which social aggregates mutually shape each other (albeit aggregates unequal in terms of power). And, moreover, these anthropological works have sought to answer quite different questions about what being human is about and why human beings do what they do, which complicates to the extreme any attempt at treating them as part of a common scholarly (or political) enterprise.[8] There are however certain epistemological currents within these works that enable one to follow what happened to the concept of value within anthropology – for instance, by following the flourishing of such debates from the 1970s to the early 1990s among a number of anthropologists who, in most cases, had an ethnographic focus on Melanesia and Polynesia.

In what could nowadays be characterised, perhaps with some utility, as a pre-postmodern form of posing anthropological questions and debating, those authors initially engaged each other upon (common) grounds partly fertilised by the contributions of labour theories of value. Seeking to understand and provide explanations for different aspects of social organisation and cultural forms, the potential and limitations of labour theories of value for such enterprise were critically discussed and differently regarded. Yet those theories nonetheless shaped key questions framing the discussions: What is exchange-value? To what extent can one speak about commensurability of substance in exchanged objects when one consults the ethnographic record, and not only the political economy manual? What is that substance, when commensurability can actually be said to exist? Could Ricardian and Marxian theories of value contribute to explaining what takes place in forms of exchange, often non-monetised, within and between non-capitalist societies? Are those forms of exchange, and the forms of production that precede them, articulating power inequalities in the social arena, whether along the lines of class, gender, age group or any other lines? The answers to these and other questions were often diverging and in some cases antagonistic (cf., for example, Sahlins 1972: 277–314 with Modjeska 1985), but the analysis of social life was generally driven by a search for causalities and explanation.

In hindsight, one could say that those anthropologists sparred in an epistemological ring whose cords, initially firm, would gradually be cut loose. This was perhaps influenced by the fact that the fight kept on going for too long with no clear scholarly victor, and rivals tired of such contests. But also, in hindsight, it is tempting to suggest that it must also have been facilitated by the fact that the production of academic knowledge could not remain timelessly impermeable to a political context in which grand narratives about the functioning of society gradually disappeared (or narrowed down to varieties of a neoliberal creed).

At any rate, durable works of that current tended to reinforce substantivist understandings of exchange in general (from barter to market exchange to gifting) as embedded in the reproduction of culturally mapped social relationships, including inter-group relationships, that nonetheless could include different types of hierarchy, inequality and exploitation (for example Gregory 1982; cf. Josephides 1985). But in parallel to these debates there gradually emerged an identifiable move towards shedding light on how models of personhood, agency and sociality are construed and brought into being by such transactions (Munn 1986; Strathern 1988; Humphrey and Hugh-Jones 1992). Concerns with value as that substance associated with material processes of production (in its classical political-economic definition) were gradually displaced as a potential pivot for understanding and explaining diversities and similarities across social aggregates. To date, that drift characterises and conditions central currents of anthropological approaches to value.

Efforts aiming to renew and refocus these debates abound, but without substantial reorientation. Though it is impossible to pinpoint a single influence within them, it is evident that echoes of Kluckhohn's (1951) definition of (social) values as conceptions of the desirable are far more sonorous than Marx's contributions. This, of course, has implications for the type of questions that anthropologists can answer with the conceptions of value they articulate: let us recall that Kluckhohn aimed to contribute to a theory of action in a field in which functionalist theorisations of society predominated, whereas Marx theorised for the understanding of capitalist societies in a light that unveiled them as driven by conflict, not organic cohesion. Needless to say, with the tools of Kluckhohn and those of different types of functionalism, one cannot aim to answer the questions that Marx considered fundamental to understand the functioning of modern society – questions that continue to emerge when one looks at the state of affairs across the world.

In the context of renewed debates, some anthropologists have been pursuing the generation of distinctively anthropological theories of value (Graeber 2001; Pedersen 2008; Otto and Willerslev 2013). Others have resorted to theory on 'social' and 'economic' value to facilitate the generation of an anthropology of economy (Gudeman 2001), and yet others have set as a driving motivation the anthropological theorisation of social reproduction within capitalism – nonetheless reproducing a conceptualisation of value as a bounded social terrain for the definition of worth (Narotzky and Besnier 2014).[9] This varied production certainly demonstrates the salience that the concept of value has gained in the discipline, but it also becomes an illustration of the meagre overall results.

This was ingeniously suggested (and with a sense of humour at that) by Pedersen (2008) in his comments on one of these efforts coordinated around the concept of value. He compared the risks of such repeated but conceptually and theoretically uncoordinated knocks on the door of 'a value theory' with the risks of 'burning out' of which intravenous drug users are well aware: too many careless shots around the same spot might end a cycle of regular highs with a dramatic collapse of the vein. In anthropological approaches to the theory of value something similar might have been happening: many a wonderful high has taken place, but the theory is more and more looking as if it were no such thing.

Let me follow on from this shooting up metaphor to situate our own effort more concretely. Otto and Willerslev (2013), who coordinated another stimulating round of knocks on the door of value in anthropology (eventually, 'value as theory'), concluded that, as it were, in order to at least defer the burning out of the vein (at this pace, avoidance seems impossible), one could identify two spots for injections to take place. This might be just as well in order to take temporary control of one's highs, for there would be two main different types of drugs in circulation: theory-driven and ethnography-driven (anthropologies with value as theory).[10] However, in their case one is left with the impression that, even if the deferral of a burn-out were possible, the interim result might not be all that productive: it is as if we were in one of those stories about soul mates whose paths continuously cross but who never get to realise a happy ending; alas, if only, one day, they had stopped to talk with that other!

So in terms of this shooting up metaphor, this volume informs users about a basic point from the outset: whatever the degree of alteration of your state of consciousness might finally be, the production of *a* theory of value (or value theory or value as theory) *is not* a particularised aim here. On the contrary, from the common grounds demarcated in the previous section, we seek to facilitate engagements with current global issues: with identifiable forces in a totalising system that stimulates the projection of (exchange-)value onto anything and with the examination of the ways in which cultural forms and human sociality affect and are affected by these forces – which are differently experienced and responded to by people across the world, as we will see.

Parts and Wholes

The reading I propose for these anthropologies of value requires additional elaboration on a question that this introduction has so far only partially unfolded. This question relates to the grounds upon which we converge and the shaping of seminal concepts with which we work. The idea behind the epigrammatic title of this introduction suggests that people everywhere, and in virtually every 'culture' across the world, are realising, if they have not already done so, that (exchange-)value can potentially be discovered in or projected onto anything – even nothingness. This being the case, critically reflecting on the frames within which cultural patterns are shaped and within which the meaning of what people do is relationally produced becomes indispensable. Let us do so by looking, for instance, at the works of Turner (2008) and Graeber (2001), which have been influential within the new currents of efforts aiming to generate a distinctively anthropological theory of value.[11]

Turner's contributions certainly opened avenues for an overarching anthropological enterprise around a conceptualisation of value, partly by resorting to what he denominated the anthropological dimension of Marx's work. In Turner's view, that dimension would have been more developed in the so-called philosophical period of Marx – his early, pre-*Capital* period. For his own discussion of value, which he aimed to make applicable to the study of pre-capitalist societies, Turner abstracted ideas from Marx's writings in connection with notions of human agency (always resulting from creative tensions between its subjective and objective, material and ideal, individual and social dimensions) and invited reflection on 'the ways ideological representation tends to objectify itself as the producer rather than the product of that activity and its social forms' (2008: 44). What Turner thus recovered for the study of society was dependent on the study of 'production', creatively adapting Marxian contributions and making them exportable to non-capitalist societies: one would just need to identify what counts as production in a given society, which would be ethnographically inseparable from how such a society 'defines the need (or needs) that serve as the focus (or foci) of its productive activities' (2008: 45). Turner proposed that this focus be understood as an exploration of the 'meta-need' of any social system, equivalent to the accumulation of capital in capitalism unveiled by Marx. Even in pre-capitalist societies, Turner nevertheless argued, this meta-need would tend to be practically articulated by relationships of exploitation: some social group/s extract surplus (of whatever value is generated and pursued in the culturally bounded productive process) from other groups. This extraction would be made possible because those who exploit have control of key means of production – again, of whatever is produced in those systems in order to satisfy its culturally defined needs.

That was the way Turner presented the centrality of his conception of value: in most if not all societies, that 'surplus tends to be appropriated, not merely as a brute product, but in *a form of value*' (Turner 2008: 45, my emphasis). One thereby gets a closing of the gap between ideological representation and value, but the latter concept becomes totally removed from the Marxian matrix that was nevertheless used to frame contributions to the conceptualisation of (social) production, surplus, agency and exploitation. This proposal has in any case been influential among a whole current of anthropologists, particularly those who work with groups presented as living in non-capitalist socio-cultural spheres.

From a comparable angle, the overall foundation of Graeber's theoretical proposition (2001) is a conceptualisation of value in relation to the way in which actions become meaningful to people by their being situated within a particular social totality (in Graeber's terms, generally 'a culture'). Value is in the end what drives and orients people's actions in such a totality, something that, to some extent, would conceptually crystallise what is ideologically defined as socially worthwhile within it. As it were, in this type of work Kluckhohn and Turner come together – and Marx becomes ever more distant.

In both Turner's and Graeber's proposals, then, one finds conceptualisations of value that open up the possibility for overarching anthropological theories: the study of value becomes possible in any 'culture' or 'society', for there could be none without some sort of collective frame of meaning. However, there are crucial limitations in such anthropological enterprises as avenues for the understanding of the 'world of humankind'. These limitations become apparent if one considers that the suggestion contained in our entitling epigram does speak of a real contemporary phenomenon – and, hopefully, that will be the case when reading the essays contained in this volume. While seeking to open up the way for a universalisable anthropological theory of value, those enterprises always end up equating the totalising sphere of ideational 'production' within which actions take on meaning with a given 'culture' or 'society', thus setting limits to our possibilities of understanding central aspects of humankind and what culture means within it. Such proposals thus become comparable in central respects to some of the precedents that they wanted to replace within anthropological theory: they reinforce (they cannot escape) the idea that autonomous 'cultures' or 'societies' (defined along ethnic, national, religious, etc. ... terms) are the ultimate totalising, bounded spheres within which whatever organising principles of 'value' (or culture) operate.

This problematic form of analytically bounding the social sphere of totalisation for the analysis of action cannot be resolved by the emphasis on 'the politics of value' to which Graeber draws attention (2001: 88–89). It is thus acknowledged that, to some extent, conflict drives and characterises social life, but, from that angle, struggle would spin around the establishment of what value is within a given cultural sphere. Conflict and political struggle thus remain equally confined to autonomous 'cultural' and basically ideational spheres – say, a Kayapo sphere, or a Malagasy sphere. Such approaches cannot explain (and do not seek to explore) the causes that motivate social change – even if the latter is understood in terms of changes in the production of value such as they conceptualise it. And they certainly obscure possible explanations of why, when looking across 'cultures' nowadays, one can find comparable processes and cultural patterns that people themselves present as forms of adapting to, resisting or trying to suppress a certain social force – one which, from an analytical angle, one could associate with the 'laws of motion' of capitalism. Comparing what happens around the widespread processes of commodification (or, for that matter, deliberate de-commodification) becomes very telling in that respect. Because such adaptation, resistance or reorientation is often expressed by and takes place through the activation, transformation or creation of particular forms of sociality, as the chapters in this volume illustrate.

We do share the premise so crucially and rightly defended by anthropologists that cultural forms influence human interaction, its experience and regulation. But with this volume we would also like to contribute to shedding light on precisely how cultural forms operate in the mediation of concrete social relationships, and in order to do so it becomes important to seek alternatives for theories of culture (or value) that remain silent around issues such as capitalist expansion, exploitation of some social aggregates by others, or exploitation of some classes of people by other classes of people within a given social aggregate (cf. Castree 1996–97). It is against this background that we consider that there is no incompatibility in the combination of a minimum common Marxian ground for the convergence of our anthropologies of value and the diversity of theoretical approaches to conceptualise human sociality and cultural practice beyond that. That common ground enables us to pursue the understanding of something central about 'drives for action' and the interpretation of meaning across social aggregates: Why can commodification appear everywhere as a process (even if in different degrees)? And why is it – or can it be – everywhere also resisted as an identifiable force? The otherwise diverse theoretical approaches precisely enable us to answer these questions ethnographically and anthropologically, focusing on (culturally mediated) responses to such a force. In short: the world economy can be seen as a totalising sphere (one continuously generating flows of interaction), but one that is inhabited through cultural diversities between and within the social aggregates that result from processes of interconnection.

Cultural Mediations

Here is another caveat for readers. You may be disappointed if you approach this book seeking to confirm preconceptions about the current character or directionality of 'societies', 'nations' or 'cultures' around the world. Binary conceptual oppositions such as 'global north' and 'global south', 'west' and 'east', 'west' and 'the rest', 'commodity economies' and 'gift economies', or 'core' and 'periphery', continue to be used by some analysts to suggest that one of any of those poles is more pervaded or more historically consonant with the cultural and philosophical premises that sustain capitalism. A reading of the chapters in this volume destabilises such suggestions – as others have with their scholarship.[12] As a matter of fact, it brings into question the validity of such binary oppositions as the basis of preconceived generalisations about culturally mediated engagements with capitalism. Most contributions in this volume present a robust ethnographic grounding and, establishing channels of analytical communication between different world regions, they reveal that both spheres in any of those pairs (however they may be defined) harbour 'double movements' that generate creative tensions between systemic forces and counter-cyclical human practice. The book's structure has been precisely designed in acknowledgement of that reality, grouping chapters in two sections. The first presents a 'global south' in which many subjects can and do actively seek avenues for more advantageous incorporation into the world system (for instance, embarking on processes of commodification). The second section reveals a 'global north' where subjects, on occasion reacting to the ways in which the core of the world system produces its own internal peripheries (just as the periphery of the world system produces its cores), actively seek to oppose or practically attenuate with their forms of sociality some of the effects of capitalism – for instance, by embarking on processes of de-commodification.

We of course take the 'double movement' concept from Polanyi's thesis in *The Great Transformation* (2001 [1944]), which continues to be fruitfully reclaimed for social theory production and anthropological debates (Hart and Hann 2009). Within these debates we share in the view that the responses of 'society' to the expansion of the (allegedly self-regulating) 'market' aiming to attenuate the latter's dissolving effects are not circumscribed to statutory legalised institutions, but to be found in a variety of forms of sociality and organised political activity.

Examinations of how tensions and double movements are both produced and experienced by people in different parts of the world become stimulating avenues to reflecting on how to create better futures in a globalised world. All over this world one finds sources of affluence, but also dystopian images like those that revolutionaries and poets worriedly envisaged over a century ago. But all over the world, too, one finds groups of people who seek to maintain or to create anew forms of sociality that contest the premises of a market-regulated existence. Even though financialised capitalism has generated complex dynamics that Polanyi could not fully foresee, and despite the fact that his conceptualisation of double movement might present divisions between those who consider it best to approach it as a form of collective consciousness and those who want to seek its traces where such movement becomes objectively institutionalised (Robotham 2009), Polanyi's contributions remain a wellspring of ideas for social analysis.

Structuring Sections

In structuring this volume we resort to the terms 'global south' and 'global north' precisely to bring to the fore some of their crucial limitations as analytical concepts. Unless one were to use these terms as mere geographical categories (which is precisely the only usage that is wholly discarded in their varied conceptualisations in the social sciences), they hide as much as they reveal about the world we live in. These terms are variously conceptualised,[13] for instance as spheres naming countries with high and low human development indexes (north and south, respectively); or as spheres amalgamating countries that donate (global north) or receive foreign aid (global south); or as naming the conglomerate of countries with large formal economies and public sectors versus the conglomerate constituted by countries where such sectors are lacking. Different criteria are used to define those spheres, but at any rate substantial difficulties with these concepts derive from using countries (nation-states) as the units of analysis on which to apply the criteria of classification: this transforms global south and global north into easily misleading concepts. It is not only that the diversity of classifications makes some countries oscillate between south and north, depending on the defining criteria of that particular classification. It is not either a question of the inadequacy of these units to shed light on structural imbalances between potentially shifting cores and peripheries in integrated world economies, as Wallerstein (1976) and other advocates of world system theory rightly contended. Major difficulties also derive from the fact that social inequalities and cultural differences within countries, which can be as prominent as those between countries situated in the 'southern' and the 'northern' sides of those divides, are wiped out – and with them the possibilities of adequate characterisations and explanations of humankind within that system that is recognised as globalised. These difficulties are exponentially multiplied when such units of analysis are presented as corresponding with equally bounded cultures – and, as a matter of fact, 'cultures' are very often transformed into independent units of analysis to characterise and explain this globalised world and its inequalities. A more or less tacit tendency in these cases is to suggest that people in the global north (sometimes nominated 'the West') share a culture and that it is consonant with the functioning of globalised capitalism, whereas in the global south one would find cultural commonalities of a different, and rather anti-capitalist, type.

Against these trends, and also in relation to the already discussed limitations of theories of value that equally transform 'cultures' into independent units of analysis, this volume contributes to testing the idea that, south and north, we live in times in which people behave as if they knew that, potentially, there is exchange-value in everything. This of course does not imply that there are no economic and political structural differences between core and peripheral areas of the world system, as many aggregate indicators demonstrate; but it does suggest that people, everywhere, increasingly seem to generate and interpret their socio-cultural creations in relation to the laws of motion and the silent compulsion of that system. It is therefore not surprising to find that those laws, sometimes coded as 'neoliberal globalisation', generate political approximations between actors of the south and the north, since all of them become exposed to new forms of accumulation by dispossession (Kasmir and Carbonella 2008; Glassman 2006). But it is also understandable that, as this volume illustrates, there is a 'global south' in which subjects, some of them occupying disadvantaged positions within their peripheral countries, actively transform or try to transform things with use-value into things with exchange-value. Ethnographic studies carried out in Cook Islands, Papua New Guinea, Fiji, Venezuela and Cuba will illustrate in this volume how such processes are nevertheless embedded in specific (but dynamic) cultural forms and frames.

In turn, we present a 'global north' where one finds subjects who actively protect what they consider important about humanity and nature from some of the effects of capitalist market dynamics – on occasion trying to de-commodify things and spheres of life. In this north the reader will be able to find subjects whose social activity projects the principles of a gift economy – something that some analysts conceive as the attribute of societies in a pre- or a-capitalist south. In this section of the volume we include studies addressing populations from Canada, Iceland, Ireland, New Zealand and the United States of America (USA).

The Chapters

The first part of the volume, grouping studies carried out in the so-called global south, opens with the chapter by Jane Horan, who explores the dynamics surrounding the public sale of a *tivaivai* (a type of quilt) in the Cook Islands. *Tivaivai*, made by women and normally circulated as gifts, have been important objects within the islanders' ceremonial economy and pivotal to the mapping and maintenance of their social relationships. The transformation of *tivaivai* into commodities has generally been considered inimical to the maintenance of such relations as the foundations of the islanders' sense of collective body. Women have often expressed variants of the idea that 'It's not right to sell your *tivaivai*', as Horan notes. The exceptional degree of publicity around the sale of the *tivaivai* that she addresses in this chapter therefore constituted an unprecedented milestone. Horan explains why this process, which opened the path to a more systematic commodification of *tivaivai*, could be successfully consummated in a way that did not debase the social standing of the producer/seller nor the cultural importance granted to the object itself. Key to understanding that outcome is the position of authority of the woman who produced and sold the *tivaivai*, and her skilful command of local and intercultural codes of power. In parallel, through this chapter one gains insights into some of the forces that push Cook Islanders to transform the production of *tivaivai* into a commercial product: as the seller of the *tivaivai* laments: 'The reality is that we live in a *papa'ā* [European] world, we need money.'

In chapter 2, John Cox examines the emergence and functioning of a Ponzi scam in Papua New Guinea (PNG). In dialogue with theories of value creation in the spheres of exchange and consumption, Cox reveals that the success of this scam partly rested on the way in which it intertwined the promise of financial gain with local idioms of Christian commitment. This intertwining enabled participants to conceptualise themselves as promoting national development and salvation while pursuing individual profit, and the scam thus became an avenue through which the local population gave expression to two salient models of personhood identifiable in contemporary PNG: a model of a Christian self-controlled moral self and a model of an economically entrepreneurial (moral) self. Cox illuminates how these models of personhood become enmeshed in class cleavages within contemporary PNG: within the moral project of the Ponzi scam, both models coalesce in the search for a more egalitarian society (and one less threatened by conflict) that middle-class actors ideally conceive as an extension of their socioeconomic standard among less privileged sectors of society.

Also working in Papua New Guinea, Olivia Barnett-Naghshineh, in chapter 3, explores the process through which *asbin*, a winged bean that played an important role as a gift within local ceremonial economies, is at present cultivated primarily to be sold as a commodity, gradually becoming a marginal cash crop in the process. Her ethnography around Goroka in the Eastern Highlands Province provides a grounding to understand the political-economic changes that stimulate that process of commodification, but also how the local population strive to reproduce ceremonial economies as avenues for the re-creation of social relatedness and notions of personhood not guided by selfishness. In this context, Barnett-Naghshineh emphasises that money, in parallel to playing its role as mediator of market relations, has been incorporated as a gift in ceremonial economies, in an illustrative example of the way in which the local population seeks to reproduce the social fabric of the region through their own culturally mediated forms. People from Goroka say that 'It is money time' (*Nau em taim bilong mani*), as Barnett-Naghshineh reminds us. This expression evocatively captures both the current centrality of money in the maintenance of social relatedness through ceremonial economies and the perceived degree of incorporation of the region (and its people) into the world economy.

In chapter 4, Geir Henning Presterudstuen analyses how local understandings of the relationship between people and the environment in Fiji, as epitomised by the concept of *vanua*, have been affected by the commercial uses currently given to land within an expanding market economy. The social structure of contemporary Fiji has been strongly conditioned by the tense balance between Fijian landownership, foreign capital and Indian labour – what an influential Fijian political figure aptly characterised as the three-legged stool upon which the country's social formation rests. In this formation there is an increasing importance of the tourist industry, as well as growing demands for socioeconomic development by large sectors of the population. Against this background, Presterudstuen revisits the meaning of the concept of *vanua* and analyses its current permutations among the Fijians. *Vanua* encapsulated the idea of a mutually constitutive tie between place and people in the island, and also named forms of cultural appropriateness associated with collective identity – *cakacaka vakavanua* can be translated as 'acting in accordance with the land'. However, the cultural contents of the *vanua* category and its practical expressions have been transformed in response to growing incorporation into the world economy. Presterudstuen resorts to the concept of 'entification' to explain that process, in parallel shedding light on the mechanisms through which part of the Fijian population has de facto constituted itself as landed class and on the ways in which traditional forms of collective land ownership are being adapted to the conditions of a market in which land is commercialised.

In my own chapter (chapter 5) I examine the transformation of waterfalls into rent-capturing commodities in the Venezuelan *Gran Sabana* (Great Savannah), and discuss the source of value in this transformation. I show that the emergence of this type of rent-capturing commodity, in which members of the Pemon indigenous people are actively participating, is dependent on a type of collective labour that I denominate cultural labour. This type of labour is defined as the collective creational powers of one's group ancestors in relation to a commodified thing. When people speak about it, it tends to be accompanied by an emphasis on how the forms of life of one's own group (presented through the idioms of culture and tradition) contribute to the conservation of that particular commodified thing. I argue that this type of commodification can partly be interpreted as a response that attempts to stop or attenuate the negative impacts of historical processes of dispossession, but also that it is essentially inscribed as a dynamic of contemporary capitalist expansion.

In chapter 6, Marina Gold analyses the effects of the creation and partial liberalisation of a housing market in socialist Cuba. The revolution of 1959 included guaranteeing housing as a citizen's right and de-commodified that arena of social life. Ownership over houses was recognised and mechanisms to regulate their transference and exchange were in place, but outside a capitalist market logic. However, in 2011, in the midst of a number of economic and political adjustments, legislation was passed that enables Cubans and foreign residents to sell and buy houses through such market mechanisms. Gold examines the results of that transformation in relation to new forms of *cuentapropismo* (self-employment) that have emerged around the house market, showing that such employment and the market remain densely embedded in bundles of non-marketised social relations. These relations become indispensable for the successful development of new enterprises and, in parallel, constitute a context in which selfish behaviour and the public display of economic affluence is discouraged. Gold thus provides stimulating insights into the dynamics that shape a moralised understanding of market relations in Cuba and demonstrates how notions of revolutionary commitment continue to discursively pervade social praxis in the country. In the new context, allegiances to a revolutionary ethos are now giving room to entrepreneurial selves that are nevertheless conceptualised as pillars of a sustainable socialist society.

With this analysis of a process of commodification of houses in a socialist country we close the examination of socio-cultural dynamics in the global south. We then move to explore its alleged structural (and for some, socio-cultural) opposite in the global north. This transition is initiated in chapter 7, in which Moira White revisits Ernest Shackleton's Imperial Trans-Antarctic Expedition of 1914.

Shackleton's adventurous ordeals are by now salient in the annals of expeditionary history, and have also been popularised by a number of celebratory films and books. White brings original insights to the analysis of that event and to our discussion of value by focusing on the fate of penguins that one of the expeditionary ships eventually brought to New Zealand. Through detailed archival research, White documents how penguins, part of the faunal specimens that the expedition aimed to collect, moved from constituting the source of life-saving meat for shipwrecked sailors to becoming appreciated gifts and symbols for visual consumption in a variety of exhibitions once they arrived in Dunedin (New Zealand). The dynamics that shape that trajectory bring insights for those interested in the discussion of aspects of 'the social life of things' (Appadurai, 1986), but they also unveil the cultural codes that shaped what one could denominate a gift economy among members of social elites of the period. Thus White's chapter constitutes a very stimulating opening for our discussion: we are reminded of the existence of such apparently non-capitalist cultural codes among people and social classes who nevertheless were pivotal in the active expansion of the capitalist market economy (in parallel to British imperial expansion) in the early twentieth century.

In chapter 8, Fiona McCormack explains why the emergence of fishery quota systems, an expression of the establishment of property rights over natural resources that responds to the principles of the so-called 'tragedy of the commons', constitute a paradigmatic example of the way in which neoliberal ideology and the financialisation of capitalism have generated profound socio-environmental transformations in different parts of the world. With fieldwork experience in New Zealand, Iceland and Ireland, McCormack structures her analysis in three main sections: the first scrutinises the political processes through which fishing rights have been transformed into particular types of property; the second explains how those rights have become part of complex webs of marketisation and financialisation in which the focus has been on the creation of value in the sphere of market exchange, with dramatic results in many cases and always obscuring a growing inequality linked to the conditions in the sphere of production; the final section, based on ethnographic work in Dún na nGall (Donegal, Ireland), illustrates the ways in which the structural processes associated with the creation of fishery quota systems impact on localised fishing communities – often very negatively. McCormack presents moving illustrations of the way in which these communities, exposed to structural forces they cannot control and which have translated into forms of dispossession and economic displacement, often live an existence permeated by a sensation of loss. She nevertheless shows how out of this situation a narrative of nostalgia has emerged – as a critique of present conditions and as a tool for potential social change.

In chapter 9, David Boarder Giles presents an illuminating analysis of waste as a fundamental element in the ongoing production and expropriation of surplus value in contemporary capitalism. Giles uses his lengthy anthropological experience among Dumpster divers and with the Food Not Bombs anarchist soup kitchen in Seattle (USA) to shed light on a particular type of shadow economy generated by post-Fordist models of capital accumulation. At the core of these economies is waste, and 'shadow commodities' that are part and parcel of what Giles denominates 'abject capital'. The latter rests on the systematic disposal of those commodities, which becomes essential for the maintenance of commodity markets – including food markets. Disposal annuls the exchange-value of commodities while they nevertheless still can be (and sometimes are) used, generating a systemic contradiction. Giles explains how the existence of that type of capital remains creatively ingrained in the logics of contemporary capitalism: it has given rise to mechanisms of 'abject recapture', through which economic agents seek to recirculate (and ultimately to recapitalise) the commodities and surpluses that have been thus disposed of through alternative market avenues. However, Giles also demonstrates that not every social agent lives these contradictions of capitalism thinking of how to make money out of them. His work among people who politicise access to and redistribution of waste under different (and often overtly anti-capitalist) socio-cultural mechanisms provides a stimulating platform for discussing the contradictions of contemporary capitalism and potential alternatives.

In the closing chapter, Fern Thompsett discusses alternatives to the marketisation of university education and the parallel process of 'enclosure of knowledge', phenomena that continue to expand worldwide, but also generate growing discontent. Specifically, Thompsett focuses her attentions on the emergence of 'free university' projects, from her own experience as an activist in Australia and through her research in Canada, Mexico and the USA. She characterises 'free universities' as projects of collective study with four basic characteristics: they do not have state affiliation, are open to everyone and free of charge for participants, generate physical, offline gatherings of people and include goals of emancipation. Thompsett discusses the challenges that these projects face in capitalist societies, where there seem to be only small interstices within totalising market logics, and places emphasis on the way in which activists, in addition to rejecting the enclosure of knowledge and the rationality that leads to the marketisation of education, find common grounds in their efforts to create spaces as forms of commons and to de-commodify of human labour. Thompsett thus opens avenues to understand the anti-capitalist potential of free universities, but also their present importance as expressions of a double movement in core areas of the world system.

In relation to the idea condensed in the title of this introduction, the sum of these chapters results in an invitation to reconsider why value, as conceptualised by Marx, remains a useful tool for anthropology as a discipline – and for the analysis of social and cultural forms in the contemporary world more generally. Marx's conceptualisations have been generally neglected, or turned upside down, within the renewal of anthropological approaches to value. This is a pity, and is often the outcome of misleading mechanical associations of Marx's approach with an 'economic' one (as opposed to a 'social' one), or arises from mistaken assimilations of an economic understanding of value with something referring to the degree to which objects are desired (see note 8). However, Marx's contribution remains in some respects a still irreplaceable analytical tool precisely for its eminently social character. He certainly conceptualised value in relation to the notion of commodity, the creation of wealth and (primarily) the sphere of production, but he did so within an epistemological frame that enabled a holistic analysis of 'modern society' (the society of capital) and a discussion of its politics. With capitalism globalised as a world economy, the analytical avenues he opened are still in very good shape for those seeking to explain, among other things, what the title of this introduction hints at.

Notes

1. I am grateful to Geir Henning Presterudstuen and Sergio López for comments and suggestions on earlier drafts of this chapter, and, very specially, to Lisette Josephides. I also thank very sincerely the contributors to this volume, who have brought my ideas on contemporary anthropology and the concept of value within it to a place that I would have never found without them. Of course, I am solely responsible for any errors that this introduction may contain.
2. Let us once more remark what is well known: only the first volume of this work was published during Marx's life, specifically in 1867 (with its last partially revised edition published in Paris in instalments between 1872 and 1875). The first edition in English would come still later, in 1887. Volumes two and three saw the light for the first time in 1885 and 1894 respectively, with Marx resting in Highgate cemetery since 1883. Engels was in charge of the publication of those latter volumes, which were edited out of drafts that Marx had left behind, some of them incomplete. Those three volumes constitute the contents of *Capital*, as it has been known since, in its many subsequent editions and translations.
3. Of course, classical economists had already developed labour theories of value, and Marx explicitly built his own upon (and in dialogue with) those theoretical foundations. However, Marx's contribution was distinctively shaped in *Capital*: he developed his own approach in order to reveal (and be able to critique) the 'laws of motion' of capitalism, and not as a theory primarily designed to explain the determination of prices. Marx made clear his intentions when remarking that Adam Smith and David Ricardo had had their attention 'entirely absorbed in the analysis of the magnitude of value' (Marx 2008: 483, note 1) as a result of what Marx considered to be a more determinant limitation: they had failed to fully grasp the historically situated character of capitalism as a mode of

production, tending to present it as one 'eternally fixed by Nature' (Marx 2008). For Marx, classical economists had developed tools to rationalise the events that they studied without fully engaging in the search for causalities, which opened the doors to critical political economy.

4. Nature, which is certainly indispensable, was nevertheless conceptualised as a non-produced condition of production. For a creative discussion of the way in which Marxian theory of value could be expanded as a 'value theory of nature' with which to shed light on the organisation and division of nature within capitalism, see Coronil (1997: specifically ch. 1).
5. For a discussion of the reasons why Adam Smith's work came to dominate the classical canon and an overview of contributions of other classical economists whose positions were in key respects closer to those advanced by Marx in *Capital*, see Perelman (2000).
6. Not that this expansion was a one-sided cultural move, as it were, with the history of a European core gradually imposed upon peripheries. The histories of people involved in and affected by such expansion were mutually constituted, as Eric Wolf, among others, emphatically contended (1990 [1982]). It is worth noting that Fernando Coronil, in one of the most stimulating takes of an anthropologist on the Marxian theory of value, rescued a comparable idea when trying to theorise 'localised' histories: capitalism was presented as a global process that 'mutually forms centers and peripheries', rather than one that 'expands from active modern regions and engulfs passive traditional societies' (1997: 8). Some of the new drive of capitalist expansion (such as certain forms of commodification and financialisation) are not always dependent on territorial ingredients, but they bring social actors of cores and peripheries into mutual constitution as much as the previous ones.
7. It is of course the case that concepts such as use- and exchange-value were not coined by Marx either, but, as noted above regarding the labour theory of value, they gained a new conceptual shape when situated within the theoretical field established by *Capital*.
8. In the view of Graeber, in the social sciences there are the three main streams within which 'value' would have been conceptualised (2001: 1–2): value conceptions of the desirable; value in relation to the degree to which objects are desired; and value as meaningful difference. This would roughly correspond to conceptualisations of value within sociology, economy and linguistics, and they would be to a considerable extent 'refractions of the same thing'. There are two questionable aspects in this classification: one is that scholars who can be situated within any of those streams have in fact been trying to answer different questions, in some cases aiming to find the right tools to explain how people define the world in which they live and differently interpret and guide their action within that definition, and in others looking at the causes and consequences of those differences in the definition of the world. The other important difficulty is that such classification presents 'value in the economic

sense' in a manner that overlooks Marxian contributions to social theory, for Marx's theory of value could actually not find room in such 'economic sense'. In Graeber's classification, 'value in the economic sense' comes close to what Appadurai defined as 'a definite sum of value, which results from the commensuration of two intensities of demand' (1986: 4). In both cases, 'economic value' is displaced to the sphere of exchange as the sphere of definition of what value is about, therefore disregarding the sphere of production (in a material understanding of production) as significant for the definition (and thereof the analysis) of value.

9. Of these efforts, those that have covered more ground in the elaboration of a theory have been produced by authors who, other merits aside, embarked on the task individually (Gudeman and Graeber); those who tried to do so coordinating collective endeavours that were not accompanied by collective authorship nor by clearly demarcated epistemological grounds have obviously faced challenges that transform the production of *a* theory into a remotely achievable goal.
10. Even if, for argument's sake, one were to accept that division as a meaningful classification of anthropological knowledge, that would not bring a response to the challenges posed by the ambiguities and differences in conceptualisation of value and in the type of 'anthropological question' they so aim to address: one realises that in both spheres (the so-called theory-driven and ethnography-driven) there is in turn a multiplicity of (a priori or a fortiori) such conceptualisations among contributors. This is not at all a problem in itself, of course, but it does become a difficulty if the goal is to try to define (and try to provide some explanation for) a certain question or set of questions.
11. Let me take this opportunity to make here a posthumous tribute to the inspiring work of Terence Turner, who passed away in November 2015. And let me make the critical engagement with his work that follows in this chapter a grateful part of that tribute.
12. The destabilisation of such suggestions has of course a long tradition within anthropology, arguably as long as the history of anthropological perspectives that has contributed and continues to contribute to stabilise said suggestions. As for the former, worthy of note are the contributions of Chris Hann and Keith Hart (for example, 2011) in reclaiming the humanist heritage from scholars such as Mauss, who inspiringly unsettled certain projects of classifying societies along lines such as interest-driven or altruism-driven, since disinterest (and codes of mutual obligation) and interest are to be found in any social aggregate – the core of capitalism included. Such unsettling was fertile for the production of anthropological knowledge, but also for that search for better futures for humanity with which Mauss associated such production. Kasmir and Carbonella (2008) made a lucid critique of the limitations implied in maintaining the labels 'global north' and 'global south' as categories of analysis of contemporary capitalism, often veiling the interconnectedness of struggles

by labourers against dispossession in different parts of the world (that is, by labourers in the global north and in the global south).

13. For a succinct overview of this question, see Eriksen (2015).

References

Appadurai, A. 1986. Introduction: Commodities and the politics of value. In A. Appadurai (ed.) *The Social Life of Things: Commodities in Cultural Perspective*. Cambridge: Cambridge University Press.

Castree, N. 1996–97. Invisible Leviathan: Speculations on Marx, Spivak, and the question of value. *Rethinking Marxism* 9(2): 45–78.

Coronil, F. 1997. *The Magical State: Nature, Money, and Modernity in Venezuela*. Chicago: University of Chicago Press.

Eiss, P.K. and D. Pedersen. 2002. Introduction: Values of value. *Cultural Anthropology* 17(3): 283–90.

Eriksen, T.H. 2015. What's wrong with the global north and the global south? Available at: http://gssc.uni-koeln.de/node/454 (accessed 31 October 2015).

Fernández Liria, C. and L. Alegre Zahonero. 2011. *El orden del Capital*. Madrid: Akal.

Glassman, J. 2006. Primitive accumulation, accumulation by dispossession, accumulation by 'extra-economic' means. *Progress in Human Geography* 30(5): 608–25.

Graeber, D. 2001. *Toward an Anthropological Theory of Value: The False Coin of Our Dreams*. New York: Palgrave.

Gregory, C. 1982. *Gifts and Commodities*. New York: Academic Press.

Gudeman, S. 2001. *The Anthropology of Economy*. Oxford: Blackwell.

Hann, C. and K. Hart. 2011. *Economic Anthropology: History, Ethnography, Critique*. Cambridge: Polity Press.

Hart, K. and C. Hann. 2009. Introduction: Learning from Polanyi. In K. Hart and C. Hann (eds) *Market and Society: The Great Transformation Today*. Cambridge: Cambridge University Press, pp. 1–16.

Humphrey, C. and S. Hugh-Jones (eds). 1992. *Barter, Exchange and Value: An Anthropological Approach*. Cambridge: Cambridge University Press.

Josephides, L. 1985. *The Production of Inequality: Gender and Exchange among the Kewa*. London: Tavistock.

Kasmir, S. and A. Carbonella. 2008. Dispossession and the anthropology of labour. *Critique of Anthropology* 28(1): 5–25.

Kluckhohn, C. 1951. Values and value-orientations in the theory of action. In T. Parsons and E.A. Shils (eds) *Toward a General Theory of Action*. Cambridge, MA: Harvard University Press, pp. 388–433.

Marx, K. 2008. *Capital: A New Abridgement*. Oxford: Oxford University Press.

Modjeska, N. 1985. Exchange value and Melanesian trade reconsidered. *Mankind* 15(2): 145–62.

Munn, N. 1986. *The Fame of the Gawa: A Symbolic Study of Value Transformation in a Massim (Papua New Guinea) Society*. Cambridge: Cambridge University Press.

Narotzky, S. and N. Besnier. 2014. Crisis, value, and hope: Rethinking the economy. An introduction to supplement 9. *Current Anthropology* 55 (Suppl. 9): S4–S16.

Otto, T. and R. Willerslev. 2013. Prologue – Value as theory: Value, action, and critique. *Hau: Journal of Ethnographic Theory* 3(2): 1–10.

Pedersen, D. 2008. Introduction: Toward a value theory of anthropology. *Anthropological Theory* 8(1): 5–8.

Perelman, M. 2000. *The Invention of Capitalism: Classical Political Economy and the Secret History of Primitive Accumulation*. Durham, NC: Duke University Press.

Polanyi, K. 2001 [1944]. *The Great Transformation: The Political and Economic Origins of Our Times*. Boston, MA: Beacon.

Robotham, D. 2009. Afterword. In K. Hart and C. Hann (eds) *Market and Society: The Great Transformation Today*. Cambridge: Cambridge University Press, pp. 272–83.

Sahlins, M. 1972. *Stone Age Economics*. Chicago: Aldine-Atherton.

Smith, A. 2012 [1776]. *An Inquiry into the Nature and the Causes of the Wealth of Nations*. Ware, Herts.: Wordsworth Editions.

Strathern, M. 1988. *The Gender of the Gift*. Los Angeles: University of California Press.

Turner, T. 2008. Marxian value theory: An anthropological perspective. *Anthropological Theory* 8(1): 43–56.

Wallerstein, I. 1976. The world system perspective on the social sciences. *British Journal of Sociology* 27(3): 343–52.

Wolf, E. 1990 [1982]. *Europe and the People without History*. Berkeley: University of California Press.

PART I

Emerging Value in the 'Global South'

1

On the Capacity to Change the Structural Parameters of Value

The Sale of One Particular Cook Island *Tivaivai*

Jane Horan

Introduction

If, as the title of one of David Graeber's latest articles on value states, 'it is value that brings universes into being' (2013: 219), it takes a very skilled individual to coalesce expertise in value into what is tantamount to gain in a capitalist sense. The intertwining of economic value (as in gaining money) with so-called cultural value at the boundary of what Gudeman calls the realm of market and the realm of mutuality (2001, 2008, 2009) becomes a slippery, tricky process that has the potential to debase and undermine not only people, but significant valuables and cosmological universes as well. Or not. Because if the parameters of what is valued and how are expertly elaborated, the outcome can be a new version of the universe. Such capacity tends to be the reserve of only very specific individuals who can work with, manage, command even, the parameters of value as a structural reality, which is inevitably about versions of power (Graeber 2013: 226; cf. Turner 2006). This chapter is about one particular Cook Islands[1] woman, Māmā Vereara Maeva-Taripo, who has this capacity. The detail is about how Māmā Vereara very publicly exchanged, for an unprecedented sum of money, one specific, special (cf. Kopytoff 1986) *tivaivai taorei* (unquilted quilt)[2] that she had designed and made with help from her *tivaivai* group. *Tivaivai* are the paramount valuable in the Cook Islands ceremonial economy and are not meant to be sold, because of their capacity to express the core Cook Islands values of *aro'a* (love) and kinship. What this detail speaks to is *how* value not only brings universes into being, but also *how* the command of such value (and values and valuables) elaborates those universes via the capacity to wield versions of power, to the extent that this becomes a driver of social change as a response to broader capitalist forces.

'Value', according to Turner, is a 'relational aspect of a structure of interdependent productive activities, rather than a positive, inherent property of the labor invested in products' (2008: 46). It is therefore a 'special form of representation, which requires a medium of representation' (2008: 49; cf. Graeber 2001: 75–77, 2005). For Cook Islanders, the most significant medium of representation is *tivaivai*, and these appear at major life and ceremonial events in the Cook Islands ceremonial economy. These are made to be gifted publicly (for the most part) to close kin and important non-kin. The gifting of such valuables maintains, underlines and/or creates the most important relationships in Cook Islanders' lives. *Tivaivai* are used to wrap and adorn people going through ritual events like weddings, funerals, male rite of passage events called haircuttings (*pākoti'anga 'o'ora*), key birthdays, graduations and anniversaries. They are also gifted to church ministers at the conclusion of their tenure, as well as to chosen high-level dignitaries at public ceremonies. These textiles are also used to decorate and dress the venues in which such events take place. *Tivaivai*, made and used in this way, are the paramount valuable because they have come to be the materialisation – literally and figuratively – of core values for Cook Islanders. These are about kinship and the centrality of family in the individual and collective Cook Islands worldview, and the process of doing *aro'a*, which is glossed as love and is about actions rather than just words (Buse and Taringa 1995: 76).

By gifting and/or making *tivaivai* a woman shows herself to be – in the eyes of the assembled crowd of other Cook Islanders at public ceremonial events – the best version of a Cook Islands mother, wife, church member, Cook Islander. Hence, *tivaivai* are implicated in a performance of value. As a consequence, the making and use of *tivaivai* provides access to, and the axis of, the acquisition of prestige as *mana* (power) for all who gift them, but in far more exalted ways for those few skilled makers and users who have the ability to influence others because of their expertise in the performance of value, which includes the design and cutting of *tivaivai* as well as the largesse to teach others and help them make and/or acquire *tivaivai*. Māmā Vereara is one of these individuals because her actions to do with *tivaivai* through the course of her life are *recognised* as being worthy of the conferment of *mana* by others.

In April 2001, Māmā Vereara openly and explicitly sold her spectacular *tivaivai taorei* for the extraordinary price of NZ$10,000. Not only was the sum exceptional, but that the sale was conducted so overtly was unprecedented as well. Even before the sale, Māmā Vereara was arguably the most high-profile *tivaivai* maker and expert in *tivaivai* (called a *ta'unga*) in the Cook Islands and beyond, and is recognised as one of the most influential women in the Cook Islands community, ever. The people who paid the NZ$10,000 for the *tivaivai* were the owners of the most exclusive tourist resort on the main island of Rarotonga (The Rarotongan Beach Resort and Spa), Tata Crocombe and Elizabeth (Liz) Raizis. The exchange of money for the *tivaivai* was conducted in a very public manner at a Trade Fair, and an article was written about the sale in the *Cook Islands News* (Bataillard 2001), a newspaper publication that is widely read by Cook Islanders throughout the Cooks and the wider diaspora.

What is significant is that neither Māmā Vereara as a woman of esteemed *mana* and therefore the capacity to influence others, nor *tivaivai* generally as the paramount form of valuable, were undermined or debased through the very public process of the sale. The reason, I argue, is about Māmā Vereara's capacity to command and manage the parameters of value, because, as it transpired, her *mana* and status were enhanced through the process, and *tivaivai* generally acquired a new benchmark in monetary value. The specific *tivaivai* sold became even more renowned, and the intricacies of the way value, values and valuables in relation to *tivaivai* and what they are and do, were expanded and elaborated. This is not about the agency of objects (Gell 1998), which amounts to a fetishised notion of the intrinsic value of *tivaivai* (cf. Turner 2008; Graeber 2001), but rather about the power of Māmā Vereara to manage and command value in Turner's (2008: 46) sense, and how value as a way of seeing the world is augmented in the face of financial opportunity and pressure.

The Sale and 'Sale' of Tivaivai

I have routinely heard Cook Islanders say that *tivaivai* are never sold:[3] many women said things like 'I would never sell my *tivaivai*,' 'It's not right to sell your *tivaivai*' or 'You need your *tivaivai* for your children, why would I sell them?' The inference being that such a blatant association of money with *tivaivai* that takes place in straight mercantile exchange places the textiles, and the women that make and use them, squarely in the midst of the tension between the realms of mutuality and market (Gudeman 2008). The tension is about the implication that mercantile exchange is conceptualised as effectively pulling valuables away from the all-important performance and expression of core values and into the realm of the market, where the ideology of what *tivaivai* are is too able to be dissipated and the relationships expressed by the values materialised by *tivaivai* are explicitly, potentially irrevocably nullified. This is dangerous territory so the boundaries between the realm of mutuality and the realm of market are rigorously, ritually managed during all the range of events that constitute the Cook Islands ceremonial economy (Horan 2011, 2012, 2013, forthcoming).

However, money, generally associated with the realm of the market, is given as a gift at most types of public ceremonial events, but especially at haircutting ceremonies and through funerary processes. But in all instances, the actual 'face' of money as 'the great leveller, that … does away with all distinctions' (Marx 1961: 132; cf. Bloch and Parry 1989: 6)[4] is strenuously denied. This is done by always wrapping[5] notes in envelopes and writing one's name on the front of the envelope to explicitly emphasise that the main purpose of the gift is to forge a social connection.[6] Who gives what and how much is assiduously recorded in 'family books' and it is this information that becomes the basis upon which social relationships are conducted in terms of obligations to be reciprocated or to be received at future events. While money is ranked below *tivaivai* ritually, the gifting of it is done in Cook Islands ceremonial events in such a way that 'its flow elicits the distinctions that create … social life' (Robbins and Akin 1999: 15). But money clearly has use in the realm of market, to the extent that the increasing focus on money as the gift (Loomis 1983; Horan 2012) is a pragmatic response to the broader political economy that Cook Islanders live in.

As I became increasingly involved in *Va'inetini* (*tivaivai*-making groups) in South Auckland, I became aware of the fact that *tivaivai* – despite the rhetoric to the contrary – were relatively routinely exchanged for money, in contexts and under circumstances that *looked* very much like mercantile exchange. I would arrive at one of the *Va'inetini* meetings and would hear about how a particular woman had sold a *tivaivai* during the week to another who *really needed one* for her child, grandchild, niece or nephew for their haircutting, wedding, 21st, etc., or how another woman had sold a *tivaivai* because she 'needed money to go on a *tere parti*'.[7] A number of the *Va'inetini* had *tivaivai* under construction for sale at their public *tivaivai* shows to 'fundraise for the group', with the inference being that the Māmās could make better and more *tivaivai* with the proceeds from such sales. So if a given woman really needed a *tivaivai* she would be able to ask around, somebody would inevitably need money, and *if the cause was right* it would be seen as appropriate to sell a *tivaivai*. Women I spoke to who had sold or bought *tivaivai* all tended to speak in these terms; the *right cause* was always about needs to do with ceremonial obligation and family, and, providing nobody was trying just to make money, what was implicit was that the sale of the *tivaivai* would help both the buyer and the seller operate as a good Cook Islands woman, mother and/or aunty. The acquisition of such a *tivaivai* and what it would be used for or what the money would allow the seller to do, situated the transfer of money within the realm of mutuality. The rhetoric of need inherent in such transactions made the notion that '*tivaivai* are never sold' contextually correct: if selling means a fully mercantilised market transaction, *tivaivai* are, for the most part not sold, because Cook Islands women are effectively asserting a particular, limited meaning of selling, which they explicitly contrast with the forms of transactions they enter into when money is exchanged for *tivaivai*.[8] The rhetoric is ultimately about the tension between the realm of mutuality and the realm of market (Gudeman 2008). While such transactions were not covert, they tended not to be done with any fanfare, let alone in a blaze of publicity.

I argue that the way *tivaivai* have been – and continue to be – exchanged for money has changed and permutated at the behest of other capitalist forces at play in Cook Islanders' lives, in part because of the precedent set when Māmā Vereara exchanged her *tivaivai taorei* with the Crocombes in 2001. Ultimately, the assemblages that *tivaivai* and money have come to form are a consequence of the logics of a Cook Islands version of human economy which is about the way value (and valuables and values) work. Graeber contends that 'what distinguishes human economies is merely that they recognise that the chief business of any social system – or indeed any system of production and distribution of material goods – is the creation and mutual fashioning of human beings' (2012: 412; cf. Hann and Hart 2011: 9), whereby 'forms of value emerge to regulate a process which is ultimately about the creation of people' (Graeber 2001: 142). The relationship among the nexus of value, values and valuables becomes the story of the relationship among the actions of people, embodied cosmologies, the ideological rhetoric of how things should be done and the forms that coveted valuables take, as well as the way specific nuanced processes of power take place (Turner 2006, 2008; Graeber 2001, 2013).

Cook Islands women buy *tivaivai* in South Auckland now because more and more women are time-poor, or have decided that they do not want to make *tivaivai*, but they still need them for obligations. What makes the 'sale' of the *tivaivai taorei* made by Māmā Vereara more than a sale was the way that the process and the circumstances, along with the specific protagonists involved, coalesced to effectively reconfigure the parameters of value that *tivaivai* inhabit as semiotic media of value, and as part of the evolving dialectical tension between the realm of market and the realm of mutuality.

The Reality of the Sale of Mama Vereara Maeva's Tivaivai Taorei

On Tuesday 10 April 2001, an article written by Nancy Bataillard appeared in the *Cook Islands News* in Rarotonga, with the headline 'Intricate tivaevae [sic] fetches huge price'. The article read like this:

> An exquisite and intricate tivaevae taorei (quilt) displayed at last week's South Pacific Trade Fair has sold to Rarotongan Resort manager Tata Crocombe and his wife Elizabeth. Crocombe was reluctant to reveal the actual price he paid, but it is understood to be more than NZ$10,000.
>
> And it seems he may have scored something of a bargain. Cook Islands Association Non-Government Organisation (CIANGO) president Vereara Maeva said that particular tivaevae had previously been ordered by a wealthy United States resident who had been prepared to pay NZ$30,000. The quilt was supposed to be delivered to the US in June.
>
> 'But I thought I'd rather sell it to our local people. I knew the Crocombes would use it to promote our own hotel and our country' said Maeva.

The article recounted how Māmā Verara had designed the *tivaivai* and how it had taken her and her *tivaivai* group 'two years to sew, and another year for Māmā Vereara to finish it off'. The article continued by quoting Māmā Vereara:

> It is not an easy job. If I had been paid NZ$50.00 an hour to do it I probably would have earned about NZ$37,000 a year. We made it in three years – you add that up … the sale of the expensive tivaevae should encourage the women who make them. The money is in their hands.

The article recounted how five women, including Māmā Vereara, had been asked to put *tivaivai* up for sale at the Trade Fair and continued:

> Although it's the first time Maeva had ever sold her tivaevae commercially she says she didn't do it for the money but to promote her organisation and the Cook Islands. The five women in CIANGO[9] [at the stall at the Trade Fair] sold almost all of their craft. It is understood the Crocombes also bought a number of other tivaevae to display in the hotel.
>
> 'It's amazing that locals are buying too. I would like to thank those who bought our things and a big thank-you maata to Tata Crocombe and his wife for their support' says Maeva. (Bataillard 2001)

The article appeared on the third page of the newspaper and was widely read, or at least news of the sale spread rapidly. When I arrived in Rarotonga the week after the Trade Fair to begin a month-long stint of fieldwork, everyone I spoke to was talking about it. When I got back to Auckland at the end of May, the sale – and the amount paid – was widely known there too.

When I interviewed Liz Raizis of The Rarotongan Beach Resort and Spa (referred to as The Rarotongan), she said that she and her partner Tata Crocombe considered that *tivaivai* were the 'quintessential expression of Cook Islands culture' and that it was their aim to make a dedicated exhibition space at the resort to showcase Cook Islands culture generally and *tivaivai* in particular.[10] They were intent on giving visitors a Cook Islands experience at their resort and they considered that this included having access to *tivaivai* because the textiles are so important to the way Cook Islanders see the world. Raizis said that they wanted to move away from the generic resort experience, so the hotel at the time was on a drive to place more uniquely Cook Islands objects in the hotel complex. For example, they had also bought copies of works by local artists, in which *tivaivai* featured prominently, to hang in the resort rooms. When I asked her why the resort had bought the *tivaivai* at the Trade Fair, she noted how hard it was to buy *tivaivai* normally, and that they were just not for sale routinely, 'especially quilts of that calibre.' She said that the women who had gone to the Trade Fair had 'psychologically' got their heads around selling. She and Tata Crocombe had been on the lookout for *tivaivai* to buy for some time and the Trade Fair constituted a unique opportunity to buy, so buy they did. She said that when they saw Māmā Vereara's *tivaivai taorei* for sale they knew it was special and unique. Liz Raizis talked about why they purchased Māmā Vereara's *tivaivai taorei*:

> you know that is truly an historic piece, it is truly a work of art, so there is no doubt that was a high price to pay but we just felt … strongly that

> it was a truly special piece, that kind of thing does not come on to the market very often and it would be a corner stone of any exhibition, or celebration that we would want to put together … I know that she felt very relieved and comforted to know that it would remain in the Cook Islands, and it would be owned by a Cook Islander, and I think those are very important things. (Liz Raizis, personal interview, Rarotonga, 22 May 2001)

That particular *tivaivai taorei* already had a singularised (Kopytoff 1986), special character to it even before its sale. The first time I saw this *tivaivai* was when it was in pieces and under construction in Māmā Vereara's living room in Aorangi in November 1999.

I had gone to interview her on my first stint of fieldwork in the Cooks, and she told me at the time that the first version of the *tivaivai* had been used to wrap one of her sons at burial after he had died in an accident, and she was thinking about giving this version to another son who lived with her. When I next saw this *tivaivai taorei* in October 2000, it was finished. I was back in Rarotonga for a few days and happened to be there when the National Council of Women were holding their annual conference. A craft competition was held in conjunction with the gathering and Māmā Vereara had submitted her now finished *taorei* as her entry. Māmā Vereara's *tivaivai*

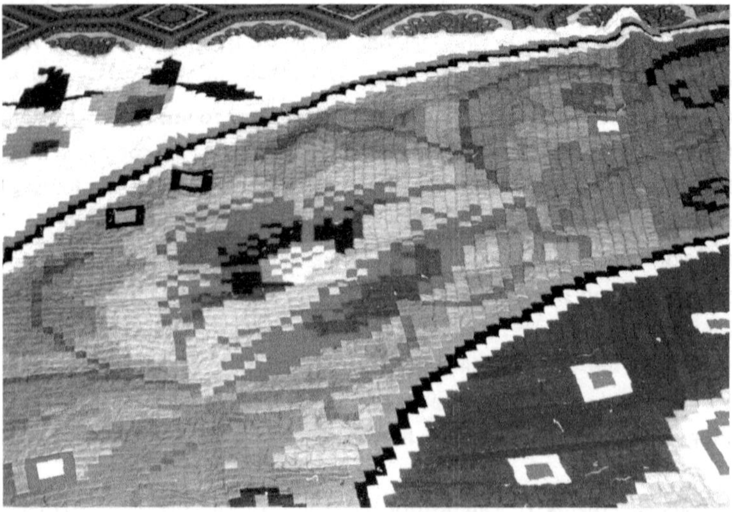

Figure 1.1 Māmā Vereara's *tivaivai taorei* under construction in November 1999

taorei was the outright winner of the competition, effectively judged the best *tivaivai* in the Cook Islands that year.

The craft competition was held in the National Auditorium, which was across the roadway from the Pukapuka Hostel where the conference was being held. I remember walking into the auditorium and seeing this large *tivaivai taorei*. It was displayed by being arrayed over the angled seating, so it was not easy to have a close look at it, but my overall impression of the *tivaivai* was that it was a magnificent, beautifully executed piece of work. The other *tivaivai* displayed were also extremely fine examples of the various types of *tivaivai* and were done by some of the most talented makers from around the Cooks, but Māmā Vereara's *tivaivai taorei* stood out. The circular floral pattern was unusual and complicated, the colours were beautiful, and for such a large *taorei*, it was balanced and even.[11]

Clearly, the *tivaivai* itself was special, but it seems to me that the *tivaivai* constituted the whole package, so to speak, because of *who* Māmā Vereara Maeva-Taripo is. It was no coincidence that the Crocombes decided to buy *that tivaivai* from *that* particular *tivaivai* maker for the largest amount ever transacted for a *tivaivai*. Māmā Vereara is not by any means the average *ta'unga*. She is arguably the most high-profile maker of *tivaivai*, and Cook Islands woman in the Cooks, the Cook Islander diaspora, and even the world. Her public service accolades are numerous, and when I mention

Figure 1.2 Māmā Vereara Maeva, Māmā Kimiora Samuel and Māmā Tokerau Munroe sitting in front of Māmā Vereara's winning *tivaivai taorei*, at the craft display during the National Council of Women's conference in October 2000

her name to any Cook Islands woman in New Zealand, Australia, or the Cooks, they all know who she is.

Māmā Vereara was born on Aitutaki in 1940. Originally trained as a school teacher, she worked for the Public Service until 1996 and then got involved in a non-government organisation (NGO) work. She set up the Cook Islands chapter of the National Council of Women in 1984, an extraordinary feat that required uniting women from one end of the Cooks to the other. She told me the story of how she lobbied successive prime ministers until her vision for Cook Islands women prevailed. Her light-hearted humour and droll delivery of the story of her run-ins with successive prime ministers and other powerful men made me laugh, and the way she told the story made it sound as if the eventual outcome was inevitable. But her comedic story-telling ability belied the steely resolve she possesses and her astute knowledge and command of Cook Islands power structures. She was president of the National Council of Women from 1987 to 1996 and has since held many positions in various NGOs, and she holds a *Rangitira* title under Tinomana Ariki on Rarotonga. Māmā Vereara is a renowned *tivaivai ta'unga*, she is as famous for her generosity in teaching others to do *tivaivai* (as she and her now deceased first husband and family travelled around the Cooks, as her husband was posted from one island hospital to another in his capacity as a medical doctor) as she is for her NGO work. She is charismatic, kind, acutely intelligent, an astute political operator and highly regarded by most.

So the sale of *that tivaivai* for *that* price by *that* particular woman was as much about who the maker was, what she had done in her life, and the profile she had among Cook Islander women in the Cooks and beyond as it was about the *tivaivai* being a large and beautiful *taorei*. But even more significantly, alienating that particular prize-winning *tivaivai* in the particular way it was sold at the Trade Fair, as chronicled in the media, had ramifications in realms previously unreached. Being sold in the way the *tivaivai* was, and being bought by the owners of one of the most exclusive resorts in the Cook Islands for the centrepiece of their collection in a relative blaze of publicity, the *tivaivai* morphed into a valuable art commodity. Effectively, a reordering of the regimes of value (Appadurai 1986) had taken place, and it was not just about the price of *tivaivai*, but also fundamentally about the way *tivaivai* operate as the axis of prestige of *mana* for Māmā Vereara. The process also became about 'the nature of persons as it is defined at the shifting boundaries between subject and objects, boundaries whose particular configurations may define a historical epoch' (Keane 2001: 66).

The transaction was so weighted because *tivaivai* are semiotic media of value that effectively perform and demonstrate the circulation of value (Fajans 1993) as they are made and used in the Cook Islands ceremonial economy, and exemplify good Cook Islands womanhood.

I argue that Māmā Vereara's status as a *ta'unga* was reoriented along with the overall structural parameters of value as these pertain to *tivaivai*. For Māmā Vereara Maeva, to sell that *tivaivai* in that way to the Crocombes had the potential to be denigrating and devaluing for *tivaivai* as a whole, yet it was also potentially extremely compromising for her. However, the way Māmā Vereara and the Crocombes handled the process meant it ended up exalting the art form into a hitherto unattainable realm. Because of the public way the process was conducted and the ameliorated version of the usual rhetoric that suffused the process, it moved beyond a simple transaction into one that was about the reordering of the regime of value that *tivaivai* occupied. Māmā Vereara was really the only person who could have done this without compromise.

The Crocombes were aware of the implications of doing business with such a high-profile purveyor of *tivaivai*, and how their payment constituted a reordering of the structural parameters of value. Liz Raizis said to me:

> When we bought that piece, Tata was well aware at the time that it would set a new benchmark; we weighed that into the equation as well ... he is also pleased and delighted that it would, because it meant that it would help create a market for *tivaivai* that up until now people haven't known that there would be people prepared to buy it, [and at] ... a responsible price, and that they could actually sell it right here in Rarotonga ... And it meant that people would really realise that these are valued things. (Liz Raizis, personal interview, Rarotonga, 22 May 2001)

They knew what they were buying and what it meant to buy from Māmā Vereara. They knew that one form of value associated with *tivaivai*, its price in the realm of market, was inexorably elevated but still within a universe that was sufficiently about Cook Islands versions of mutuality rather than market process, hence Raizis' assertion that a new benchmark was being set.

The rhetoric around the sale and the fact that Māmā Vereara was allegedly offered NZ$30,000 for it by an overseas (i.e. non-Cook Islander) buyer was part of this revaluing of *tivaivai*; this other price is attached to the *tivaivai* as much as the NZ$10,000 sale price, and was part of the rhetoric that situated the new conditions under which the sale was taking place. The two price tags are both part of that particular textile's new realm of value, and arguably part of a new realm of value for *tivaivai* generally. The fact that Māmā Vereara was at the Trade Fair with *tivaivai* for sale reinforced her assertion that she wanted her special *tivaivai taorei* to stay in the Cook Islands. What was more important was that by being alienated for that brief moment, that *tivaivai taorei* effectively became publicly, specifically inalienable once The Rarotongan took ownership of the *tivaivai* and it became the star of their collection. Keane notes that such reordering can involve a 'certain dematerialization of the human world, a denial of the ways in which human subjects are enmeshed with material objects' (2001: 66), but in this instance that *tivaivai* became the materialisation of an extended set of values (cf. Turner 2006) that incorporated money in a new way. The *tivaivai taorei* became the most publicly valuable *tivaivai* in an economic sense as well as cultural sense because it was a prize-winning *tivaivai* – made by Māmā Vereara. The dialectic between the realm of mutuality and the realm of market was reconfigured, but it was a fine line to tread. It seems to me that either by design or not, the sale was astutely managed in the media by Māmā Vereara and the Crocombes. By accepting such a substantial sum of money, she could have appeared 'greedy', a word I often heard used by Cook Islanders when they spoke about issues of money at events and in gifting. But that this did not happen was because of the way Māmā Vereara and the Crocombes were portrayed in the article and, in particular, the way Māmā Vereara talked about the number of hours it had taken her and the women to sew, and how low their hourly rate was (Bataillard 2001).

The wording of the article in the *Cook Islands News* stands as a public record, evoking a for-the-times version of the rhetoric that suffuses such exchanges of money and *tivaivai*. The same but different: as befitted the new set of opportunities, realities, location of the 'universe', referencing ritual exchange – albeit in a new way. There was a performance of values within the extending parameters of the structural construction of value, and a trading of valuables: from Māmā Vereara, along with her *tivaivai*, came her prestige, her profile, and her *mana*, and from the The Rarotongan came the promise of exalting the *tivaivai* by collecting it and ultimately displaying it in the hotel complex, and the money. Māmā Vereara was publically honoured, and she received a substantial sum of money. I argue that while the money that changed hands was probably not wrapped in an envelope bearing the Crocombes' name and that of the hotel in bold print on the exterior, the social relationships enacted through the exchange were tantamount to this format as seen in other ritual exchanges. The newspaper article stands as the record of the relationship, a 'public book' so to speak, with a requisite set of ongoing obligations. But the new assemblages were untried and potentially unstable.

Boundary Maintenance (and Expansion)

When I went to see Māmā Vereara not long after the sale, she was a little uneasy about talking about what had transpired. The context was complex. Such new assemblages of money and *tivaivai* in this context became about redefining the truly human in Graeber's sense (2012). The last thing Māmā Vereara wanted personally and as a public figure was to be associated with making *mere* money out of *tivaivai*. Her unease and defensiveness were revealed implicitly in the specifically circuitous route that our conversation took in the half hour or so I spent with her in her CIANGO office that afternoon. She spoke of the sale in terms of doing a great service to The Rarotongan which was in turn actively exalting the profile of *tivaivai* for Cook Islanders in the eyes of visitors to the islands, and therefore *tivaivai* as a whole (once again, the rhetoric of mutual benefit). The insider/outsider distinction made between the NZ$10,000/NZ$30,000 prices was underlined and her defensiveness was lest the transaction be reduced to merely a sale.

This was new territory for the transacting of *tivaivai* in regard to the sums of money involved and the public mode of sale, but it was new territory for Māmā Vereara too. She told me that 'true women make *tivaivai* ... we laugh at women who don't make *tivaivai* [but] ... it hurts me to see our culture as a commercial enterprise.' She said '*papa'ā* [Europeans] don't understand the value of *tivaivai*,' that it 'disappoints' her when she sees a *tivaivai* hung on a wall and not on a bed. She said the 'single greatest threat to *tivaivai* and its value is the commercialisation of *tivaivai* ... But the reality is, that we live in a *papa'ā* world, we need money.' She asserted that by selling *tivaivai*, women's talents were at least being appreciated, but the negatives were the commercialisation of culture and 'the essence, the value of culture [is] gone with money'. The push and pull of Polanyi's (1944; see also Hart and Hann 2009) double movement, adroitly *and* appropriately located within the rhetoric and reality of the burgeoning structural parameters of value via the fetishised focus on the use-value of *tivaivai* as bedspreads, belied her sanctioned, pragmatic Wagneresque invention of culture (Wagner 1981 [1975]).

That the sale put a price, and a high one at that, on the previously ambiguous realm of *tivaivai* production was significant. The process meant that the monetary value (cf. Turner 1979; Graeber 2001: 1–2) of *tivaivai taorei* in particular was publicly organised by Māmā Vereara, on her terms specifically and in Cook Island terms generally. She indicated in the *Cook Islands News* article that other *tivaivai* could be measured in price against the one she sold. When I was back in Auckland a few months later, I heard conversations to that effect, which showed exactly how that had happened.

I often visited another *Va'inetini* in South Auckland that met regularly at a pre-schooler *Punanga Reo* (language nest). The women there all had children, grandchildren, nieces or nephews at the centre, and were as often as not looking after the children while their sons and daughters were in paid employment. The Cook Islands early education teacher who ran the centre saw it as a logical progression that the Māmās would meet to make *tivaivai* in the same environment, in and around the children, while the latter learnt Rarotongan, because fostering language was about fostering culture. The group had a small amount of funding from Creative New Zealand to make and market framed pieces of embroidered and piecework *tivaivai*. One day, in late July 2001, I was driving Māmā Tu and Māmā Vaerua to the regular Wednesday meeting of the Tiare Maori Va'inetini when they both suggested that we go to the Mangere Town Centre on the way, to see the launch display of the framed pictures in the middle of the shopping centre.

The *Punanga Reo* women had about ten framed pieces of *tivaivai* mounted on easels; there was also a trestle table that had two *tivaivai tātaura* with matching pillows for sale, as well as various pillow cases, a *tivaivai manu*, and some hand-crocheted table cloths. Above one of the easels was a sign that stated the name of the group, and where their funding had come from. The conditions of sale, as in 'cash up front', were listed beside this. There was another small notice that said the designs were all 'copyright'. Each frame had a card taped to the corner which listed the title, the name of the person who cut and designed it and the name of the sewer. The prices were not shown, but one of the Māmās had a folder with a list of the prices of each frame. The prices were set by each woman, and varied widely according to what the individual woman thought her work was worth. One *tātaura* piece of embroidered flowers was priced at around NZ$400, another *taorei* piece which one of the women had sewn the night before the framing was to take place because they needed an extra piece to make up the numbers was priced at NZ$1,800. I asked the woman why it was priced so high and she said that 'one like that sold in Raro for NZ$10,000'. Keane (2001: 66) contends that 'the growing availability of alternative regimes of value can give heightened visibility to certain cultural assumptions' or, as in the case of *tivaivai*, extend the regimes of value that it operates in, which is exactly what happened here. The framed piece did not sell for NZ$1,800, the woman eventually dropped the price, but that the women were getting a sense of the monetary value of *tivaivai* was exactly as Māmā Vereara had anticipated when she was quoted as saying 'The money is in their hands' (Bataillard 2001). This was the emerging market for *tivaivai*.

Conclusion

When I was in Rarotonga in 2010 for the Pacific Arts Association Symposium, the meeting organisers commissioned an exhibition of *tivaivai*. Some twenty quilts were assembled from various sources, including The Rarotongan Beach Resort and Spa. Māmā Vereara's *tivaivai taorei* was the centre piece of the exhibition. This was the first time I had had a chance to look at the *tivaivai taorei* that sold for NZ$10,000 up close properly, and I was amazed to see that there was an error in the pattern at the centre of the large *tivaivai* where a set of four squares were out of sequence. While the error was small, it was now obvious to me – as it would have been to others. Because of the symmetry of the *tivaivai*, such an error would always be negatively noted by other Cook Islands women. That the *tivaivai* was less than perfect should have dictated a lesser value in a commercial process too. But that this was not the case was because the imperfection was merely a small feature of the profile and context of that particular *tivaivai taorei*; who made it, who bought it, why and how, were what singularised that *tivaivai*. Māmā Vereara's capacity to circulate value and operate within what Turner (2006, 2008) calls the structural parameters of value via *tivaivai* as semiotic media of value, on multiple levels, meant that she possessed the capacity to influence because she was recognised as having significant *mana* to be able to do so. That she was ultimately able to translate this into money, without generating animosity or detracting from herself as an expert in *tivaivai*, was about her *mana*, which was derived from her capacity to be recognisably efficacious in the universe brought into being by the Cook Islands parameters of value, her performance of Cook Islands values, and her skill in the production and use of *tivaivai* as valuables.

Acknowledgements

I would like to thank Māmā Vereara Maeva-Taripo and Liz Raizis for agreeing to speak to me about the extraordinary *tivaivai taorei*. I am also grateful for the post-doctoral scholarship awarded to me by the Kate Edgar Educational Trust which provided financial support while I wrote this chapter.

Notes

1. The Cook Islands lie 3,270 km to the north-east of New Zealand, in a broad band of 15 low-lying atolls and mountainous islands that sit between Tahiti to the east of the group and Samoa to the west. In terms of population spread, only about 20,000 (Cook Islands Statistics Office 2006) Cook Islanders reside in the island homelands, while some 61,839 Cook Islanders live in New Zealand (Statistics New Zealand 2013). Of these, at least half live in Auckland, which is the biggest Polynesian city in the world, and also the biggest Cook Islands city in the world. Communities of Cook Islanders live in various cities in New Zealand, Australia and the United States, as well as other Pacific islands like Tahiti, and operate via the ritual economy as a nexus.
2. *Tivaivai* are ostensibly made as bedspreads, and while the textiles' obvious use-value is as a bed covering, to the extent that many women do decorate the beds in their homes with the textiles on at least special occasions or when guests stay, this is now far less common for Cook Islanders in New Zealand in particular. Now, *tivaivai* tend to be kept as heirlooms, partly because they are not so durable any more, because the cotton fabric used to make the textiles is of lesser quality and doesn't bear up to routine use, but also fewer women are making the textiles, so to be given one is enormously significant. But, more importantly, I argue (Horan 2012) that the most significant use-value of the textiles is as a 'wrapping' in ceremonial events, either as the gift or as decoration of the ritual venue, because of what *tivaivai* do to maintain or create relationships. There are three main types of *tivaivai*. The simplest form is the *tivaivai manu*, comprising an appliqued pattern layer cut from a single piece of cloth and sewn to a base layer. *Tivaivai tātaura* also comprise a top pattern layer sewn to a base layer, but several different coloured fabrics are used and the textile is embellished with varying amounts of embroidery. The most elite *tivaivai* are considered to be the *tivaivai taorei*. These are made in the patchwork style and the finest examples consist of thousands of tiny squares laboriously hand-stitched together in an intricate symmetrical pattern.
3. The ethnography in this chapter is derived from the fieldwork I did for my PhD thesis. It was conducted in Auckland with several visits to the Cook Islands and Australia between November 1999 and November 2002. However, because I

live in 'my field' I have ongoing friendships and research relationships with a number of my participants.

4. Simmel in turn, has argued that the impersonality and anonymity of money coalesces well with the impersonal and inconsequential relationships which are characteristic of the marketplace that operates under such principles. He contended that money changes the way people think, is anathema to bonds of kinship and the other ascriptive criteria that hold people together, ultimately sundering person from object (Simmel 2011 [1907]: 332–37; cf. Bloch and Parry 1989: 5). Simmel contended that while the gift of an object effectively carried with it an element of the giver (cf. Mauss 1990 [1925]), exchange relations are 'more completely dissolved and more radically terminated by the payment of money' (Simmel 1978: 376, quoted in Bloch and Parry 1989: 5). According to Simmel, money destroys community, depersonalising and neutralising social relationships with a distancing objectivity that is supposedly in marked contrast to non-monetary processes (Simmel 2011 [1907]; cf. Bloch and Parry 1989: 6).
5. Cook Islanders wrap that which is valuable to signify and notify: people and ceremonial event venues with *tivaivai* and other lesser textiles (Kaeppler 2007), and money as a lesser valuable in an envelope.
6. The only exception would be the *'ei* (neck wreath) that are used to bedeck the initiate during a haircutting or at a 21st birthday celebration, which are generally made from coloured artificial flowers and sweets, and can feature cash notes of various denominations as part of the adornment. But in this instance money is a form of decoration (Graeber 1996) rather than money out-in-the-open (Horan forthcoming).
7. A *tere parti* is a group of people travelling together for reasons such as attending a family reunion or sport competitions.
8. Going rates for the various *tivaivai* at the time were: tacked but not sewn *tivaivai manu* were sold for around NZ$250, a fully hand-sewn, finished *tivaivai manu* is priced in the vicinity of NZ$600–NZ$800 and up to NZ$1,000, but one woman told me she sewed a *tivaivai manu* for a friend for NZ$400. A *tivaivai tātaura* would go for around NZ$1,000–NZ$1,200 or more, depending on the amount of embroidery on it. *Tivaivai taorei* are seldom offered for sale, but one that I did see for sale was a smaller handmade *taorei* made from diamond shapes and was offered for NZ$800.
9. The five women who were asked to sell *tivaivai* at the Trade Fair event were not all in the same *tivaivai* group, but their individual groups were affiliated to CIANGO, which is more of an umbrella organisation that represents a range of NGOs (non-government organisations) in bigger Pacific-wide and world-wide forums, as well as helping the so-called 'on the ground' groups function logistically. CIANGO is a not-for-profit organisation and is a laudable institution in its goals and aims. Māmā Vereara Maeva at the time was employed as the president of CIANGO.

10. To put the purchase of the *tivaivai* by The Rarotongan in context, the collecting and displaying of exemplary Pacific Islands quilts by exclusive tourist resorts was a precedent set by the best resorts in Hawai'i. A form of patronage of the local arts, such collecting was also an effective marketing and profiling strategy that added prestige to the resort and allows guests to get a sense of the locale. Having *tivaivai* gave the resort *mana* too.
11. The quality of a *tivaivai* is judged by both the maker and others, by the evenness and neatness of the sewing, as well as the choice of colours and the pattern execution. I routinely saw women at *tivaivai* shows walk up to a *tivaivai* being displayed and flick the corner over to look at the evenness of the sewing on the reverse side. When a *taorei* is sewn by a group of women, the challenge is to maintain the same tension and seam allowance to avoid puckering and unevenness. That there was no evidence of this in Māmā Vereara's *tivaivai* was testament to her skill and that of the other women who helped her sew it.

References

Appadurai, A.1986. Introduction: Commodities and the politics of value. In A. Appadurai (ed.) *The Social Life of Things: Commodities in Cultural Perspectives*. Cambridge: Cambridge University Press, pp. 3–63.

Bataillard, N. 2001. Intricate *tivaevae* fetches huge price. *Cook Islands News*, 10 April.

Bloch, M. and J. Parry. 1989. Introduction: Money and the morality of exchange. In J. Parry and M. Bloch (eds) *Money and the Morality of Exchange*. Cambridge: Cambridge University Press, pp. 1–32.

Buse, J. (with R. Taringa). 1995. *Cook Islands Maori Dictionary*, edited by B. Biggs and R. Moeka'a. Ministry of Education, Government of the Cook Islands; School of Oriental and African Studies, University of London; Institute of Pacific Studies, University of Auckland; Pacific Linguistics, Research School of Pacific and Asian Studies, The Australian National University.

Cook Islands Statistics Office. 2006. *Cook Islands Census of Population and Dwellings 2006*. Available at: http://www.stats.gov.ck/statistics/censussurveys/censurvnav.htmCook islands (accessed 20 July 2010).

Fajans, J. 1993. Introduction, exchanging products: Producing exchange. In J. Fajans (ed.) *Exchanging Products: Producing Exchange*. Oceania Monographs, University of Sydney, pp. 1–14.

Gell, A. 1998. *Art and Agency: An Anthropological Theory*. Oxford: Clarendon Press.

Graeber, D. 1996. Beads and money: Notes towards a theory of wealth and power. *American Ethnologist* 23: 1–32.

—— 2001. *Toward and Anthropological Theory of Value: The False Coin of Our Own Dreams*. New York: Palgrave.

—— 2005. Value: Anthropological theories of value. In J. Carrier (ed.) *The Handbook of Economic Anthropology*. Cheltenham: Edward Elgar, pp. 439–54.

—— 2012. On social currencies and human economies: some notes on the violence of equivalence. *Social Anthropology* 20(4): 411–28.
—— 2013. It is value that brings universes into being. *Hau: Journal of Ethnographic Theory* 3(2): 219–43.
Gudeman, S. 2001. *The Anthropology of Economy: Community, Market and Culture*. Malden, MA: Blackwell.
—— 2008. *Economy's Tension: The Dialectics of Community and Market*. New York: Berghahn Books.
—— 2009. Necessity or contingency: Mutuality and market. In C. Hann and K. Hart (eds) *Market and Society: The Great Transformation Today*. Cambridge: Cambridge University Press, pp. 17–38.
Hann, C. and K. Hart. 2011. *Economic Anthropology: History, Ethnography, Critique*. Cambridge: Polity Press.
Hart, K. and C. Hann. 2009. Introduction: Learning from Polanyi 1. In C. Hann and K. Hart (eds) *Market and Society: The Great Transformation Today*. Cambridge: Cambridge University Press, pp. 1–17.
Horan, J. 2011. *Tivaivai* and value in the Cook Islands ritual economy: The creation of value, values, and valuables in a diasporic community. In W. Little and P. McAnany (eds) *Textile Economies: Power and Value from the Local to the Transnational*. New York: Altamira Press, pp. 57–76.
—— 2012. *Tivaivai in the Cook Islands Ceremonial Economy: An Analysis of Value*. PhD thesis, University of Auckland.
—— 2013. *Tivaivai* and the managing of 'community' funding in Auckland, New Zealand. In F. McCormack and K. Barclay (eds) *Engaging with Capitalism: Cases from Oceania, Research in Economic Anthropology*, vol. 33. Bingley: Emerald Group, pp. 83–106.
—— (forthcoming) Cook Islands *tivaivai* and the haircutting ceremony in Auckland: Ritual action, money, and the parameters of value. In A.-K. Hermkens and K. Lepani (eds) *Women's Wealth in the Contemporary Pacific: Gender, Value and Moral Economies*. Canberra: ANU-EPress.
Kaeppler, A. 2007. Containers of divinity. *Journal of the Polynesian Society* 116(2): 97–130.
Keane, W. 2001. Money is no object: Materiality, desire, and modernity in an Indonesian society. In F.R. Myers (ed.) *The Empire of Things: Regimes of Value and Material Culture*. Santa Fe: School of American Research Press, pp. 65–90.
Kopytoff, I. 1986. The cultural biography of things: Commoditization as process. In A. Appadurai (ed.) *The Social Life of Things: Commodities in Cultural Perspective*. Cambridge: Cambridge University Press, pp. 64–91.
Loomis, T.M. 1983. The Cook Islands haircutting ritual as practised in New Zealand. *Journal of the Polynesian Society* 92(2): 215–32.
Marx, K. 1961. *Capital*, vol. 1. Moscow: Foreign Languages Publishing House.
Mauss, M. 1990 [1925]. *The Gift: The Form and Reason for Exchange in Archaic Societies*. New York: W.W. Norton.

Polanyi, K. 2001 [1944]. *The Great Transformation: The Political and Economic Origins of Our Time*. Boston, MA: Beacon Press.

Robbins, J. and D. Akin. 1999. An introduction to Melanesian currencies: Agency, identity and social reproduction. In D. Akin and J. Robbins (eds) *Money and Modernity: State and Local Currencies in Melanesia*. Pittsburgh: University of Pittsburgh Press, pp. 1–40.

Simmel, G. 2011 [1907]. *The Philosophy of Money*, with a Foreword by C. Lemert. London: Routledge.

Statistics New Zealand. 2013. *Census QuickStats about culture and identity/Pacific peoples ethnic group*. Available at: http://www.stats.govt.nz/Census/2013-census/profile-and-summary-reports/quickstats-culture-identity/pacific-peoples.aspx (accessed 17 May 2014).

Turner, T. 1979. Anthropology and the politics of indigenous peoples' struggles. *Cambridge Anthropology* 5: 1–43.

—— 2006. Kayapo values: An application of Marxian value theory to a non-commodity based system of production. Unpublished manuscript.

—— 2008. Marxian value theory: An anthropological perspective. *Anthropological Theory* 8(1): 43–56.

Wagner, R. 1981[1975]. *Invention of Culture*. Chicago: University of Chicago Press.

2

Value and the Art of Deception

Public Morality in a Papua New Guinean Ponzi Scheme

John Cox

Introduction

Ponzi scams typically work by paying early investors with money from new recruits. This creates a short-term spectacle of wealth that draws in new investors with a sense of urgency and excitement. However, the pyramid then quickly collapses, leaving later investors bewildered at the loss of their money. Whereas popular accounts have ridiculed these dupes for their greed and gullibility, anthropologists have seen scams as windows into broader social and economic transformations (e.g. Verdery 1995; Apter 1999; Bornstein 1999; Tsing 2000; Smith 2007; Musaraj 2011).

In this chapter, I use the example of U-Vistract, the large and enduring Ponzi scam (or 'fast money scheme' in the local idiom) from Papua New Guinea (PNG), to show how scams articulate underlying social dynamics. Indeed this process of articulation is fundamental to the practice of deception: scams must draw on existing social norms in order to appear legitimate to their investors.

In the PNG case, the success of U-Vistract can be attributed in part to its capacity to assemble a spectacle of wealth (by paying cash to early investors). However, the scheme's plausibility rested on a parallel ethical project. In this latter aspect of the scheme, members were encouraged to imagine themselves as engaging in ambitious financial practices that would bring about the Christian renewal of the nation. In doing so, investors were deceived, not so much by their individual greed for money, as by their underlying aspirations for communitarian development.

In order to explore the dynamics of this prolonged and manipulative process of deception critically, I turn to Robert Foster's (2007, 2008, 2013) work on value, brands and commodity chains. Foster argues that the value of corporate brands is created not simply by clever marketers but also by the 'consumption work' (Miller 1987) of consumers. The concept of consumption work recognises that surplus value is not only created by labour in the process of production but is also generated by the affective use-value created by consumers (Foster 2008: 14). Inspired by Foster's approach, I outline several implications of seeing U-Vistract as a 'brand', the value of which is jointly created by the fraudsters behind the scheme and their unwitting 'investors'.

Ponzi Scams and Fast Money Schemes in PNG

Ponzi schemes create a spectacle of wealth, paying early investors large amounts of money. As was the case with the PNG fast money schemes, word spreads quickly. Before too long, there are queues of people waiting to deposit their money. The spectacle of queues itself adds to the momentum: more and more join from curiosity or a fear of missing out on the millions available. These latter investors do not realise that they have been duped into funding the payments to earlier investors and that their deposits will not be returned to them. This is a conventional account of Ponzi schemes. Though not altogether wrong, it misses much of the social texture of the events described.

Ponzi and pyramid scams have operated in PNG since the colonial period (Stent 1977) and have recently resurfaced in numbers in Port Moresby (Radio Australia 2015). However, they came to particular prominence in 1999 as a wave of 'fast money schemes' washed over the capital, Port Moresby, drawing in thousands of investors, not least the educated middle class and their patrons in politics and the higher levels of the public service (Cox 2013). Many of these 'elites', as town-dwellers with education are routinely known, were part of the scams' 'inside track' (Verdery 1995) and did receive early payments. The success of wealthy or powerful individuals became widely known and authenticated the schemes for thousands of later investors.

In the late 1990s, fast money schemes were not actually illegal in PNG. Most of the schemes in question began under the patronage of the Skate government, which exempted the schemes from the Financial Institutions Act, permitting them to take deposits from investors without supervision. The promises of 100 per cent or 200 per cent returns per month were 'too good to be true' but also too good to ignore. As I shall argue later in this chapter, the schemes also cloaked themselves in Christian prosperity rhetoric that made them too (morally) good *not* to be true.

In the following two sections I explore the dynamics of value production within fast money schemes, first in the economic sphere (where real money was recirculated to early investors in these Ponzi schemes) and then in the moral sphere (where unpaid investors were groomed to think of themselves as participating in a Christian project of national renewal). In referring to these 'spheres' my intention is to foreground the kind of discourses that animated different phases of this long-running Ponzi scam. I do not mean to imply that there are separate 'economic' and 'moral' spheres, a notion that anthropologists have shown to be deeply flawed (Akin and Robbins 1999; Parry and Bloch 1989).

Economic Spectacle

As Tsing (2000) has argued of the Bre-X mining fraud in Indonesia and Canada, scams rely on spectacle for their power to lure investors. The public nature of their performances of wealth is seen to imply transparency and legitimacy. The outrageous can be made plausible if presented as a public display of technical expertise or mastery of resources.

In the case of U-Vistract, the nature of the spectacle has changed a number of times. It began within the Bougainvillean community in Port Moresby, initially targeting well-to-do Bougainvilleans on the pretext that the scheme would rebuild the province of Bougainville after the ten-year civil war there (Regan 2010). The founder, Noah Musingku, sought out 'high level' Bougainvilleans, including the main political leaders, and made personal appeals that they found hard to refuse (Cox 2013). They in turn recruited relatives back in Bougainville. Soon the scheme also spread to non-Bougainvillean workmates, neighbours, in-laws and fellow church members, particularly those from Port Moresby's large Pentecostal congregations where the 'prosperity gospel' is a familiar teaching (Cox 2014b; see below).

The spectacle of early investors being paid large amounts of money generated a rush of new investors who were not on the 'inside track' and whose money was eventually lost. As the government closed the fast money schemes down, investors were summoned to large public meetings such as the one at Sir John Guise Stadium in 1999, where amid prayer and other elements of Christian worship, angry investors were reassured, told to have patience and then informed that the 'delays' in payment were the result of actions by a greedy, interfering and corrupt government (*The National* 1999).

In 2002, two years after being declared insolvent, U-Vistract created another public spectacle by opening 'The Royal Bank of Papala' in the downtown Port Moresby offices formerly occupied by the Bank of Hawaii. The Royal Bank of Papala was swiftly raided by police and Bank of Papua New Guinea officials and closed down. However, the story circulated widely and was reinterpreted by U-Vistract as evidence of the government's hostility to the scheme. These reiterations of public events reconfirmed for many that Musingku and his henchmen really did have some financial expertise.

The scam's critique of the PNG government extended into new declarations of sovereignty. U-Vistract was able to exploit the perennial lack of legitimacy of the PNG state (e.g. Clark 1997; Robbins 2004a; cf. Oppermann 2015) and its poor record of service delivery (Cox and Phillips 2015; Howes et al. 2014). Taking advantage of the post-conflict fragmentation of law and order in Bougainville, where the sovereignty of the PNG state is still not recognised everywhere, Musingku introduced the idea of the 'Kingdom of Papala'. The Kingdom of Papala was invented first as a Christian spiritual realm 'like the Kingdom of Heaven', and then as a physical base for the money scheme in Bougainville. This became a complicated way of weaselling into the confidence of the Bougainvillean separatist leader, Francis Ona (Cox 2013; Hermkens 2013). Ona had been an important leader of the armed conflict against the Panguna mine and the PNG government. In 1990, he had made a 'unilateral declaration of independence' as the 'Republic of Me'ekamui'. In 2004, apparently persuaded by promises of millions of Kina, Ona allowed himself to be crowned king of the 'Royal Kingdom of Me'ekamui', just as Musingku appointed himself 'King David Pei II' of the Royal Kingdom of Papala (Regan 2010). The money scheme had become a kingdom and, in gaining Ona's patronage, now had the protection of a powerful party to the Bougainville peace process.

These apparently implausible claims of sovereignty became an outrageous spectacle that allowed Musingku to set up operations in South Bougainville beyond the reach of law enforcement authorities. This has been augmented by the introduction of a new (pseudo-)currency, the Bougainville Kina (Cox 2014a). The spectacle of launching a currency – supposedly backed by (unmined) gold reserves – seems to have reassured Bougainvillean investors, rather than becoming what in cognitive dissonance theory is denominated a 'disconfirmation event' (Stone 2000): an event that disproves the claims of a cult or similar group.

Abstract Systems, Expertise and Patter

Spectacle alone is not sufficient to induce investors to part with their money. Public spectacle must be matched with more intimate performances of expertise. In the case of financial products, few investors are confident in their own financial knowledge and defer to the 'financial patter' of those seen to be experts. There is considerable mystification at play here, particularly in regard to claims that this risky financial machinery is the product of highly technical rational calculation by dispassionate and fully informed expert financial decision makers. As the anthropology of finance has shown, such calculations often emerge from highly sexist cultural environments where competitive machismo is a key driver of decisions (Miyazaki 2006; Zaloom 2006; Ho 2009). Nevertheless, financial institutions are widely perceived as rational 'abstract systems' too complex for anyone but designated experts to negotiate (Giddens 1991).

For fast money schemes like U-Vistract to represent themselves as abstract systems, they needed to perform as if they were formalised systems like banks. They therefore mimicked some of the formal processes expected of banks, such as filling in forms and providing account statements. At the scheme's height, they rented offices and impressed people with computers, a display of technological mastery that has now migrated to the internet. U-Vistract's recently decommissioned website (ibom.biz),[1] where it is rebadged as the 'International Bank of Meekamui' (IBOM), has been a testament to the scam's powers of mimesis. The website is professionally produced and repeats the anodyne patter of financial institutions everywhere: 'world class financial solutions at your doorstep'. It also contains testimonies from supposedly successful investors and even staff, as well as back issues of the *Papala Chronicles*, a newsletter containing stories of payments, new forms of investment such as 'treasury bonds' and so forth.

Photocopies of U-Vistract propaganda were circulated to investors without internet access through the scam's agents in Port Moresby and the provincial towns of PNG. These agents were usually Bougainvilleans who would build up a network of local contacts, acting as 'access points': people who help the public to negotiate the complexity and formality of abstract systems (Giddens 1991). In the early phases of the scam, local agents focused on recruiting high-profile investors who would be paid and then spread the word that the schemes really worked. After payments stopped, the role of local committees shifted to keeping investors happy by disseminating U-Vistract magazines and leaflets. Agents would organise meetings of investors to deliver the latest 'updates', reassuring them that their money was safe and would be paid to them very soon.

Personal contact with investors allowed U-Vistract to string their unpaid clients along, perhaps for years. Sometimes they would solicit new contributions for specific causes. In Madang, U-Vistract ran two additional rounds of collections within the already scammed community of investors. In 2005, they took money from existing clients to build 'the broadband network' in Bougainville that would supposedly allow them to pay investors electronically (Cox 2015). In 2008 and 2009, patient investors were asked for 'stamp duty' to process 'school fees' payments that never eventuated (Cox 2013).

Scott (1998) has made the argument about the necessity for people to become legible to the gaze of the state in order to benefit from modernist development programmes. Where Scott sees the state as the primary actor in imposing a regime of legibility, others have noted that, in many cases, people seek to make themselves legible to the state. An example from PNG is the seeking of health care in public hospitals where patients seek to make themselves visible to doctors and nurses as worthy of medical treatment (Street 2014). This process equally applies to other abstract systems beyond government such as banks (and their counterfeits). Indeed, U-Vistract investors often described banks as part of 'the government system' (cf. Foster 2002). However personable someone acting as an 'access point' may be, customers must still render themselves worthy. Indeed *the more personable* an access point is, the greater the reciprocal obligation on the customer to show that they deserve to receive the services provided. As the next section shows, U-Vistract investors had to demonstrate that they were the kind of modern persons eligible to benefit from the scheme: good Christians of moral intent.

Good Christians and Personal Disciplines

As I have argued elsewhere (Cox 2014b), U-Vistract exemplified, elicited and exploited two related modes of worthy personhood that are idealised in contemporary Melanesia. The first of these was the self-controlled Christian moral self (Robbins 2004a). The second was the thrifty (or entrepreneurial) modern financial self (Zaloom 2006; Bainton 2011; Schuster 2015). In its ingenious rhetoric and its surveillance of investors, U-Vistract combined these two tropes in ways that reassured investors that they were worthy persons who had made sound financial decisions that would ultimately be rewarded. These practices allowed U-Vistract to build its brand by incorporating the affective labours or 'consumption work' (Foster 2007; Miller 1987) of its (consumer/investor) clients.

New investors wanting to join had to produce a letter from their pastor or priest attesting to their good character. Failure to meet these expectations became an excuse for why the scheme had not paid anyone. In U-Vistract propaganda 'updates', members were told that 'the accounts of some investors and helpers were stopped because they broke the rules of the organization by engaging in immoral activities ...' or, in the same article, 'customers and investors who misuse their money and break moral rules of the Ministry have only themselves to blame if their accounts are stopped' (*Papala Chronicles* 2005). In such statements, the scheme drew on a familiar repertoire of Christian moralising often used publicly in PNG (Eves 2008). Such warnings and exhortations allowed non-compliant members to be dismissed and established a paternalistic relationship between the scheme and its investors wherein the latter had to prove their moral worthiness as self-controlled Christians.

A second theme is the application of Christian self-control to modern financial disciplines. Money can provide a moral jeopardy, tempting people to waste their resources on sinful activities. However, in the 'prosperity theology' that has widely infiltrated Pentecostal and many other churches in PNG (and beyond), money is seen as a blessing from God rewarding faithful believers for their piety. Such blessings also create obligations to use money to advance God's work in the world through tithing (routinely donating a tenth of one's income to the church) and other disciplines (Cox and Macintyre 2014). These disciplines of the contemporary Melanesian 'financial self' differ in many ways from the calculating and competitive risk-taking stockbrokers described by Zaloom (2006), but they do promote the idea that one must embrace financial risk in order to achieve returns on investments (Cox 2014b).

As Robbins (2004b) notes of the prosperity gospel in relation to older ideas of the thrifty Protestant ethic, this is a shift away from the Weberian principles of steady accumulation through saving over time (Weber 1958 [1930]). Such sober principles were promoted by the Australian colonial government in its later years as it tried to encourage saving among its Melanesian subjects in the hope of debunking 'cargo cult' expectations (Foster 1998). As Lindstrom (1993) has demonstrated, 'cargo cult' has a remarkable range of historical meanings and can be a powerful term of disparagement, either of Melanesian villagers or of financial speculators.

Others have shown how contemporary discourses of development deploy 'cargo cult' as a paternalistic way of blaming development failures on the laziness of recipients (Cox 2009; West 2001).

The new financial self is entrepreneurial and actively takes risks in anticipation of spectacular rewards. For Pentecostal Christians, the 'invisible hand of the market' is the benign hand of God revealing His plan for action in the world to the benefit of faithful Christians. The faith of financial speculators, such as those studied by Zaloom (2006) and Ho (2009), combines competitive masculinist work practices with an ideology of 'the market' as a transcendent and efficient distributor of wealth. By remaking this modern financial self as a Christian self (using the prosperity gospel), U-Vistract concealed the most morally troubling elements of self-centred capitalism and redirected its members' attention to a more worthy project: redeeming the nation (Cox 2014b).

Scales of Deception: National Development, Global Finance and Christian Reform

Scams are fundamentally about money. It is a commonplace observation that they prey on people's hopes of becoming wealthy. Yet it is a mistake to naturalise or to universalise assumptions that everyone wants to be rich. Anthropology, including many of the contributors to this volume (e.g. Barnett-Naghshineh, Horan, Presterudstuen), can produce an immense back catalogue of peoples whose economic desires are grounded in social reproduction and which critique greed and selfishness, associating these vices with wealth.

Such moral critiques of wealth are ubiquitous in PNG. They range from private conversations about the failure of relatives to contribute adequately to ritual activities or household expenses, to more public letters to newspapers or posts on blogs or Facebook that decry the ill-gotten gains of wealthy politicians and their cronies, all presumed to be corrupt. They also extend to church leaders denounced as hypocritical for their love of money; Pentecostal pastors often being a target. 'They have classes on how to make money', I was told by the (Catholic) manager of a microfinance programme referring to Pentecostals. This person thought running classes on making money was an improper activity for a church, although he himself ran very similar programmes teaching the disciplines of handling money referred to earlier (Matbob 2010; Schuster 2015).

In a 'sleight of hand' (cf. Gewertz and Errington 1999), U-Vistract turned its investors' attention from the fact that they had not been paid to the anticipation that they would be paid soon and, when they were, they would have so much money that they would not know how to spend it. As explained in *Papala Chronicles*, this placed them in a moral jeopardy. Money without appropriate discipline could lead to sinful activities, such as men leaving their wives and families (Cox and Macintyre 2014).

Like Foster's corporate brand managers, U-Vistract's directors put considerable effort into managing relationships with their clients. This is the work of surplus value creation based on the appropriation of affective labour that is of primary interest in this chapter. In addition to moral warnings, U-Vistract managed the affective connections of its investors by cultivating a positive moral vision. The scheme's moral vision had several interrelated elements. Each drew on existing themes within the broader modern social imaginary (Taylor 2004) of middle-class PNG. As Tsing (2000) describes of a mining scam in Indonesia and Canada, the art of deception can be seen as the conjunction of several intersecting 'scale-making projects'. For U-Vistract, this included a national scale, a global scale and a personal scale.

The national scale focused on the ongoing project of egalitarian 'grassroots' development across the nation. As I have documented elsewhere (Cox 2013), PNG's middle class are highly conscious of their own economic precarity (Standing 2009) in the face of climbing costs of urban living (Barbara et al. 2015; Sharp et al. 2015). They are also troubled by rural poverty, even while romanticising subsistence horticulture and village life (Golub 2014). These concerns are articulated in many public debates and private discussions and provided U-Vistract with an existing discourse to incorporate into its propaganda. Broadly speaking, this discourse bemoans the lack of services in rural areas and attributes this failure of development to corruption among public officials, especially MPs. In PNG's 'evangelical public culture' (McDougall 2013; cf. Eves et al. 2014), this critique often takes a Christian turn, with accusations of selfishness and moral laxity providing the primary interpretative framework for understanding corruption.

The global scale exploited the idea that international financial markets generate enormous wealth but are inaccessible to ordinary Papua New Guineans. This would be remedied by U-Vistract, which presented itself as a Christian reform of global financial systems designed to share the wealth of the global economy with the world's poor, beginning in PNG. U-Vistract acknowledged a global value chain of financial investment within which it promised to include its members. It then developed a parallel narrative of reform that blended popular critiques of the World Bank and other international financial institutions with ideas of Bougainville as a place of mineral wealth, Bougainvillean resistance to neocolonial capitalist exploitation, social credit theories of money and Pentecostal prosperity theology. I will not develop an analysis of these intriguing combinations here but I include below a short clipping from one of Musingku's speeches (in Peii 2005) in order to give some of the flavour of these narratives:

> Friends, co-workers and fellow citizens, Bougainville is the only nation in the world with an unborrowed currency system. She is not caught up like the rest of them in this international debt-engine/machine. She has no debts to anybody, no debts to PNG, no debts to the World Bank, IMF, ADB, Australia, etc. Whilst the rest of the world are caught up in this international debt-engine Bougainville is enjoying her freedom which she earned when she repulsed all foreign systems out from her land during the *'Bougainville-Crisis'*.

Figure 2.1 Extract from one of Musingku's speeches

This re-appropriation of the global economy was a scale-making project that offered an explanation of PNG's failure to flourish despite its endowments of natural resources that many believe should make it a 'rich country' (Cox 2013). Its explicitly Christian character also set the scheme in the context of a transnational Christian oecumene (Marshall-Fratani 2000; McDougall 2003), wherein Melanesians may imagine themselves as members of a fully modern community free from the cultural failings or corruption of their own nation (Cox and Macintyre 2014; Robbins 2004a).

The Domestic Moral Economy: Middle-Class Obligation and the Deserving Poor

At a personal scale, acquisition of wealth is related to the problems of moral jeopardy mentioned above. Christian investors were expected not to spend their money on self-centred or sinful consumption. Rather, they were to reinvest it in the moral project of developing the nation. Investors were encouraged to imagine themselves as Christian patrons, generously giving to the deserving poor and so legitimising their own privileges. I have discussed some aspects of this previously (Cox 2011; Cox and Macintyre 2014) but here I elaborate on two examples of Christian patronage: one an investor's account of being groomed by the scheme and the other an example from *Papala Chronicles*, wherein motifs of the deserving poor are used to legitimise U-Vistract.

The first example is best told in the words of a policeman from Madang named Isaac. Having been introduced to U-Vistract by a Bougainvillean colleague, Isaac invested some K24,000 over several years. He began with K1,000 of his savings: 'It was a lot of money. That's my savings – it took me three to four fortnights to save this money which I invested.' Each payday, Isaac deposited K200 or K300. This was up to half of his salary of K600 per fortnight. In doing so, he demonstrated a financial discipline that many associate with the Seventh-day Adventist church, a church of which he is an elder.

> It's from a Christian man. It's sort of a religious type of scheme and then it's coming here to help people, the poor people and then bring the poor people up to a standard where people can live in a same level … So, at the first place when they introduced it, they didn't want the money put in first, they wanted [to recruit] the poor people and [investors] must be recommended by the pastor and all this so that everybody can have the money. [This is in order to] reset the balance in the society (and all these things) where we live.
>
> And the money we get, we have to pay tithes, offering and then pay the pastor's house, mission schools and all these things. That's what they told us. We can't get the money and, you know, make problem with the family or, like putting the money into beer. They said 'no'. Those are some of the rules that U-Vistract has set. They told us, 'If you get the first payment and then come back and misuse this money, with beer and women and all these things, you will never come and join us, you just get your money and go!' That's what they said. Because it's sort of a Christian type of scheme. That's what they said. So all the things and the principles that they said – the guidelines and all these things – they are from Christian principles where we thought this was true. They were

doing it with prayer, asking in God's name, opening the door of the office with worship and all this.

In this extended interview, conducted in 2009 in Madang, Isaac shows how U-Vistract appropriated Christian practices of tithing and normative moral conduct. The scam mapped out the proper path of Christian expenditure and contrasted this ideal with another powerful trope: that of sinful (and male) drunkenness and family violence (Cox and Macintyre 2014).

Also worth noting is the discussion of the poor and the explicitly egalitarian hopes of 'resetting the balance of society' or bringing the poor up to the 'same level' as the urban middle class. This hope, which indexes the national traditions of development mentioned earlier, confirms middle-class citizens as normative modern Papua New Guineans who 'set the standard' for their less privileged compatriots (cf. Errington and Gewertz 2004: 109). However, it also implies that middle-class Papua New Guineans are more troubled by the plight of the poor and less threatened by them than Gewertz and Errington (1999) implied in their magisterial study of class distinctions in PNG. U-Vistract was successful in convincing middle-class Papua New Guineans like Isaac that, by investing in the scheme, they would be putting themselves in a position to take direct action to alleviate poverty or to 'do' development. As I shall show later, the scheme nurtured these ideals and fantasies as a way of building its brand, which depends on 'its recognition by consumers or users as a symbol of their own creative activities …' (Foster 2008: 18).

Isaac's anticipation of the poor being brought up to the level of the middle class was reflected in U-Vistract propaganda, such as the widely circulated magazine, *Papala Chronicles*. Below is a typical example. Ruth Kuripasi, a Bougainvillean woman, is profiled as being 'on the threshold of becoming an instant millionaire' (in Sapan 2005).

Here Ruth's investments in U-Vistract are presented as a work of faith. In this context, the portrayal of Ruth as 'simple' or 'simple minded' reflects not only middle-class condescension and stereotyping of the poor (Hau'ofa 1987), but Christian motifs of childlike trust and privileging faith over knowledge. Ruth's 'faith in God for the financial blessing she and her family are about to enjoy' qualifies her as a model Christian and therefore as a deserving recipient of U-Vistract's bounty. Underscoring her 'deserving poor' status, Ruth models proper Christian expenditure: she plans to

Papala Chronicles *Issue 17* "Home Views" *eek Ending, Friday 14th October 2005* 3

Thank God for my millions

BY TONY SAPAN

Fourty(40) year old Ruth Kuripasi of Kakotokori village may be a simple Siwai mother who could hope for nothing more than the average village based mother can hope for, for her young family of school age children.

Having faith and hope for a better future for her young family is strengthened by her undivided belief that what ever she and her family can hope for in life, is from none other than God Almighty, the creator of all things.

Ruth is on the threshold of becoming an instant millionaire and she knows it without any reasonable doubt that she will become one as long as she locks her faith in God for the financial blessing she and her family are about to enjoy.

She has just invested K100,000 from her Access Account at the Royal International Bank of Meekamui into treasury bills on the way to become a millionaire as long as she is prepared to stake not only her life but that of her entire family on the investment. For this she heaps praise on the good Lord for this life long blessing.

Happy Ruth Kuripasi and Emily Hurokori

She acknowledges the support and guidance of the King of the Royal Kingdom of Papala, His Royal Highness King David Pei II for the support, guidance and motivating to her and her fellow villagers into investing what ever little they had into this life long investment in God's bank of abundance.

Ruth may be simple minded, but knowing that what her family is in for in terms of the financial blessings they are about to enjoy through her connection with the U-Vistract and its Founder and Principal Director is the best thing that has ever happened in her entire family.

A devote United Church follower Ruth Kuripasi has plans to put some of the money she hopes to earn from her RCBM treasury bills investment into assisting orphans and widows in her village.

"Any other worthwhile village development initiatives that are implemented for the common good of all citizens including programs to enhance the spiritual well being of citizens, will also get my full support" Ruth said.

Ruth is among the first recipients of this life long financial blessing courtesy of the God given UV monetary and banking system to come out publicly to express her thanks for the assistance. *pc*

Little millionaires

...cont from page 1

Rossie was only a suckling when her father was killed by the BRA in 1996.

Other two little ones to become millionaires are Charlie Michael (11 years) and Ishmael Sipari (aged 9) both from Motirui village

Figure 2.2 'Thank God for my millions'

assist the 'orphans and widows in her village'. Orphans and widows are of course the biblical prototype of the deserving poor but also a visible reality in post-conflict Bougainville. With stories such as this, written in English and circulated to a middle-class audience around PNG, investors could see their hopes of egalitarian development being reflected back to them even as they saw them being realised through U-Vistract. As Graeber (2001: 105) puts it, 'The object of desire becomes an illusory mirror of the desirer's own manipulated intentions.' The illusory national development imagined by U-Vistract and its followers had the added convenience of not requiring urban investors to sacrifice any of their privileges or have their own finances worn down by the requests for assistance from village kin that many find so burdensome (Gewertz and Errington 1999; Cox and Macintyre 2014).

Scams, Brands and Value Chains

Foster (2007, 2008, 2013) has written about corporate branding and the affective relationships that consumers develop with such brands. He argues that these relationships are a form of labour. According to Foster, through their affective labour or consumption work, consumers have in fact become key producers of value for such commodities and that this value is represented in the brand:

> consumption work can be understood as a form of concrete labor that brands objectify; that is, a brand subsumes multiple, private, and diverse instances of consumption work and makes that work available in objective, socially recognized form: the brand and brand-name product. (Foster 2013: 51)

The value produced by consumers' affective labour accrues principally to the corporations that have legal ownership of particular brands. Corporations themselves are conscious of this value-creating relationship with their customers. Some are beginning to describe their brands as 'love marks' in an attempt to reflect the importance of affective relationships between consumers, commodities and the corporations that (co-)produce them. These relationships operate as a form of 'keeping-while-giving' (Weiner 1992).

There is a close parallel to the processes of affective co-production that Foster describes and the workings of PNG fast money schemes that I have described above. Like the value of corporate brands, fast money schemes are not simply produced by workers, in this case the fraudster Noah Musingku and his cronies. Rather, the dupes of such scams also have a role in co-producing value as they engage with the promises of wealth offered by the schemes. In exploring these dynamics, my intention is not to blame the victims (and is certainly not to exonerate the fraudsters), but to show how the illusion of value is jointly created by both parties (even if unwittingly) within the workings of the art of deception.

The first step in applying Foster's value chain analysis is to establish that fraudulent investment is a type of commodity. Scams have an insubstantial nature, pretending to be what they are not, relying on deceit and illusion and so generating a spectacular 'economy of appearances' (Tsing 2000). There is of course a material base to such economies of appearances, even if this is merely paper forms to be filled in, computer print-outs or websites.

However, scams lack some of the material qualities of the kinds of 'things' whose circulation and exchange has inspired a generation of scholars since Appadurai's (1986) collection. Similarly, while there is some labour on the part of the fraudsters in terms of producing propaganda, organising meetings and courting investors, the illusory rewards that fast money schemes promise their investors is primarily work of the imagination, not the 'sweat of thy brow' (Genesis 3:19).

Instead of focusing on the materiality or labour-derived value of scams, I turn to what might be considered their use-value as a way of arguing that scams are a type of commodity. This argument is specific to the fast money schemes I have studied but could also be adapted for financial products more generally. The purchase of fraudulent financial products in a sense is the purchase of nothing at all, a mere deception. However, for the purchasers, the receipts and account statements or the reassuring meetings and newsletters have a kind of use-value. This use-value is not practical but is affective in nature. It makes the members of the scheme feel differently about their financial situation (and possibly other elements of their lives through flow on effects) because of their purchase of an (albeit fraudulent) investment product. The apparently worthless receipts and fake account statements that investors receive take on a powerful symbolic value as they are mistaken for representations of money 'as a repository of value' and therefore objects that symbolise 'accumulation in and of itself' (Turner 2008: 51; cf. Corrigan 1997: 34). However, they are not merely misrecognised tokens of a 'universal commodity' but are 'singularised' (Kopytoff 1986: 76) by being incorporated into investors' moral narratives of self and nation.

What I am describing as an affective use-value here also relates to Foster's description of consumption work by consumers that generates value for corporate brands. As corporations appropriate their consumers' consumption work into their brands, so scams appropriate, nurture and profit from their victims' expectations. Investors in U-Vistract have lost their money and so are victims of deception. Nevertheless, by buying into the promises of the scam, they unwittingly find a certain moral use-value in the hopes for personal and national prosperity. Part of the affective use-value as experienced by U-Vistract members is that they feel less excluded from the global financial system: through investing in U-Vistract, they have the illusion of being included in the circuits of wealth that other nations are already benefitting from. Thus their purchase of an illusory market commodity still gives them 'purchase' in the market economy, in the sense of being able to imagine themselves as participating in economic life from an advantageous position. Investing in U-Vistract then provides an example of Turner's reading of Marx's fetishism of commodities, where capitalism produces its own fundamental deceptions:

> the media of representation of value tend to become objects of accumulation in their own right and thereby promote the development of forms of social consciousness based on the alienation of subjective awareness of the real source of value in human (social) productivity. (Turner 2008: 54)

For U-Vistract investors, these fantasies of accumulation were reconfirmed in participation in lively Pentecostal church services celebrating the prosperity gospel, in moral self-surveillance and practices of tithing (Cox and Macintyre 2014: 144–47) and in reading the scheme's propaganda and imagining a prosperous PNG freed from corruption and poverty (Cox 2011). Like Fijians who bet on Australian horse races, for many investors U-Vistract is 'a key activity through which [they] perform modernity' (Presterudstuen 2014: 262). U-Vistract investors believed that they were participating in something global, where the source of value was exogenous and where they could escape from a more constraining Melanesian moral economy.

Chains of Accrual, Renewal and Distribution of Value

I wish to develop two further points from Foster's analysis of value chains that can be used to understand the processes of value creation that are at work in fast money schemes. These relate to questions of to whom the value created in a value chain accrues, how value is distributed across the chain and how the value needs to be continually renewed.

The first point that I wish to develop is Foster's insight that, in collaborative works of value creation, surplus value is distributed unevenly. Corporations do not only profit from appropriating the manual labour of producers of commodities, nor simply from sales of increasing volumes of commodities, they also appropriate the consumption work of consumers whose affective attachment to branded commodities builds the market value of the brand. The brand then becomes an objectification of consumption work (Foster 2007: 718). Consumers may purchase ownership of particular commodities but, in the process, corporations build the prestige of their brands, appropriating the value that the consumers have helped to create.

Drawing on Melanesianist anthropological traditions (Munn 1986; Weiner 1992; Godelier 1999) Foster (2008: 16–17) argues that 'the sale and use of branded commodities appears ... as a form of keeping-while-giving'. The exchanges of the classic *kula* trade allow the rise (or fall) of the fame of the givers of valuables. They do so by establishing 'trustworthy connections between kula partners' (Foster 2008: 18), which allow the value created through these exchanges to increase and to return to the giver. A similar process is at work in corporate brands, where the value created in commercial exchange accrues to the corporation, both in the sale of the commodity to the consumer and in the building of the value of the brand itself. This accrues principally to the corporation as owner of the brand, rather than the consumer, and so marks a break from the *kula* analogy. Whereas corporations derive profits from selling products and owning brands, consumers may enjoy the use-value of a brand, particularly where the consumption of a particular branded product raises the status or prestige of the user.

The value of a brand, like *kula* valuables, can rise or fall. Brands require continual renewal as symbols of the creative labours of consumers in order to maintain consumers' engagement in the process of value creation (and purchase of commodities). As Foster (2008: 18) puts it, 'the value of a brand is never assured'. For this brand value to be sustained it cannot become detached from the sale of commodities and so requires continual renewal in the minds of consumers in order to elicit further purchases. For the renewal of the brand to be effective, consumers must continue to see the brand 'as a symbol of their own creative activities' (Foster 2008: 18). To Foster's 'creative activities', I would also add that consumers often purchase particular brands so as to associate themselves with a particular set of social values in the eyes of others (for example, in wanting to appear fashionable to their peers) or because they see the brand as embodying their own moral, religious, political or social values (as in the case of 'fair trade' coffee). Of course, the latter need not exclude the former (West 2012). In the U-Vistract case, the brand allowed consumers to feel that they were responsible Christian citizens, demonstrating both their competence in financial management and their good intentions for the development of the nation.

Foster's argument provides a convincing explanation of why U-Vistract has kept re-inventing itself. It is a brand that requires renewal in order for its consumers to see their own agency reflected in it. Originally 'the Bank for Bougainvilleans', targeted at the Bougainvillean diaspora in Port Moresby, it opened up to allow others to become members. This, however, was in the 'spectacle' phase, when new investors were responding to stories of payments and joined the scheme in numbers. As the scheme ran out of excuses for why the money they had promised to pay people had not materialised, they renewed the brand by increasing the Christian messages around the scheme and by introducing the concept of the 'Kingdom of Papala'. This kingdom was initially presented as a 'spiritual realm, like the Kingdom of Heaven' but provided something of a base in pseudo-sovereignty when Musingku went to Honiara and tried to scam the Solomon Islands government using the rubric of the 'Royal Assembly of Nations and Kingdoms'. After this offer was rejected Musingku, on the run from PNG authorities moved back to Bougainville and again rebranded the scheme as 'the Royal Kingdom of Papala', supposedly a 'Twin Kingdom' with the 'Kingdom of Me'ekamui', Francis Ona's separatist group. Since then the scheme has come up with a number of new names. Its main website presents it as 'the International Bank of Meekamui (IBOM)', a moniker which has had some success in scamming American and Australian investors through complicated fraudulent networks. IBOM has also announced the launch of a new (fake) currency, the Bougainville Kina (Cox 2014a). It reports to its dupes that they have accounts worth millions of dollars of this actually worthless and unexchangeable pseudo-currency.

These complicated twists and turns make little sense to those convinced that the U-Vistract brand (or its Kingdom of Papala or IBOM rebrands) are simply fraud. However, to those investors still engaged in the work of maintaining a use-value for the brand (by continuing to believe that one day they will be paid), this continual rebranding is an effective sign that 'things are happening'. The 'updates' shared with local clients' committees become 'news' – information linking its hearers to a broader Christian narrative of the purposeful unfolding of time (Robbins 2004a: 165ff.). In this way, the scheme manages to prolong the symbolic use-value (Corrigan 1997) of its brand with its consumers, even though the benefit has already been accrued. With the collapse of the scheme's ability to make payments to its investors, any exchange-value of the brand is lost (to both fraudsters and investors, even as the former continue in their attempts to recruit new victims). Only the affective value now remains to be appropriated. For the fraudsters to continue to extract value from the U-Vistract brand, they must continually renew it by rebranding the scheme and so appropriating the affective labours of their investors.

The second observation of Foster's (following Appadurai 1986) that I wish to explore here is that as value is created and appropriated across large distances, a far-flung moral economy is created that links producers, corporations and consumers into a shared social world. Accounts of this moral economy may diverge radically, depending on the position of participants within it. In the case of corporate branding, this may allow corporations to accrue value for themselves by exploiting both producers and consumers' ignorance of how a product is used or made (Foster 2008: 20).

U-Vistract provides a fascinating case of this exploitation of participants' gaps in knowledge. This is not simply because the scheme lies to people and so deliberately creates ignorance through its own acts of deception. The 'how' of U-Vistract's operations is intriguing because of its awareness of how financial globalisation creates an international moral economy that Papua New Guineans are aware of but, for the most part, feel they do not benefit from. In its patter about investment, U-Vistract invoked global institutions, such as the New York and London stock exchanges or the World Bank. For PNG's middle class (and many others besides), these are institutions where great wealth is created and kept: they are the very places in the global economy whence one would expect money to originate. Yet knowledge of these nodes in the global financial system creates a problem of moral economy: if there is so much wealth in the global economy, why are Papua New Guineans missing out? Many middle-class Papua New Guineans believe that any surplus value produced by the nation's economy is being appropriated by foreign capitalists (with the assistance of corrupt local elites).

U-Vistract nurtured this (entirely reasonable) moral critique of capitalism through two narratives about global finance. The first positioned the scam as a mediator between PNG investors and international institutions. I explained earlier how the scheme presented itself as an 'access point' that would connect PNG investors with the 'abstract systems' of global finance. The second narrative was a more aggressive critique of these institutions that presented U-Vistract as a radical Christian reform of the international financial systems that are keeping the majority of the world's population poor. According to U-Vistract, these oppressive international agencies (and their PNG cronies) need to be replaced by new institutions such as the 'International Bank of Meekamui'. I have discussed the contours of this idiosyncratic 'financescape' earlier and elsewhere (Cox 2011, 2013, 2014b; Cox and Macintyre 2014), but here my point is to place this moral critique of global capitalism within the context of other capitalist value chains which also require a degree of ignorance or divergence of understanding in order for surplus economic value to be accrued. U-Vistract's genius was to exploit its investors' moral sensibilities and hopes for a more prosperous and more egalitarian nation, creating value for the scam in ways similar to those described of corporate brands. In both cases, the accrual of value to the owners of brands depends on the affective labours of consumers.

Conclusion

Scams create the illusion of wealth through deception. Like global commodity chains, the distribution of this wealth accrues unequally, with the profits captured by the owners of the scam. As I have argued above, the value of the U-Vistract brand is not a simple theft of clients' money but is also an appropriation of their affective labours. In the case of U-Vistract, this affective labour was elicited from its 'investors' in two ways. First, the scheme created an economic spectacle that demonstrated its efficacy in conjuring and distributing resources. As is the case in all Ponzi schemes, this spectacle was short-lived but it created a platform for building the U-Vistract brand through further efforts to create more enduring relationships with its members. This second phase of appropriating affective labour relied on contact with members, continually renewed through personal relationships, clients' committee meetings, Christian worship, distribution of literature, calls for new contributions. This periodic rebranding of the scheme gave the illusion of a 'forward momentum' (Miyazaki 2004) that renewed the hopes of the doubtful. As Foster describes of the interconnections between consumers, corporate brands and value chains, these relationships allowed investors to see their own affective labours reflected in U-Vistract as they worked at being worthy financial selves and good national and global Christian citizens. These hopes and practices represent the moral use-value that is the only return on their investments that U-Vistract members were going to see. In the meantime, U-Vistract had taken their money and used their moral engagement with the brand as a means of concealing this deception by diverting investors' attention away from the scam to the failings of the PNG government or their own moral shortcomings.

Notes

1. On 4 July 2015, the ibom.biz website suddenly closed, having been the face of the U-Vistract scam for ten years. Musingku has set up several other websites and has posted a video explanation of the closure on www.international bankofmeekamui.com. Possible reasons for the closure may include a falling out between Musingku and the Dutch national who originally set up the site or perhaps the server responsible has realised that they are hosting a scam website.

References

Akin, D. and J. Robbins (eds) 1999. *Money and Modernity: State and Local Currencies in Melanesia*. ASAO Monograph. Pittsburgh: University of Pittsburgh Press.

Appadurai, A. (ed.) 1986. *The Social Life of Things: Commodities in Cultural Perspective*. Cambridge: Cambridge University Press.

Apter, A. 1999. IBB = 419: Nigerian democracy and the politics of illusion. In J. Comaroff and J. Comaroff (eds) *Civil Society and the Political Imagination in Africa*. Chicago: University of Chicago Press, pp. 267–307.

Bainton, N. 2011. 'Are you viable?' Personal avarice, collective antagonism and grassroots development in Papua New Guinea. In M. Patterson and M. Macintyre (eds) *Managing Modernity in the Western Pacific*. St Lucia: University of Queensland Press, pp. 31–59.

Barbara, J., J. Cox and M. Leach. 2015. The emergent middle classes in Timor-Leste and Melanesia: Conceptual issues and developmental significance. State Society and Governance in Melanesia Discussion Paper 2015/4. Canberra: Australian National University.

Borenstein, E. 1999. Public offerings: MMM and the marketing of melodrama. In A.M. Barker (ed.) *Consuming Russia: Popular Culture, Sex and Society since Gorbachev*. Durham, NC: Duke University Press, pp. 49–75.

Corrigan, P. (1997) *The Sociology of Consumption: An Introduction*. London: Sage.

Cox, J. 2009. Active citizenship or passive clientelism: Accountability and development in Solomon Islands. *Development in Practice* 19(8): 964–80.

—— 2011. Prosperity, nation and consumption: Fast money schemes in Papua New Guinea. In M. Patterson and M. Macintyre (eds) *Managing Modernity in the Western Pacific*. St Lucia: University of Queensland Press, pp. 172–200.

—— 2013. The magic of money and the magic of the state: Fast money schemes in Papua New Guinea. *Oceania* 83(3): 175–91.

—— 2014a. Fake money, Bougainville politics and international scammers. *State, Society and Governance in Melanesia In Brief* 2014/7. Canberra: Australian National University.

—— (2014b) 'Fast money schemes are risky business: Gamblers and investors in a Papua New Guinean Ponzi Scheme', *Oceania* 84(3): 289–305.

—— (2015). Israeli technicians and the post-colonial racial triangle in Papua New Guinea. *Oceania* 85(3): 342–58.

Cox, J. and M. Macintyre. 2014. Christian marriage, money scams and Melanesian social imaginaries. *Oceania* 84(2): 138–57.

Cox, J. and G. Phillips. 2015. Sorcery, Christianity and the decline of medical services. In M. Forsyth and R. Eves (eds) *Talking it Through: Responses to Sorcery and Witchcraft Beliefs and Practices in Melanesia*. Studies in State and Society in Melanesia. Canberra: ANU Press, pp. 37–54.

Errington, F. and D. Gewertz. 2004. *Yali's Question: Sugar, Culture and History*. Chicago: University of Chicago Press.

Eves, R. 2008. Cultivating Christian civil society: Fundamentalist Christianity, politics and governance in Papua New Guinea. *State Society and Governance in Melanesia Discussion Paper* 2008/8. Canberra: Australian National University.

Eves, R., N. Haley, R. May, J. Cox, P. Gibbs, F. Merlan et al. 2014. Purging parliament: A new Christian politics in Papua New Guinea? *State Society and Governance in Melanesia Discussion Paper* 2014/1. Canberra: Australian National University.

Foster, R.J. 2002. Your money, our money, the government's money: Finance and fetishism in Melanesia. In R.J. Foster (ed.) *Materializing the Nation: Commodities, Consumption and Media in Papua New Guinea*. Bloomington: Indiana University Press, pp. 36–60.

—— 2007. The work of the new economy: Consumers, brands and value creation. *Cultural Anthropology* 22(4): 707–31.

—— 2008. Commodities, brands, love and kula: Comparative notes on value creation in honor of Nancy Munn. *Anthropological Theory* 8(9): 9–25.

—— 2013. Things to do with brands: Creating and calculating value. *Hau: Journal of Ethnographic Theory* 3(1): 44–63.

Gewertz, D. and F. Errington. 1999. *Emerging Class in Papua New Guinea: The Telling of Difference*. Cambridge: Cambridge University Press.

Godelier, M. 1999. *The Enigma of the Gift*. Chicago: University of Chicago Press.

Golub, A. 2014. *Leviathans at the Gold Mine: Creating Indigenous and Corporate Actors in Papua New Guinea*, Durham, NC: Duke University Press.

Graeber, D. 2001. *Toward and Anthropological Theory of Value: The False Coin of our Own Dreams*. New York: Palgrave.

Hau'ofa, E. 1987. The new South Pacific society: Integration and independence. In A. Hooper, S. Britton and R. Crocombe (eds) *Class and Culture in the South Pacific*. Auckland and Suva: University of Auckland and University of the South Pacific, pp. 1–15.

Hermkens, A.-K. 2013. Like Moses who led his people to the promised land: Nation- and state-building in Bougainville. *Oceania* 83(3): 192–207.

Ho, K. 2009. *Liquidated: An Ethnography of Wall Street*. Durham, NC: Duke University Press.

Howes, S., A.A. Mako, A. Swan, G. Walton, T. Webster and C. Wiltshire. 2014. *A Lost Decade? Service Delivery and Reforms in Papua New Guinea 2002–2012*. Canberra: the National Research Institute and the Development Policy Centre.

Kopytoff, I. 1986. The cultural biography of things: Commoditization as process. In A. Appadurai (ed.) *The Social life of Things: Commodities in Cultural Perspective*. Cambridge: Cambridge University Press, pp. 64–91.

Marshall-Fratani, R. 2001. The global and local in Nigerian Pentecostalism. In A. Corten and R. Marshall-Fratani (eds) *Between Babel and Pentecost: Transnational Pentecostalism in Africa and Latin America*. Bloomington: Indiana University Press, 80–105.

Matbob, P. 2010. Banking: Inculcating the culture of saving. Bringing hope to rural dwellers. *Islands Business*, February.

McDougall, D. 2003. Fellowship and citizenship as models of national community: United Church Women's Fellowship in Ranongga, Solomon Islands. *Oceania* 74(1/2): 61–80.

—— 2013. Evangelical public culture: Making stranger citizens in Solomon Islands. In M. Tomlinson and D. McDougall (eds) *Christian Politics in Oceania*. New York: Berghahn Books, pp. 122–45.

Miller, D. 1987. *Material Culture and Mass Consumption*. Oxford: Basil Blackwell.

Miyazaki, H. 2004. *The Method of Hope: Anthropology, Philosophy and Fijian Knowledge*. Stanford, CA: Stanford University Press.

—— 2006. Economy of dreams: Hope in global capitalism and its critique. *Cultural Anthropology* 21(2): 147–72.

Munn, N. 1986. *The Fame of Gawa: A Symbolic Study of Value Transformation in a Massim (Papua New Guinea) Society*. Cambridge: Cambridge University Press.

Musaraj, S. 2011. Tales from Albarado: The materiality of pyramid schemes in post-socialist Albania. *Cultural Anthropology* 26(1): 84–110.

The National. 1999. Praying for reprieve. 23 September.

Oppermann, T. 2015. Fake it until you make it: Searching for mimesis in Buka village politics. *Oceania* 85(2): 199–218.

Papala Chronicles. 2005. U-V not a finance company. *Papala Chronicles* 18: 4.

Parry, J. and M. Bloch (eds) 1989. *Money and the Morality of Exchange*. Cambridge: Cambridge University Press.

Peii, D. 2005. Welcome speech at meeting of the National Government of Bougainville. *Papala Chronicles* 20: 8.

Presterudstuen, G.H. 2014. Horse race gambling and the economy of 'bad money' in contemporary Fiji. *Oceania* 84(3): 256–71.

Regan, A. 2010. *Light Intervention: Lessons from Bougainville*. Washington, DC: United States Institute of Peace Press.

Robbins, J. 2004a. *Becoming Sinners: Christianity and Moral Torment in a Papua New Guinea Society*. Berkeley: University of California Press.

—— 2004b. The globalisation of Pentecostal and charismatic Christianity. *Annual Review of Anthropology* 33: 117–43.

Sapan, T. 2005. Thank God for my millions. *Papala Chronicles* 17: 3.
Scott, J.C. 1998. *Seeing Like a State: How Certain Schemes to Improve the Human Condition Have Failed*. New Haven, CT: Yale University Press.
Schuster, C. 2015. *Social Collateral: Women and Microfinance in Paraguay's Smuggling Economy*. Oakland, CA: University of California Press.
Sharp, T., J. Cox, C. Spark, S. Lusby and M. Rooney. 2015. The formal, the informal and the precarious: Making a living in contemporary Papua New Guinea. *State, Society and Governance in Melanesia Discussion Paper* 2015/2. Canberra: Australian National University.
Smith, D.J. 2007. *A Culture of Corruption: Everyday Deception and Popular Discontent in Nigeria*. Princeton, NJ: Princeton University Press.
Standing, G. 2011. *The Precariat: The New Dangerous Class*. London: Bloomsbury Academic.
Stone, J. (ed.) 2000. *Expecting Armageddon: Essential Readings in Failed Prophecy*. New York: Routledge.
Taylor, C. 2004. *Modern Social Imaginaries*. Durham, NC: Duke University Press.
Tsing, A. 2000. Inside the economy of appearances. *Public Culture* 12(1): 115–44.
Turner, T. 2008. Marxian value theory: An anthropological perspective. *Anthropological Theory* 8(1): 43–56.
Verdery, K. 1995. Faith, hope and caritas in the land of the pyramids: Romania, 1990 to 1994. *Comparative Studies in Society and History* 37(4): 625–99.
Weber, M. 1958 [1930]. *The Protestant Ethic and the Spirit of Capitalism*. New York: Charles Scriber's Sons.
Weiner, A. 1992. *Inalienable Possessions: The Paradox of Keeping-while-giving*. Berkeley: University of California Press.
West, P. 2001. Environmental non-governmental organizations and the nature of ethnographic inquiry. *Social Analysis* 45(2): 55–77.
—— 2012. *From Modern Production to Imagined Primitive: The Social World of Coffee from Papua New Guinea*. Durham, NC: Duke University Press.
Zaloom, C. 2006. *Out of the Pits: Traders and Technology from Chicago to London*. Chicago: University of Chicago Press.

3
Asbin
A 'Has Been' of Papua New Guinea Highlands Gift Exchange?

Olivia Barnett-Naghshineh

Introduction

I first came across *asbin* (the name for winged bean in Tok Pisin, the lingua franca of Papua New Guinea [PNG]) in the kitchen of wealthy friends in Goroka. I saw a pile of small, grubby-looking tubers on a sideboard in the otherwise glistening kitchen and asked what it was. My friend explained they were a *tumbuna* (meaning ancestral or pre-colonial in this context) crop, considered special because you can eat four different parts of the plant – the leaves, flowers, beans and tubers. A woman from my friend's village had gifted them. Despite a kitchen full of pricey imported luxuries, my friend was hugely grateful for the bunch of *asbin* she had received on her previous visit home.

Later I realised this friend was not the only one putting a high premium on this food-gift; many people in Goroka, capital of the Eastern Highlands Province in PNG, enthusiastically burst into storytelling when *asbin* is mentioned. This crop's tubers were once considered the most important gift to exchange and contributed to the status of the women who grew it. But the gift exchange of these tubers (the only part that is cooked and given in prestige contexts) is now in decline. Meanwhile money has become not just a requirement to satisfy daily needs, but also a key component of the ceremonial economy. Based on the understandings and experiences of contemporary change of my interlocutors in Goroka, I argue that as money becomes an increasingly essential part of the ceremonial economy, the impetus to grow *asbin* has waned. A highly nutritious and historic crop grown for hundreds, if not thousands, of years, and once so important that it was the ultimate currency, is thus coming closer to being extinct.

In this chapter I use oral histories of those living in Goroka and their reflections on contemporary change to give my interpretation of what has led to this crop losing its place in the ceremonial economy: people, women especially, can use their time and effort in a number of ways in a cash economy, plus the ability to use money and commodities as gifts has meant that growing *asbin* is no longer considered worthwhile. Three main sections will structure my arguments. First I introduce *asbin* and explain how it is produced and exchanged, by whom and for what purpose. The second section will outline the development of the cash economy in Goroka and the Eastern Highlands, linking this process to the introduction and growing importance of money in the local economy. Section three discusses why *asbin* is no longer grown and why people are making this choice, relating this to modern education and changing aspirations.

Let me first of all clarify my use of tenses throughout this chapter. *Asbin* is still grown in some parts of the highlands and from time to time in Goroka. Therefore I use the present tense when giving the descriptions that my interlocutors provided, and the past tense to refer to my fieldwork.

Introducing Asbin: *Em Gat Value*

As it grows, *asbin* looks like any normal bean plant growing up against stakes in rows separated by neat drains, sometimes bearing fruit or flowers. The scientific name for *asbin* is *Psophocarpus tetragonolobus* and it is commonly cultivated in parts of the world where protein is not in abundance (Kahn 1976). It grows throughout South East Asia but only develops its edible tubers at altitudes of 1,300m to 1,850m (Bourke 1982). The Eastern Highlands, ranging from 1,500m to 2,000m above sea level, and Goroka, located in a valley at about 1,700m, are thus ideal areas for its cultivation. Production is seasonal, meaning it is only consumed once in an annual agricultural cycle and generally planted in the driest months, with a nine-month gestation period. During this time, the bean plant is pruned methodically as the removal of the flowers, beans and leaves, leads to large tubers (if picked at the correct moments). Highlanders also say *asbin* is good to grow because it enriches the soil (*grisim graun*) for other crops, making sweet potatoes grow especially well.

Asbin is no longer gifted as it once was but is still said to have 'value'. People in the highlands use the term 'value' to talk about some objects and not others. 'It's got value' (*em gat value*) was a simple but weighty statement, used in a context that suggested an appreciation by all. The Tok Pisin term '*value*' refers to objects that are considered a gift, or something that is exchanged publicly. In this sense it refers to an inalienable quality that relates the object directly to the person giving it and a collectively recognised status (Mauss 2000 [1925]). Money is also said to have 'value', which I interpret to mean something similar. Money is now part of the ceremonial economy in which objects are exchanged as part of socio-political relations between groups and individuals (Gregory 1982: 19). Money has become a pervasive medium of exchange for obtaining certain luxury goods, thus contributing to its status as a ceremonial item due to its utility in other economic realms. As I will show, the reverse is true for some food crops, which become commodities because of their ceremonial status.

To a non-highlander, *asbin* could look insignificant: small, brown, and dirty after being cooked in the *mumu* (earth oven). Yet once the skin is peeled off one finds an ivory-coloured, soft and nutty inside. Many people told me that 'if you eat *asbin*, you won't need rice or sweet potato, it will fill you up until you sleep!" And indeed I did found *asbin* moreish and filling – it became my favourite food to buy in the market and be given in villages.

In a place where growing food requires hard labour and dedication, it is unsurprising that giving food that fills the stomach (and has high levels of protein and iron),[1] is highly welcome. But aside from this, *asbin* is representative of the skill and generosity of those who grow it. It was even said by some people to improve the multi-tasking abilities of those who consume it because of its multiple edible parts. Its power and status meant *asbin* could finish any conflict and ease tensions between people when exchanged. It was the ultimate food-gift.

Asbin is distinctly a woman's crop – it is taboo for men to grow it. Men are responsible for growing other ceremonial crops, including taro, sugarcane and bananas. Traditionally, the sisters and mothers of a husband give *asbin* seeds to his new wife. Today seeds are sold in small batches in the Goroka and Mount Hagen markets for little money (about PGK1, equivalent of USD0.33, for a small pile).

The production and consumption of *asbin* is thus one that requires a healthy set of social relations and has a clear gender division of labour. 'For a small food, it is a lot of hard work,' said Ben, a migrant to Goroka originally from Unggai district. Production was widely understood by both men and women to be difficult and fiddly. Being able to grow *asbin* is thought to be 'a gift' that only some have, said Ben. It takes skills, knowledge and attentiveness (and possibly a bit of magic) that not everyone possesses. The harvesting requires the help of other women. In turn, it is taboo for women to do the *mumu*, therefore cooking requires the labour of men.

Women are responsible for much of the food production and feeding of their households, and pigs, in the highlands (Godelier 1986; Sexton 1986; Strathern 1988; Sillitoe 2001). Traditionally they do not inherit land, which is held by clans and subdivided into plots for male-headed households. While men are largely responsible for organising public ceremonial exchanges between clans, women can nonetheless receive recognition and appreciation for the production of gifted items. *Asbin* is significant because not only do women gain much of the credit for growing it, but they can also gift it, either between themselves, with other families and kin groups or as part of their community. Whereas with pig kills, women gain recognition for looking after pigs but rarely host feasts or exchange pigs personally, which is how men have traditionally gained public and political status in the highlands (Meggit 1974; Godelier 1986: 14; Josephidies 1985: 172; Hide 2003).

Some people saw *asbin* as equal to pig or 'lamb flaps',[2] meaning that in the context of the ceremonial economy (and the politics of relationships that are negotiated within this), it is a gift of equal status and power. *Asbin* comes in multiple sizes but are generally about an inch or two in breadth and can be up to about four or five inches long. Some are long and slim while others are short and round. The size and shape of the tubers matters and can signal the status of the person receiving it, in relation to the giver, and contributes to the renown of the producer/giver. This is similar to the way that pig meat is distributed, with certain cuts of meat going to people of more or less status (previously the worst parts were always given to women), or according to those who had contributed to previous exchanges (Brown 1978).

Asbin differs from pig as a gift in that women are able to gift *asbin* themselves, and are also the only ones able to grow the crop due to garden taboos. *Asbin* fundamentally depends on the hard work and skill of talented women. In this way, the production of *asbin* is even more reliant on women's labour than pig production, although both require dedication and attention. In her book *The Production of Inequality*, Josephides (1985) argues that women's labour is alienated in the process of production, allowing men to gain politically from the wealth items that their wives work to produce. In the case of *asbin*, women consider this to involve a huge amount of labour, particularly compared to other crops, but they also gain public status from being able to grow it and gift it to people, while men gain recognition when cooking *asbin*. A lecturer at the University of Goroka, for instance, was proud to say he organised a large *asbin mumu* in his village to prove that he could still do what is expected of a village leader, despite living in town.[3]

Taking Asbin *to Market*

During my first week in Goroka I visited a remote village where a friend was installing a water tank. In this village I got to know Mama Apo, an outgoing and talkative woman with a cheeky grin and charming manner. Her village is on a mountain ridge between Chimbu province and Eastern Highlands, too steep to grow vegetables in large amounts but high enough for some crops to grow well. The community there were excited to hear of my interest in *asbin*. Almost nine months after my initial visit, Mama Apo insisted that I harvest some *asbin* she had planted and witness how the tubers are cooked before taking them to the market.

I learnt how backbreaking harvesting *asbin* is when working in the garden – yet Mama Apo explained that her mother would have planted double the amount she had. We cut down the dead beanstalks, removed the stakes and used coffee tree branches with purposefully shaped pointy ends, so not to damage the delicate skin as we dug up the tubers. The tubers were left underground in the garden overnight and the next day some young girls in the village returned with Mama Apo to collect them. The following night the *mumu* pit was prepared by Mama Apo's husband and young men in the village. The *mumu* was left for four hours to ensure it cooked thoroughly. It is considered a bad omen if it doesn't cook and can mean the future of the relationship between the giver and receiver will be doomed. As the *mumu* was slowly uncovered we were told the *asbin* had been perfectly cooked. The plan was to take the biggest *asbin* (tied into large bunches) to the market that day. However, the distance, lack of buses and then heavy rain meant we spent a night with relatives of Mama Apo on our way to Goroka.

Mama Apo's relatives insisted on buying all of the *asbin* from us. The previous year she had given her sisters big bunches of *asbin*. This year however they knew she intended to sell them and so agreed to buy the *asbin* at their estimated normal market price of PGK30 per bundle (about 1kg);[4] this price sufficed for an exchange between kin. The fact that the relatives were using money and agreed a price is evidence that *asbin* now lies in the realm of commodities, while nevertheless remaining a highly appreciated gift. Goddard (2000) shows, in his assessment of the gift–commodity dichotomy, that it is useful to consider how objects can be part of both types of exchange, depending on the social relationship desired, building on Appadurai's (1986: 13) argument that objects have a commodity potential depending on social context. At times I witnessed *asbin* change status from being a gift to a commodity and reversed again within a single moment, the relationships and context determining its exchange status. Each of the families that had helped Mama Apo recently were gifted a bunch of *asbin* at the *mumu* pit in the village before the majority were taken to town. The young men who collected firewood were given long, thin tubers, while children were given small round ones. People in the village told me that they thought Mama Apo was a strong and generous person.

Different Forms of Asbin *Exchange*

The exchange of food (especially) is a means of extending, expanding and managing relationships between kin and associates in the highlands, and in PNG more generally (Malinowski 1922; Godelier 1986; Sillitoe 1998; Strathern 1988). Food is transformative in that social relations are shaped by it (Fajans 1988), and it can even stand in for social relationships (Lederman 1986: 17). *Asbin* can be seen in this light. It was used for bride wealth, compensations and debt repayments (public ceremonial contexts)[5] as well as for showing gratitude between individuals (smaller day-to-day and ceremonial contexts). Older people in Goroka could recall the huge effort that went into communal *asbin* exchanges, telling me how the village leader ordered all the women in the community to plant *asbin* at the same time for a feast that would be hosted nine months later. As mentioned previously, from people's narratives it seemed *asbin* was something that could be grown by women on behalf of the community, but could also be grown for their own personal exchanges. The village leader responsible for organising such a group exchange event would gain political notability for it, showing that he was able to organise his people, much like the Moka and pig kills of the upper highlands (see Godelier 1986; Read 1965; Strathern 1971; Josephides 1985; Stewart and Strathern 2005). Younger people I spoke with could not remember such exchanges – yet they knew that *asbin* was a very special food.

The appreciation and circulation of this crop meant that some even likened it to a traditional kind of money. 'Before money came, we used *asbin*', said a man in the Goroka market. However, as far as I can tell, *asbin* was never exchanged directly for other necessities between groups, as per the salt money of the Baruya (Godelier 1998), or even one-for-one exchanges, so it would not technically be considered a commodity (M. Strathern 1992; Robbins and Akin 1999). From the stories I was told, *asbin* was always in the realm of gift exchange, used to convey a desire for future relations and as recognition of those that already existed. The man may then have been referring to a correlation between *asbin* and the current use of money in the ceremonial economy.

For women, *asbin* was the ideal crop given to show personal gratitude, as the following account from a market vendor illustrates:

> If a woman is pregnant and finds it hard to go to the garden, then her neighbours will fetch her food, water and wood. She will then remember the people who helped her and once she has given birth she will plant *asbin*. Nine months later the *asbin* will be ready and she will invite those who helped her to attend a *mumu* where she will distribute *asbin* to them. They will be very grateful for this.

The giving of *asbin* would sometimes be reciprocated, but this was not expected at the point of initial exchange. For example, Bryan, an agricultural adviser from Bena district, told me:

> My mother was well known in our village for growing *asbin*. She would plant ten long rows, each with a person or family in mind, and then give them to people. These people would then come back to her some weeks later with bags of rice, tinned fish, sugar and tea. She was very well known in our community, people thought of her as a strong woman and respected her.

In this story the initial act of giving *asbin* is reciprocated with rice and tinned fish, commodities which are highly appreciated in rural areas but are imported and require money to purchase from tradestores (Kahn and Sexton 1988; Maclean 1989: 84). Thus commodities become gifts as reciprocation for *asbin*.

Furthermore, there is and was a morality around the consuming of *asbin* that means it should only be shared with others, and not grown for personal consumption. While other crops (namely sugarcane, banana and taro) share this quality of being considered special *tumbuna* crops reserved for special events, they are not equal to *asbin* in hierarchy: the latter is considered to have '*value*' equal only to pigs (or greater than pigs, depending on whose account one is hearing).

As I have shown here, *asbin* is a crop that not only creates strong relations when gifted between people but also requires strong social relations for its production. I now turn my focus to the cash economy in order to analyse how money has contributed to changes in indigenous gifting practices in general and, more specifically, affected the prominence of *asbin*.

Money, Work and the Ceremonial Economy

Money is a colonial import in Goroka. The forced extraction of men for labour and the introduction of trade stores initiated the highlands' cash economy, but eventually money became part of the ceremonial economy, gaining a particular status in the process. In this sense, encompassment within the world economy has been on eastern highlanders' terms. But 'modern' lifestyles have increased the desire for commodities and money, leading to both having a place within the ceremonial economy. As people in Goroka frequently said, '*nau em taim bilong mani*', 'now it is money time'. But it is also still a time of maintaining social relations, as people demonstrate through their continued participation in a gifting economy. The cash economy has contributed to the decreased production of *asbin*, but not eradicated gifting practices.

Eastern highlanders began interacting with outsiders when Australian prospectors ventured into what was thought to be uninhabited territory in 1933 (Waiko 1993). State money was introduced into the highlands by the Australian administration in 1947, although a range of other currencies existed in PNG previously (Sexton 1986; cf. Robbins and Akins 1999). Proletarianisation began when highlands men were forcibly taken to coastal areas to work in copra and cocoa plantations around the same time (Gregory 1982: 123). Some men were employed in local coffee plantations and, over time, children educated within local missionary stations became employees of the public administration (Errington and Gewertz 1999). In 1948, Jim Leahy, son of one of the first Europeans in the highlands, established a trade-store alongside the Goroka airstrip and flew in thousands of pounds worth of European goods, including steel axes, knives and beads (Waiko 1993). Initially highlanders did not want to be paid in money. I heard stories of men crying when this was what they were given in return for their labour, since they preferred kina shells. But eventually people understood that money could be exchanged for white men's goods. Those not in waged labour increasingly pursued income-generating activities such as coffee and food production, with the encouragement of missionaries and colonial administrators (Waiko 1993).

Since the 1950s, even those living in remote rural areas have been connected in some way with waged labour, or *wokmani* in Tok Pisin (Stevenson 1986). In Goroka it was common that those selling food would lend money to relatives whose fortnightly wage was not enough to cover their expenses. Money has become an object around which people orient themselves: by working in the gardens and selling food in town, working in formal jobs, or reselling store goods in town (Sharp et al. 2015). People sell items produced locally or mass produced elsewhere (such as batteries and electronics) in rural and urban markets. But it is not just as a facilitator of commodity exchange that money has become important in the highlands, it has also been incorporated into the indigenous base of gifting (i.e. the making and maintaining of social relations).

The intrusion of capital, resulting from colonisation, has not led to the suppression of gift economies as expected, but rather to an efflorescence of gift exchange (cf. Akin and Robbins 1999). Early anthropological accounts also showed that the number of valuables given during bridewealth ceremonies among the Siane had 'greatly increased' (Salisbury 1962).[6] Brown (1978) similarly showed that the introduction of coffee trees for commodity production allowed men to purchase more pigs, food and beer for ceremonial exchanges.[7]

Money is gifted between clans in formal ceremonial settings, such as bride wealth or mortuary rituals, and between individuals in less formal settings of card games or for bus fares (Lipuma 1999; Stewart and Strathern 2005). In order for money to be recognisable as a formal gift, it is presented in various ways, such as being pinned to long pieces of bamboo or attached to headdresses for public exchange events (Brown 1978; O'Hanlon 1993). It is also handed over in envelopes on public occasions (for comparable examples in Tonga, see Horan 2012). The meaning of money is similar to that of *asbin* and other valued food items when it is used as a gift rather than merely an exchange mechanism or commodity. Strathern argued that: 'what a gift transactor desires is the personal relationship that the exchange of gifts creates, and not the things themselves' (1988:19). In Goroka, people want (and need) money and relationships at the same time, and money is thus said to have gained 'value'. It has increased in importance for everyday activities but has also gained status within the realm of the ceremonial economy.

People in towns and villages are now accustomed to eating imported foods such as rice, salt, oil, noodles and tinned fish, as well having household goods such as soap, gas and candles (Errington et al. 2013; Kahn and Sexton 1988). This makes them vulnerable to the fluctuations in the global economy and changes in the national balance of payments when prices increase. Meanwhile costs associated with children's schooling are another reason why people need money. A friend working for a public service in Goroka explained this in the following terms, in relation to the current importance of money:

> It is about westernisation, school came inside, and people thought 'ok we need to educate our children so that they will find work and have a better life'. We turned our backs on our traditional ways and thought the new ways were better for us … I tell my children now, 'if you don't do well at school, it doesn't mean you are not intelligent, you can go back to your land.' We must hold on to our land, it is labour intensive but at least we know we have food.

This mother of four was not the only person to see the dangers of sending children to school. Often people would lament that the younger generations are no longer learning how to garden and live off the land. This type of reflection is understandable especially when unemployment is high. At the same time, land shortage is increasingly an issue in the highlands. Mirium, a descendant of the clan who gave their land for development of the Goroka market in the 1960s, explained that land is one of the reasons people rely on money more today than previously.

> The size of the family has increased and there is a serious shortage of land; a lot of conflicts come up because of land. We're in a terrible dilemma … People have migrated here as labourers and they just settle and have children. But many people have no way of growing their own food so they must find coins to buy their three meals a day in the cooked food section of the market, Goroka's version of McDonald's!

The process of transition into a market economy has meant an increase in things that require money to be purchased or accessed. One example of this is the commodification of local ceremonial foods.[8] For instance, different kinds of bananas are now sold in the market so that those in wage work or who live without gardens can still maintain their customary obligations by contributing required food gifts. As one of my adopted fathers said, 'money has become our middle man'. He was contrasting this to the days when people from high altitude areas would help people in low altitude areas through exchanging food, particularly during the dry season (Barnett-Naghshineh 2015: 118). This happens infrequently now as people sell their food instead, he told me. If their gardens are dry, people have to buy food from the market. Therefore money, and the market, has become the middleman for these transactions.

Meanwhile, health care and education also require money, as do materials for modern houses, which people aspire to have as they symbolise success. Having a house made of corrugated iron and with facilities such as televisions, stoves and electricity gives status – showing that people are living a 'good life'. As consumer items also contribute to people's social status, money has gained importance in facilitating such status. But while people in the highlands have found their lifestyles changing with modernity, they are also maintaining their traditional forms of exchange and obligations to one another by exchanging material items at key moments. Money is now integrated, or indigenised, becoming a part of this aspect of people's lives or, as people in Goroka said, 'Money has got *value* now.'

The way that money gains '*value*' in the ceremonial economy directly relates to the increasing prices of imported food and the costs of fertilisers and pesticides for commercial crop production. There has been a broad shift in the mode of production from one of subsistence agriculture and production for the ceremonial economy (Lederman 1986: 16), to one of waged labour and selling of cash crops in the market, with women having a considerable role in the latter. Money has become a gift partly because it is a requirement for survival in the contemporary world. Considering money can be generated in a number of ways, it seems to me that the justification for spending time and energy growing crops such as *asbin* has decreased, particularly as commodities and money can be used for similar purposes (Barnett-Naghshineh 2015: 121). Nevertheless, *asbin* does continue to be grown by those further away from urban centres, perhaps where commodities are less obtainable. I now turn to the explanations given by some of my interlocutors for why people no longer grow *asbin*.

The Decline of Asbin

Once I asked my friend Sally if she knew how to grow *asbin*. She is in her forties and well known in her community, especially as she is one of the first female judges in a local village court. She said she knows how to but has never done so: 'Before lots of woman would grow *asbin* at the same time and then *mumu* them together, and give them to friends. No one in my village grows *asbin* now.' When I asked why, Sally responded that maybe women no longer have the seeds and grow other things instead. Introduced crops such as potatoes, broccoli, carrots and onions get the highest prices in the market and are therefore popular to grow. Many women in Sally's community grow broccoli for the market as they live close to town. Broccoli production is costly due to expensive inputs, including the seeds, which are bought in local hardware stores. These producers must have a constant supply of cash. Other producers further out of town can struggle to grow cash crops that require costly inputs because of high transport costs or due to poor soil conditions. People in these communities are more likely to continue growing traditional crops such as *asbin* as they do not cost money to produce. *Asbin* can be grown in remote mountainous areas without using fertilisers or pesticides and is small enough to transport. The seeds are cheap if not free. Out of all of the food crops that are grown, both traditional and introduced foods, *asbin* is considered to be the hardest work but also one that attracts a good price for a small investment.

Climate change was also used as an explanation for why *asbin* is no longer grown. Rato, a local agricultural adviser to farmers, explained that the seasonality of *asbin* has been disturbed, as there is no longer a correlation between the sun, moon and seasons, making it difficult for growers to know when to perform the delicate tasks required. Yet the Director of Goroka's Department for Agriculture and Livestock (DAL) had a different explanation for the decline in *asbin* production:

> Cash crops are destabilising traditional value; now people sell their best food for money and eat low-quality foods. Some people are even selling their fresh produce to buy rice, as that's what children want to eat these days.

Some people still grow *asbin*, but, like other ceremonial crops, it has entered the realm of market exchange. Those living and working in town can consume it without having to be given it formally. There is no shame in purchasing the crop in the market, and its commodity status does not seem to have detracted from its social status. Now it is exchanged between people who do not necessarily have a relationship prior to the market transaction and do not have an ongoing relationship beyond it.

Sellers consider *asbin* to be a good crop to sell because it can fetch a high price for a relatively small amount of food. The small numbers of people who sell *asbin*, its seasonality and its traditional status contribute to the prices *asbin* can be sold for in the market. One market woman explained: '*Asbin* is an expensive food. We can make up to PGK100 in one day from selling *asbin*. It is a good food to market.' This is much more than people make in an average day in the market from selling local greens, and might be closer to the amount made from selling a pile of sweet potato (a staple).

However, many producer-sellers did not feel *asbin* was a worthy investment of time and energy. Those with experience of selling crops that go for a high price, such as pineapples or other introduced foods, were not likely to spend time growing *asbin*. For example, Julie, a watermelon seller in Goroka explained:

> I know how to grow *asbin* but I don't bother any more. It's a lot of hard work. I concentrate on watermelon and oranges; these bring in money, these are good to market.

One day I met Julie in the market when she was selling ceremonial bananas, an essential wealth item in exchanges such as bridewealth. When I asked why she was selling these in the market, she reflected:

> Before, these would finish any debt or conflict. Now most of us only want money. I didn't have any situations that needed me to contribute these bananas so I have brought them to the market.

Although Julie is talking about bananas, her message demonstrates a related process to the decline in use of *asbin*. Those who do not need ceremonial crops at a particular moment can convert them into money through the market; and those who need ceremonial crops for an event but do not have any in the garden can buy them. Thus ceremonial crops get transformed into commodities and then become gifts again. The marketisation of the economy has thus both shaped production and been shaped by historical traditions of production for gift exchange.

The status that women could gain from growing *asbin* now comes from their ability to make money, whether through waged work, business, or selling food in the market. The stories told in women's initiations during their first menstruation now include advice for selling fresh produce in the market, and not the secret songs to help *asbin* or other crops grow as in bygone eras (Gillison 1993; West 2012; Whiteman 1965). Giving and sharing remain important within Goroka sociality, especially for women who assist one another often. But being educated, having a paid job or being good at marketing are held in high esteem, partly because these women (as mothers and wives) can look after their husband's kin and lubricate their clan's social relations with cash money. Women can also be more independent and gain satisfaction from being educated and working, especially when they have their own businesses.

One woman working as a village teacher explained that she bought new mattresses and pots and pans for a friend to say thank you for supporting her daughter's initiation ceremony, when usually she would have used *asbin*. Women with a cash income are thus able to maintain their social obligations by using their wages to buy commodities. However, some in Goroka have commented with concern that the lost knowledge of traditional crops and the decrease of large-scale exchanges of *asbin* has left people vulnerable to malnutrition and famine during drought periods such as that brought on by the recent El Nino (2015 and predicted to finish in 2016).

People were dreading the possibility of a drought during my fieldwork and predicted that the market would be empty and prices of food would increase drastically. At the time of writing there has been no rain in Goroka for six months and people are struggling. People who '*wokmani*' support relatives in the village, putting a strain on waged labour and heightening inequalities between those who rely on marketing their produce and those who have other means of subsistence. Thus the shift to a cash economy comes with its costs.

Conclusion

Entering the labour market to earn an income is more common for people living in Goroka today than in previous times and money is increasingly required for purchasing the food necessary to sustain a family.[9] Making contributions to customary obligations in the ceremonial economy continues but now people purchase food, pigs and commodities (such as rice bags and noodles) to do this, using money they have made through marketing or paid work. They can also contribute money itself as a gift. Meanwhile *asbin* is not grown for the sake of gifting as much, but when it is, it comes as a very welcome surprise. Women are able to maintain their social relations today without having to do such backbreaking physical labour and can instead grow other crops and make money instead. The relational economy continues through the gifting of money, commodities and some traditional foods but the marketisation of exchange is also thought to have impacted upon people's behaviour. People in Goroka often said '*selfish pasin kamap*', which I translated to mean people have become more self-oriented and less likely to help others. This reflection suggested sadness for the loss of past times when kin relations were strong and extensive. *Asbin* serves as a reminder of times when producing objects for the sake of sharing was a major aspect of people's lives and one that required intensive labour. But times, and time, change, and those who need money for material and social requirements may be more likely to grow crops with shorter gestation periods and that require less physical exertion or help from others.

Notes

1. See (Bourke 1982) and Powell (1974) for more details on nutrition and ecology.
2. A cut of meat imported from Australia and New Zealand that has become popular in PNG. See Errington and Gewertz (2008) for more on this.
3. The ability to carry out traditional exchanges of this sort is part of a gendered political system in the village that runs alongside the modern hierarchies of the urban context, where being a politician or a doctor is another form of public status but does not necessarily mean people are capable of being leaders in the rural context.
4. PGK1 is equivalent to about NZ$2.
5. Other wealth items currently include crops such as taro, yams and bananas (and money), and previously included precious bird of paradise feathers, shells and pig teeth.
6. Other ethnographers have shown how primary commodity production, the import of steel axes, and incorporation of male labour into colonial plantation economies all supported inter-clan economies where the amounts of pigs, shells, food and money increased in exchanges (Brown 1978; Gregory 1982; Salisbury 1962; Young 1971).
7. Although the use of land for coffee production instead of food is also said to have increased people's dependence on food such as rice, and maggi noodles (Errington et al. 2013), while also providing the cash income for such commodity consumption.
8. Maclean (1989) proposed that research regarding how local foods become commodified is required for PNG. The PhD research that this chapter is part of develops this area of research.

9. Tinned fish is relatively affordable for rural people and fried chicken or fish can easily be found in fast food restaurants in town – the protein content of *asbin* becomes less significant (although the nutritional qualities of *asbin*, considered to be a 'superfood' by nutritionists due to its high number of vitamins, irons and proteins, far surpass any processed or mass produced meats).

References

Appadurai, A. 1986. Introduction: Commodities and the politics of value. In A. Appadurai (ed.) *The Social Life of Things: Commodities in Cultural Perspective*. Cambridge: Cambridge University Press.

Barnett-Naghshineh, O. 2015. Global warming or cash economy? Discourses of climate change and food in Eastern Highlands Province, Papua New Guinea. In D.C. Wood (ed.) *Climate Change, Culture, and Economics: Anthropological Investigations*, Research in Economic Anthropology 35. Bingley: Emerald Group, pp. 107–33.

Bourke, R.M. 1982. Root crops in Papua New Guinea. In: E.H. Belen and M. Villanueva (eds) *Fifth International Symposium on Tropical Root and Tuber Crops*. Los Banos, Laguna: Philippine Council for Agriculture and Resources Research, pp. 121–31.

Brown, P. 1978. *Highland Peoples of New Guinea*. Cambridge: Cambridge University Press.

Burman, R. (1981) Time and socioeconomic change on Simbo, Solomon Islands. *Man* 16(2): 251–67.

Epstein, T.S. 1982. *Urban Food Marketing and Third World Development: The Structure of Producer–Seller Markets*. London: Croom Helm.

Errington, F. and D. Gewertz. 1999. *Emerging Class in Papua New Guinea: The Telling of Difference*. Cambridge, MA: Cambridge University Press.

—— 2008. Pacific island gastrologies: Following the flaps. *Journal of the Royal Anthropological Institute* 14(3): 590–608.

Errington, F.K., F. Tatsuro and D. Gewertz. 2013. *The Noodle Narratives: The Global Rise of an Industrial Food into the Twenty-first Century*. Berkeley: University of California Press.

Fajans, J. 1988. The transformative value of food: A review essay. *Food and Foodways* 3: 143–66.

Gillison, G. 1993. *Between Culture and Fantasy: A New Guinea Highlands Mythology*. Chicago: University of Chicago Press.

Goddard, M. (2000) Of cabbages and kin: The value of an analytic distinction between gifts and commodities. *Critique of Anthropology* 20: 137–51.

Godelier, M. 1986. *The Making of Great Men*. Cambridge: Cambridge University Press.

—— 1998. Salt money and the circulation of commodities among the Baruya of New Guinea. In S. Gudeman (ed.) *Economic Anthropology*, International Library of Critical Writings in Economics 99. Cheltenham: Elgar.

Gregory, C. 1982. *Gifts and Commodities*. New York: Academic Press.

Hide, R. 2003. *Pig Husbandry in New Guinea: A Literature Review and Bibliography*. ACIAR Monograph 108. Canberra: Australian Centre for International Agricultural Research.

Horan, J. (2012). *Tivaivai in the Cook Islands Ceremonial Economy: An Analysis of Value*. PhD thesis, University of Auckland.

Josephides, L. 1985. *The Production of Inequality: Gender and Exchange among the Kewa*. London: Tavistock.

Khan, T. 1976. Papua New Guinea: A centre of genetic diversity in winged bean *psophocarpus tetragonologus*. *Euphytica* 25(1): 693–705.

Kahn, M. and L. Sexton. 1988. The fresh and the canned: Food choices in the Pacific. *Food and Foodways* 3(1–2): 1–18.

Lederman, R. 1986. *What Gifts Engender: Social Relations and Politics in Mendi, Highland Papua New Guinea*. Cambridge: Cambridge University Press.

Lipuma, E. 1999. The meaning of money in the age of modernity. In D. Akin and J. Robbins (eds) *Money and Modernity: State and Local Currencies in Melanesia*. Pittsburgh, PA: University of Pittsburgh Press, pp. 192–213.

Maclean, N.L. 1989. The commoditization of food: An analysis of a Maring market. *Canberra Anthropology* 12(1–2): 161–79.

Malinowski, B. 1922. *Argonauts of the Western Pacific: An Account of Native Enterprise and Adventure in the Archipelagoes of Melanesian New Guinea*. New York: Routledge.

Mauss, M. 2000 [1925]. *The Gift: The Form and Reason for Exchange in Archaic Societies*. New York: W.W. Norton.

Meggit, M. 1974. Pigs are our hearts! The Te exchange cycle among the Mae Enga of New Guinea. *Oceania* 44: 165–203.

O'Hanlon, M. 1993. *Paradise: Portraying the New Guinea Highlands*. London: British Museum.

Powell, J.M. 1974. Traditional legumes of the New Guinea highlands. *Science in New Guinea* 2(1): 48–63.

Read, K. 1965. *The High Valley*. New York: Charles Scribner's Sons.

Robbins, J. and D. Akin. 1999. An introduction to Melanesian currencies: Agency, identity, and social reproduction. In D. Akin and J. Robbins (Eds.) *Money and Modernity: State and Local Currencies in Melanesia*. Pittsburgh, PA: University of Pittsburgh Press, pp. 1–40.

Salisbury, R.F. 1962. *From Stone to Steel: Economic Consequences of a Technological Change in New Guinea*. Melbourne: Melbourne University Press.

Sexton, L. 1986. *Mothers of Money, Daughters of Coffee: The Wok Meri Movement*. Michigan: UMI Research Press.

Sharp, T., J. Cox, C. Spark, S. Lusby and M. Rooney. 2015. The formal, the informal and the precarious: Making a living in urban Papua New Guinea. State, Society and Governance in Melanesia (SSGM) Discussion Paper. Canberra: ANU.

Sillitoe, P. 1998. *An Introduction to the Anthropology of Melanesia: Culture and Tradition*. Cambridge: Cambridge University Press.

—— 2001. Pig men and women, big men and women: Gender and production in the New Guinea highlands. *Ethnology: An International Journal of Cultural and Social Anthropology* 40(3): 171–92.

Stevenson, M. 1986. *Wokmani: Work, Money and Discontent in Melanesia*. Sydney: Oceania Publications.

Stewart, P. and A. Strathern. 2005. The death of Moka in post-colonial Mount Hagen, Highlands, Papua New Guinea. In J. Robbins and H. Wardlow (eds) *The Making of Global and Local Modernities in Melanesia: Humiliation, Transformation and the Nature of Cultural Change*. Aldershot: Ashgate.

Strathern, A. 1971. *The Rope of Moka: Big-men and Ceremonial Exchange in Mount Hagen, New Guinea*. Cambridge studies in social anthropology 4. Cambridge: Cambridge University Press.

Strathern, A. and P. Stewart. 1999. Objects, relationships and meanings. In R. Akin and J. Robbins (eds) *Money and Modernity: State and Local Currencies in Melanesia*. Pittsburgh: University of Pittsburgh Press.

Strathern, M. 1988. *The Gender of the Gift: Problems with Women and Problems with Society in Melanesia*. Berkeley: University of California Press.

—— 1992. Qualified value: The perspective of gift exchange. In C. Humphrey and S. Hugh-Jones (eds) *Barter, Exchange and Value: An Anthropological Approach*. Cambridge: Cambridge University Press.

Waiko, J. 1993. *A Short History of Papua New Guinea*. Oxford: Oxford University Press.

West, P. 2012. *From Modern Production to Imagined Primitive: The Social World of Coffee from Papua New Guinea*. Durham, NC: Duke University Press.

Whiteman, J. 1965. Girls' puberty ceremonies amongst the Chimbu. *Anthropos* 60(1): 410–22.

Young, M.W. 1971. *Fighting with Food: Leadership, Values and Social Control in a Massim Society*. Cambridge: Cambridge University Press.

4

The Value of the Vanua

The Nexus of People and Land in Fiji's Market Economy

Geir Henning Presterudstuen

Introduction

'There we have it ... our *vanua* is worth shit! Not worth development, not worth new roads, not even worth Chinese money!'[1] Seru spat out these words while sweeping his left hand through the air, pointing towards the southern parts of the western highlands village in which he was the acting chief. His violently bad mood found direction as he continued his tirade against 'the big leaders' in the coastal cities of Suva, Nadi and Lautoka 'filling their own pockets' at the expense of the people at large. Outbursts of overt anger like this were a relatively rare occurrence in this otherwise quiet and contained village, located some three hours' drive into the Nausori Highlands from Nadi, where I spent considerable time during my fieldwork in 2009. Those outbreaks were certainly not commonplace from people like Seru, whose position in the village hierarchy required him to embody the chiefly qualities of calm leadership and wisdom. What had triggered his reaction was the final confirmation that a commercial developer of South East Asian origin had decided not to go ahead with a proposed commercial tourist development project in the highlands, opting instead for leased land closer to urban amenities and Fiji's pristine coastline.

While few villagers I had spoken to in the preceding months had expected anything to come out of the developers' interest, the disappointment was palpable in Seru. Like many other contemporary Fijian village leaders, he saw more serious forays into the tourist market as the only viable long-term plan to secure better living conditions for the village that otherwise had limited means of their own. His uncharacteristically vocal eruption, however, is interesting also for a number of other reasons. Being at once emotional, evaluative and deeply political, Seru's statement can be understood both as a sort of 'metacultural complaint' (Tomlinson 2004) and as *Realpolitik*. It hints at intra-ethnic discordance between indigenous Fijians in the highlands and their coastal counterparts, as well as the ambiguous impact tourism development has on modern Fijian society. Mainly, however, it is a clue to understanding the changing nature of Fijian villages occurring in the context of the late modern Fijian service economy and, more specifically, an ideal starting point for an analysis of how the market economy influences local understandings of the relationship between people and their environment, epitomised through the concept of *vanua*, the Fijian term for the nexus of land, culture and people. In this chapter I draw upon extensive ethnographic material collected since 2009 in urban, semi-urban and rural villages in the western division of Fiji's largest island, Viti Levu, to discuss these dynamics within a larger theoretical framework through the category of 'value'.

Development and Land Value in Fiji

For most Fijians, economic change, progress and development are understood through local engagement with tourism, and the integration of the *vanua* into the tourist economy is thus a central point for my analysis. Fiji was arguably among the first Pacific Island countries that embraced mass tourism, with the Suva Tourist Board being developed already in 1923, paving the way for extensive foreign investment in tourism which eventually facilitated an industry boom in the early 1960s. It remains the largest tourism economy in the region today (Kanemasu 2013). Indigenous Fijian involvement in these projects, however, was largely limited to casual employment until fairly recently. Only in the last few decades has the commercial use of native land become part of political strategies of both national politicians and local landowners. Though I consider this as a historical moment in the context of centuries of Fijian adaptation to the market economy, I will use it as a starting point for a discussion of how the *vanua* becomes redefined in the context of the modern tourist economy. These discourses about economic development and tourism not only facilitate a reconsideration of the *vanua* in commercial terms, but also the integration of the wider concept of Fijian tradition into the modern economy.

Given their position as owners of more than 83 per cent of the country's land and the vast majority of existing land utilised for tourism purposes, Fijian landowning units, the nature of which will be further explored below, are, one way or another, crucial in the development of Fijian tourism. As a consequence, Fiji has been highlighted as 'a productive case study through which to examine whether tourism development under a system of communal land tenure contributes to local development and poverty alleviation' (Scheyvens and Russel 2012: 2). Despite these facts and the centrality of the concept of *vanua* both in Fijian traditions and customs and in the Fijian tourist industry, there has been little critical analysis of the dialectical relationship between tourism and this concept. Timoci Waqaisavou rightly pointed out the need for such an approach to 'fully understand the synergy between the vanua and the impact of tourism on native land' (quoted in Scheyvens and Russel 2012: 11). The chief purpose of this chapter is not, however, to contribute to the literature on tourism and development studies about whether particular systems of local governance or landownership are more conducive to successful relationships between tourist operators and local communities than others. Rather, my emphasis is on the more general question about what happens to local systems of tenure when land becomes integrated into the logics of the market economy through, for instance, the tourism industry.

In my analysis I draw upon the conceptual framework found in Marx's labour theory of value to focus particularly on the process through which land becomes considered a market entity, the relationship between use-value and exchange-value and how this relates to larger socioeconomic changes. Given that Marx's theory of value is centred on the relationship between labour, commodity and exchange, however, its application to the specific issue of land development and land use in Fiji is perhaps not immediately apparent. Land is a notoriously difficult category to analyse in terms of Marxian value theory, associated both with the latter's difficulty in explaining the relationship between the natural properties of land and features that are 'produced' by human labour (Bryan 1990) and the particular nature of land in the system of production. Furthermore, the fixity of land, and how it has traditionally been deeply embedded in social relationships, makes it difficult for many to imagine it as a fully marketable commodity, a point which indeed is central to my analysis below. Polanyi (2001 [1944]) famously elaborated on this and labelled land, along with labour and money, a 'fictitious commodity' that sits particularly uneasily within a market context. But rather than seeing in this a limitation in

Marxian value theory, I seek to use these tensions to examine this complex relationship in the ethnographic specific of village Fiji. In practical terms this implies that I will draw extensively upon Marx's key categories and combine these insights with a conceptualisation of local phenomena which is ethnographically meaningful. This chapter is thus engaged in a dialectical discussion between theory and empiricism. By framing my discussion with a Marxian theory of value I seek to tease out and explain some of the key processes associated with commercial development and marketisation of land, culture and people in Fiji.

In focusing my analysis on the intersection between Fijian land and tradition, entities that both are officially considered inalienable from indigenous, communal ownership, I make the case that even things that are not commodified per se become reconfigured under the conditions of the totalising system of global capitalism. Combining an analysis of the historical construction of the concept of the *vanua* and its relationship to Fiji's two economic spheres (that, for the purpose of this discussion, can be loosely defined through binaries such as traditional/modern or moral/marketised), I demonstrate how this concept has become redefined within the context of Fijian market economy through a process that, following Thomas Ernst (1999), I label 'entification'. In order to set up this discussion, however, I will first outline the key tenets of the concept of *vanua* and the Fijian system of customary land tenure.

Vanua, *Tradition and Elite Politics*

Among most Pacific peoples land is perceived as much more than its geographical properties or substance potential. It is often the source of communal identities and is linked to notions of personhood through spiritual and ritual practices. In Fiji this relationship is comprised in the concept of *vanua*, which is at the core of the entire indigenous Fijian social structure. Literally this term may be translated to mean land, region, place or spot (Capell 1991: 255), but as an indigenous concept it has far wider connotations, socially, culturally and spiritually as well as politically (Ravuvu 1987: 14–15). As a word, it signifies larger groups of people who recognise social or political allegiances and their relationship to the land. *Vanua* has thus come to embody the social connections between people in a particular locality. Further, the relationship between Fijians and their *vanua* is all-encompassing and sacred, often summarised by the notion of *I cauviti*, meaning '[o]ne does not own the land: the land owns him. Man and land are one' (Tuwere 1992: 34). Within this framework land cannot be separated from its people and is thus inconceivable as an alienable material asset.

Vanua is, furthermore, considered integral to everything Fijian. Tradition, for instance, is articulated through the concept of *cakacaka vakavanua*, most accurately translated as 'acting in accordance with the land' (Toren 1988: 712). The consequence is that tradition is defined as culturally appropriate practice rather than merely as objectified structures of the past, and thus fulfilling one's traditional obligations is situated both spatially, in connection with the land, and temporally. Just as 'events and the presence of past events in the present are determined by the way a group or an individual is related to the past in an ongoing process of symbolic mediation' (Dickhardt 2005: 344), tradition is understood and constructed in contemporary Fiji as praxis which is beneficial to, and in accordance with, the *vanua*.

It is, consequently, through the *vanua* that individual Fijians become intrinsically linked to the social collective. Social hierarchies and respect for the chief are, for instance, directly linked to the notions of custodianship of the *vanua*. But living one's life in accordance with the *vanua* is not only about respecting the chiefly office; it also implies that every member of a kinship group works specifically for the betterment of the collectivity and to maintain social solidarity and internal harmony (Farrelly 2011: 824). The nature of the *vanua*, then, is also often understood through the concept of *sautu*, that intrinsically links 'good health and wealth' to 'a wide and healthy network of relationships' demarcated by one's communally owned land (Nabobo-Baba 2006: 74).

There are thus both normative and instrumental aspects implicit in this conceptualisation of land and the relationship between land and people. Practices that are considered to help maintain or strengthen the social totality, including ritual praxis, food production and distribution of resources within the social body are by nature respected. The *vanua*, in other words, is the core aspect of what Rutz, following E.P. Thompson, has defined as Fiji's traditional, moral economy; that is 'production, distribution, and consumption activities which occur within a matrix of social relations that are normatively prescribed, strongly obligatory, bounded by highly shared rules, meanings, and symbols, and perceived as more or less permanent or natural' (Rutz 1987: 536). Although the historicity of this particular articulation of the *vanua* is unclear, its centrality in practically all Fijians' cultural identity supports the notion that it has been a defining aspect of local social organisation since long before unification and the emergence of the modern national identity.

The all-encompassing notion of the *vanua* and the various authorities, duties and responsibilities which were implicit in this social order was renewed, formalised and strengthened by the advent of modernity in Fiji. What Peter France has aptly labelled 'the new orthodoxy' (1969), the modern legal and political order brought in by colonial administrators was built around the in-principle definition of the *vanua* as the primary level of Fijian social organisation. Contained herein was the infallible authority of chiefs as custodians of the *vanua* in its widest sense, as well as new allegiances to Christian religious authorities and colonial rulers (the chief, God and the Queen became the central nexus that regulated the modern *vanua*), but also the legally formalised native ownership over the *vanua* as land through what eventually became the Native Land Trust Act in 1940. In technical terms, this legislation also established the three key tenets that have defined Fijians' understanding of land ever since; land is owned communally by politico-legally defined categories of kinship delineations, it is *de jure* inalienable from local landowning units, and these land rights are immutable in the sense that living Fijians' are mere custodians of land for future generations, 'a trust in perpetuity, so that custom was immemorial and unchanging' (Rutz 1987: 538; France 1969).

The Native Land Trust Act remains in place and contemporary land ownership is organised according to the structure determined by blood lineage that was universalised in the early 1900s. There are six different units of ownership available. First the chief, who for the time being holds the hereditary title of *Ka Levu*, can own land. Second there is land owned by agnate descendants, according to local customary kinship systems, of a member of a tribe. Third, a *tokatoka*, a traditional family unit, can own land in their own right. Fourth, a *mataqali* – which is best translated as a clan – or fifth, a *yavusa*, which refers to a larger tribe of several *mataqali*, can own land. Finally, some structures see native land rights held jointly by several *yavusa* (iTaukei Land Trust Board 2015). The *mataqali* remains the most common unit for owning land in Fiji, while *tokatoka* or *yavusa* structures are only recognised in some regions of the republic. Fijian land, however, as defined in the Native Land Trust Act, can in principle only be owned by indigenous Fijians, who today constitute around 57 per cent of the population (Fiji Bureau of Statistics 2007).

It is one of the peculiarities of Fijian colonial history that the early British administrations governed with the explicit aim of protecting Fijian traditional life in a way that saw economic relations being subordinated to, or at least kept separate from, the existing social ethics. Most analyses of the land tenure system highlight its direct links to this particular colonial project and how it became a crucial point for securing the continued sustainability of Fijian villages and the sustained dominance of native chiefs as foreign capitalists and Indo-Fijian indentured workers and their descendants made up increasingly large numbers of the total population. Indeed, in Fiji's heavily racialised modern political history, land became heavily linked to ethno-Fijian claims of political supremacy based on traditional rights through a process which has similarities to the highly politicised storytelling procedure Ernst (1999: 90) has identified in the south-western highlands of Papua New Guinea. Storytelling, in this sense, includes the creation of a set of rights associated with a native identity, and the argument that this is founded in traditional, customary practice, and thus legitimate. Ernst has discussed this process as a form of entification:

> The appearance of continuity, as well as the potential for change, are both bound up with the word entification: the process of making 'entities' or things from what have been contingent categories. (Ernst 1999: 89)

It is obviously true that the Fijian entification of land based on perceived customary rights through tradition is used in today's context to manifest a clear power relation based on ethnicity. Storytelling, political rhetoric and legal discourse in Fiji serve to establish the native Fijians' ownership and control over 'their land' in opposition to the Indo-Fijian 'others'. However, there is another, equally obvious aspect of entification – that it, in this case, makes the *vanua* a political category just as much as a cultural one. This is, for instance, evident in a famous political analogy where Fijian chief and statesman Ratu Lala Sukuna described Fiji as a three-legged stool made up of European capital, Indian labour and Fijian land. What is particularly interesting about this ideological statement in the context of my argument is that it seems obvious that the concept of the *vanua* was already, at this early stage, transformed into, or at least linked directly to, an entity, land, and located within an explicitly economic discourse.

In this process, *vanua* became central to a localised version of what Karl Polanyi (2001 [1944]) famously labelled the 'double movement' between 'social protectionism' and 'economic liberalism'. Polanyi's analysis is a historical one, arguing that a self-regulating economic sphere disembedded from society at large was an impossibility. Such an unhinged market economy, he argued, could simply not exist without 'annihilating the human and natural substance of society' and was thus always bound to incite a countermovement of protectionist responses (2001 [1944]: 77). While the dynamics surrounding Fijian land legislation and adaptation to the capitalist economy were played out differently from Polanyi's European case studies, a 'double movement' remains an apposite description of the process through which a Fijian land lease market was developed in conjunction with a strengthening of indigenous Fijians' inalienable right to own land.[2] Understood from this point of view, notions of native land and communal property rights through kin lineages were employed both to secure the continuity of these traditional concepts of Fijian identity in order to secure a stable political situation and to pave the way for modernisation (Overton 1993: 45; Rutz 1995: 76; Ward 1995). My contention is that this is a crucial point in order to understand how contemporary Fijians understand their relationship to their land and, in simple terms, the physical aspect of their *vanua*. I furthermore arrive at this conclusion by linking the process of entification directly to the Marxian theory of value and its concepts of commodification, objectification and exchange-value, a point I elaborate below before returning to the ethnographic data about contemporary debates on the role of the *vanua* as an asset in the tourist market.

Valuing the Vanua

Briefly returning to the anecdote at the start of this chapter, the main thing that made my friend Seru's statement stand out to me as a researcher was that it explicitly referred to and questioned the worth of the *vanua*. In most Fijian discourses such questions have traditionally been considered both meaningless and irreverent. In the traditional, moral economy the concept of *vanua* is generally afforded a status that goes well beyond material or normative evaluations; its worth, it is argued, is intrinsic and indisputable.

These conceptualisations are further complicated by linguistics. There are two main expressions commonly translated as 'value' in standard Fijian language. *Yaga* is most commonly used to describe the usefulness or purpose of an object (similarly, *kena yaga* is the expression used to explain the use-value of an entity). *Talei* on the other hand, is used in contexts of valuation or appraisals and is in standard Fijian dictionaries translated into 'what they wonder at or admire' as well as 'prize' (Capell 1991 [1941]: 215). However, in the context of economic transactions *I voli*, derived from *voli* that is the Fijian word for 'to buy or purchase', is used as the word for price or cost of a thing while *I sau*, derived from vernacular terms for retaliation and reciprocity, is also often used as price. When I discussed these terms with my Fijian interlocutors it became clear that they found it difficult to talk about *vanua* in any of these terms and rather preferred the use of the English 'value', further strengthening my impression that the commodification of land was an exercise that had its root in foreign, or colonial, dynamics rather than local ones.

In the previous sections I proposed that the traditional notions of *vanua* were challenged already at the outset of modern Fiji, when land became reconfigured into a legal, political and economic entity, the Fijian asset in the tripartite nexus that came to form the basis of Fiji's modern economy (with European capital and Indian labour). In what follows I seek to build on this insight both empirically and theoretically. Ethnographically I discuss how land went from a cultural category to a market entity through a series of economic and political changes during the last decades; conceptually I set out to explain how these processes of entification and marketisation relate to, and can be understood through, value theory.

This analytical focus is particularly pertinent in Fiji, where the antagonistic relationship between traditional life 'in accordance with the land' (*vakavanua*) and the 'European way' of business and money has such a central place in the local imagination (Presterudstuen 2014; cf. Williksen-Bakker 2002). Despite the fact that Fijian villagers have been in continuous relationships with the market economy for more than a century, dominant discourses still perceive the social production of human relations, order and authority to be located outside the capitalist mode of production. The dichotomy between Fijian and European ways of life, then, is in principle understood in terms that are at once historical (traditional/modern), ideological (good/bad) and spatial (city/village) and are discursively connected to explicitly different social and economic practices, a point I return to later in the analysis.

One of the few earlier attempts at analysing the marketisation of Fijian land in the context of the dichotomy described above can be found in a seldom cited article by Henry J. Rutz. Though very sound from a scholarly point of view, Rutz's article might be one of the more poorly timed research publications in the field, something which may help explain its lack of prominence in later Fijian scholarship. His opening premise – that the key disturbances over land in Fiji were largely among indigenous Fijians – a fact that could account for 'the relative absence of overt action' (1987: 534) on the issues, appears strange to the extreme given that the article was published only weeks after Fijian ethno-nationalists justified an infamous coup d'état by the need to protect Fijian interests in general, and land rights in particular, from the Indo-Fijian numerical majority. Notwithstanding this unfortunate historical happenstance, Rutz provides an insightful analysis of the process through which Fijian customary land has become entrenched in market dynamics that is worth revisiting.

For Rutz, the structure of Fijian land ownership was always based on a number of contradictions pertaining to the status of land. While the Native Land Trust Act of 1940 was ostensibly set out to protect what I, following Rutz, have defined as the Fijian moral economy from the dynamics of capitalism, it also established a land market by making inalienable land available for lease. From this point onwards, all landowning units were able and encouraged to provide unutilised land for long-term leases (up to 99 years in duration) for plantations or agricultural smallholdings (crucial for the Indo-Fijian population who set themselves up as sugarcane farmers post-indenture) or medium-term leases for other commercial ventures or residential purposes (often 50 years) (Thornton 2009). Similarly, it set up a Native Land Trust Board (NLTB)[3] that had the specific task of administering Fijian land on behalf of its owners. This was followed by the Agricultural Landlord and Tenant Act (ALTA), enacted in 1966, that set out to 'regularise the occupation of agricultural land by Fijians and non-Fijians and to establish a set of terms and conditions to be implied in the Contract of Tenancy' (Sharma 1999: n.p.).

While it is not uncommon in colonial and postcolonial settings that customary forms of land tenure become regulated through introduced laws and principles, the effects of these dynamics are often both unpredictable and paradoxical (Farran 2009). In Fiji it basically set up a system to protect the rights of communal landowning units by taking the everyday management of land away from them, effectively making them 'toothless tigers' that are 'neither controlling nor managing their own land' (Sharma 1999). In what can be seen as a direct inversion of customary Fijian land tenure, which puts landownership in the hand of commoners, the NLTB was legally constituted overwhelmingly by chiefs (nominated by the now defunct Great Council of Chiefs and the Fijian Affairs Board) and government ministers (who also traditionally held chiefly offices). In practical terms, owing to 'increasing commodification and eventual parliamentary rule, the control of the NLTB became the material base for a modern chiefly elite' who 'were now in a key position to act as landowners'

(Rutz 1987: 540) as the larger economic context was shifting from the moral economy to market relations.

While business dealings and the Fijian way of life had long been considered two 'alternate paths' (Thomas 1997) that signified deep, cultural, racial and moral distinctions, doing business was, from the immediate postcolonial period onwards increasingly promoted as the way to modernise Fiji. Political officials and chiefs sought to implement a number of strategies, from tax breaks to affirmative action, to facilitate increased commercial participation from Fijians (Williksen-Bakker 2002). While commoners to a large extent became wage labourers in the growing market economy, chiefs and other traditional leaders used their position as landowners or representatives of communal landowning units to position themselves as an urban middle class, heavily invested in commerce and land development as well as dominating political institutions and the civil service, that is 'committed to the commodification of Fijian land' (Rutz 1987: 555). The inherent antagonism in this class relation, however, was largely contained by the mutual insistence on the moral superiority of the moral economy, *vakavanua*. Chiefs generally maintained strong cultural ties with their kin groups and villages who, in turn, came to 'depend increasingly upon the patronage and resources dispensed by government in the guise of chiefly redistribution' (Rutz 1987: 556). The result, Rutz contends, is that the moral economy is strengthened by the market in two ways: 'urban wage earners use it as social insurance, and elites use it to ensure their retention of power' (1987: 556).

Though Rutz uses the term 'commodification' to describe how land becomes a market asset in the modern Fijian economy, I find it more analytically fruitful to maintain the term 'entification' to describe this process. Commodification is a more exclusively economic term used to describe the process through which unsalable items (or services and ideas) become commensurable and saleable on the market. One could say that this is not necessarily the case with Fijian land, which to a great extent remains in the inalienable ownership of indigenous Fijian kinship units. What has happened, however, is that a previously contingent cultural concept, *vanua*, has been reduced to a commensurable entity, land, which is legally and economically definable. Analysing this as a form of entification allows a more nuanced consideration, not only of the agency Fijian chiefly elites exercised in this process but also the particular political and historical context in which it took place. Ernst writes that his use of the concept entification corresponds in meaning to what Nicholas Thomas

(1992) calls substantivisation; that is on 'the stipulation of practices and institutions by an indigenous people for purpose of their "reflecting upon and manipulating" them (p. 64) in determinate situations, particularly colonial ones (p. 65)' (Ernst 1999: 90). This seems very appropriate in the Fijian context, where land became entified through the interaction between local elites and colonial administrators and the emerging institutions of the NLTB, the Great Council of Chiefs and the Native Affairs Board. In more general terms, I suggest that this conceptualisation is useful inasmuch as entification may be considered a prerequisite for commodification and a central part of the process through which traditional, moral economies move towards marketisation.

Underpinning this economic shift in the Fijian context was an emerging discourse about the value of land in the lease market driven by growing demand for land by urban settlers, Indo-Fijian smallholders and, increasingly from the 1970s, tourist investors and developers. The process of entification, then, is integral to what we can call value-creation; that is, the social negotiation and ordering of objects, subjects, rituals and actions. Ethnographically I demonstrate this point below by arguing that the reconfiguration of Fijian land which occurred as a result of modern land tenure legislation that facilitated increased marketisation highlights this theoretical point inasmuch as it made indigenous Fijian perceive the value of the *vanua* in different terms.

As the NLTB became progressively more entrepreneurial in terms of making land available for commercial developments, the inherent contradiction 'between the value and uses of land in a moral economy as opposed to those of an expanding real estate market', and, by extension, between rural Fijian landowners and more centrally placed ones, became increasingly apparent (Rutz 1987: 542). There has long been an underlying discordance between coastal landowning units and those with landowning rights in the more remote and undeveloped hinterlands of Viti Levu and Vanua Levu. The former have historically had the strategic advantages of better access to marine resources and international trade routes, as well as having dominated the formal political hierarchy since unification. In terms of development and social equality, one of the major fault-lines in contemporary Fiji similarly runs between coastal villages and remote highland ones. The development of land as a crucial entity for large-scale commercial developments has augmented these divisions and highlighted the significant price difference between coastal and inland areas.

While much of the early cultural anxiety about modernisation and capitalism was centred on the fear of losing indigenous sovereignty over Fijian land, during more recent decades this was increasingly replaced by an anxiety associated with the use-value of the *vanua* in the context of development projects. In what can be described as another 'double movement' in the Fijian modern economy, settlements that found themselves on highly marketable land became 'targets for subdivision and land development' and became 'fertile ground upon which the moral economy confronts the market' (Rutz 1987: 543) and competing understandings of the *vanua* are played out. The discontent and frustration expressed by my friend Seru and other village leaders in contemporary Fiji are obviously causally connected to these earlier developments pertaining to the marketisation of the *vanua*, in the sense that it is in the confrontation with market dynamics that the limited material benefits of maintaining landownership and a spiritual connection to the land become obvious. The connection, I argue, is best understood through a theorisation of how Fijian villagers are forced to rethink the meaning of the *vanua* and their relationship to it under the conditions of the market economy.

The Market Value of the Vanua

Turner points out that Marx's theory of value 'is inseparable from his totalizing conception of the nature of social systems of production in the broadest sense' (2008: 44). It follows that value can only be understood as a category existing within the totality of a particular mode of production. One could perhaps say that the key analytical problem in the Fijian context, then, is that the meaning of the *vanua* in the traditional moral economy has become redefined within the totalising mode of the market economy, and that this particular confrontation serves to crystallise the problems in reconciling the two modes ideologically. That the relationship between the two remains unsettled can account for the tension that occurs when entities or agents move between the different spheres, for instance when Fijian villagers take up wage work (Presterudstuen 2014) or, more specifically relevant in this context, local landowning units negotiate lease payments or development deals for their land.

When reflecting upon Seru's outburst and discussing his viewpoints at length at a later stage, it seemed clear to me that the main source of his anger was associated with the realisation that the intrinsic worth the *vanua* had in the moral economy, among his villagers, was seemingly wholly disconnected from its market value, in the sense that they could not capitalise on it. In his words, his attempts at 'bringing the village into modern times', which he interpreted as being characterised by better facilities such as stable electricity and phone connections, as well as seeing more villagers in waged work or post-primary education, had been thwarted by not only volatile market conditions but also a structural disadvantage of him not being part of the urban 'business elite'.

A central aspect of Seru's disappointment, and that of other similarly positioned landowners who felt they missed out on the benefits of development, was that the lack of material offset for landownership conflicted with a central political narrative in Fiji. Ever since land was 'entified' the dominant discourse has highlighted that indigenous Fijians would not only live off their *vanua* but also that their inalienable right to it would guarantee real material benefits, much as European and Indian capital secured their wealth.

While the details about the specific negotiations that took place are sparse, it seems clear that a Malaysian/Chinese business conglomerate sounded out several villages in the Nausori Highlands about the potential to develop an eco-tourist resort and, according to Seru and some other interlocutors, commercial farming ventures on indigenous land. Plans had been presented at two public meetings, where villagers were provided data about potential lease income and other benefits, but in the end the developers decided the plans were not financially viable.[4]

One general point derived from these ethnographic examples, that may serve to highlight the need for developing an operative anthropological theory of value, is that systems of production and exchange presuppose and facilitate conceptualisations of value with applications outside the economic sphere. Indeed, one of the central tenets of the Marxian theory of value is that it is intrinsically connected to the social production of relations not only between people and things but also, by extension, between people and their environment and between people and people.

These dynamics are more clearly illustrated by an ethnographic example from a different village I visited regularly during my fieldwork that experienced a similar sense of losing out on the benefits of the land, albeit for different reasons. This village, let us call it Vanaka for the purpose of this discussion, is located along the south-western coast of Viti Levu, one of Fiji's premium tourist strips, generally referred to as the Coral Coast. Two kinship groups in the village controlled significant amounts of unsettled and largely uncultivated land outside the boundaries of the villages. Much of the land was described as 'swamp and mangrove' that had not been utilised for anything but launching dinghies for fishing, harvesting mud crabs or dumping rubbish for the last decades. Most villagers were thus very positive about negotiating a deal when it became known that international developers had approached the NLTB with an interest in obtaining a long-term commercial lease on the location for tourist purposes. After being promised a 'handy sum' (my friends in the village had never been given the details about the negotiations as this was 'a matter for the chief' and the NLTB) of lease money paid annually, as well as support for improvements in the village's water supply and promises of employment opportunities at the resort, the vast majority of villagers had been in favour of the development proposal.

When I visited the village, the American-owned, four star resort that was eventually developed had been in operation for nearly a decade. While every sign indicates that the resort thrives and that tourists visiting, largely middle-aged couples or small families from Australia or New Zealand, have a satisfying Fijian experience (complete with Fijian dance shows, fire-walking and food prepared in *lovo* [earth-ovens]), Vanaka villagers claimed to have received little benefit from its presence on their land. A handful of villagers had been able to find a job with the company, but many struggled to gain a foothold in a tourist labour market that has its own structural limitations. Little had come of the expected village development and most, including the village spokesman, considered the lease money to be insufficient according to the current economic climate; 'peanuts' was a common metaphor.

While the historical or cultural properties are intrinsic to the traditional importance of a particular area of land in Fiji's village economy, this does not necessarily translate easily into strictly financial terms. While the commodification of cultural practices and artefacts into marketable stories, performances and events, such as, in the Fijian context, *meke* dances or fire-walking (Pigliasco 2010), this takes place in particular commercial contexts from which many Fijians view the *vanua* as distinctly separate. Indeed, both Seru and the villagers of Vanaka operated with a valuation of the *vanua* that was immaterial, so to speak. When attempting to translate this into rent price, the result was also unquantifiable – they had a sense of what to expect in terms of development outcomes, access to employment and 'a handy sum' of rent, but no fixed price or formula for calculating this. Added to this, the process of negotiating deals and accessing lease benefits is relatively opaque and far removed from individual villagers – instead it is dealt with by chiefs and the anonymous body of the NLTB. In the village, discourses about money matters and distribution are also mediated by social mores pertaining to status, consanguinity and traditional power that make them difficult to bring up and discuss openly for most commoners.

For many, the stark contrast between the luxury resort and life in the village was proof enough that they had not managed to get enough benefits out of the lease. Some explicitly used this to reflect on the rent price of their land – 'What is it worth to bang our chest and say we are landowners when we can't make any worth for ourselves [sic]', one of my friends lamented in a sober assessment of their inability to extract more material benefits from their property. This also tied into the most dramatically negative experience many villagers had in relation to the land deal: they experienced that they had lost the use of parts of their own land and, more importantly, their own coastline from where they had extracted seafood and fish for self-sustenance for centuries. Not only were the hotel grounds gated and guarded, and thus out of bounds for villagers, but the villagers' sea access was also limited by the hotel's use of the coastline for beach and water-sport facilities for paying guests. In other words, though the villagers remained inalienable owners of the land-entity to which they are traditionally entitled by law, they were inhibited from utilising big parts of it freely.

While, in economic terms, the key issue appears to be whether the recompense from developers and tourists corresponds to the use-value of the land, this misses a key point about the value of the *vanua* in the non-market economy. Given that the *vanua* encompasses a number of central cultural concepts, including social relations and belonging, its worth is difficult to reduce into an economic category. Instead it has value by virtue of 'being there', that is, being the central concept that provides local identities and communities, and providing space that can be utilised for a wide array of social purposes, ranging from habitation and food production to ritual presentations. The case study of Vanaka village highlights that the status of land is at the centre of the ongoing tension between the traditional, moral economy and the modern market.

Conclusion

While the inalienability of native landownership once was touted as a way to safeguard Fijian sovereignty, maintain the village as the site of traditional life and protect indigenous Fijians from the dangers of modern capitalism, its very structure was full of contradictions. A key one of those is that, while land itself was protected from commercial exchange, land use became *de facto* commodified through the lease system. However, whether it is use of land rather than ownership of land that has been commodified has little practical significance for Fijian villagers, given that the result is strikingly similar – they lose control of their land. Indeed, one can say that the process of articulating exchange-value on land in itself undermines the land's use-value in the sense that it alienates Fijian landowners from their ancestral territory. This becomes doubly problematic given that ancestral land lies at the centre of Fijians' socio-cultural universe.

Local discontent with the outcomes of land leases is consequently played out around the issue of value. In his landmark work on the emerging conflicts associated with land use, Henry J. Rutz argued that such disputes were always concerned about living costs and house prices in Fiji's growing urban centres and 'not the social value or moral issues of rights per se, although at times discontents about market prices might become mystified as moral issues' (1987: 535). The data presented in this chapter modifies this statement on an important point. In the current era of mass tourism, the distinction between the moral economy and the market has become increasingly blurred. In fact, the discontent expressed by my interlocutors in the Nausori Highlands and Vanaka village indicates that discourses about value are explicitly situated in the interrelation between the two economic spheres. In short, Fijian villagers increasingly perceive themselves and their environment as being affected by the market economy, an economic and social sphere over which they have limited control. Still, an increasing number of Fijian village leaders seem to share Seru's sentiments about commercial development and engagement in the tourism industry being the only possible path into economic security and social progress. In terms of what I have identified as the Fijian 'double movement' between social protectionism and commercialisation of land, then, one may say that these landowners find themselves in the paradoxical situation of pushing for the dynamics that will eventually alienate them from their *vanua*.

Notes

1. Field conversations and interviews were conducted in English or a mixture of local Fijian dialects and English, and, where necessary, translations are my own. All references to my interlocutors are pseudonyms.
2. Here I follow Colin Filer (2014) and Filer and Michael Lowe (2011) in conceptualising the notion of 'double movements' as a more flexible and historically

or ethnographically specific dynamic than the more narrow definition provided by Karl Polanyi.

3. This institution is now known as the iTaukei Land Trust Board. Given the references to this institution is largely historical I will maintain the NLTB acronym when referring to the board.
4. Although the nature of these financial dealings makes details difficult to confirm, this version of events was verified by a financial broker who had acted as an adviser to the company in question.

References

Bryan, D. 1990. 'Natural' and 'improved' land in Marx's theory of rent. *Land Economics* 66(2): 176–81.

Capell, A. (ed.). 1991 [1941]. *The Fijian Dictionary*. Suva: Government Printer.

Dickhardt, M. 2005. *Viti*, the soil from Eden: On historical praxis as a mode of connecting in Kadavu. *Oceania* 75(4): 342–53.

Ernst, T. 1999. Land, stories and resources: Discourse and entification in Onabasulu modernity. *American Anthropologist* 101(1): 88–97.

Farran, S. 2009. Land as a fundamental right: A cautionary tale. *Victoria University of Wellington Law Review* 40(1): 387–402.

Farrelly, T.A. 2011. Indigenous and democratic decision-making: Issues from community-based ecotourism in the Bouma National Heritage Park, Fiji. *Journal of Sustainable Tourism* 19(7): 817–35.

Fiji Bureau of Statistics. Key Statistics 2010. Available at: www.statsfiji.gov.fj (accessed 10 October 2015).

Filer, C. 2014. The double movement of immovable property rights in Papua New Guinea. *Journal of Pacific History* 49(1): 76–94.

Filer, C. and M. Lowe. 2011. One hundred years of land reform on the Gazelle Peninsula: A Baining point of view. In V. Strang and M. Busse (eds) *Ownership and Appropriation*. Oxford: Berg, pp. 149–70.

France, P. 1969. *The Charter of the Land: Custom and Colonization in Fiji*. Melbourne: Oxford University Press.

iTaukei Land Trust Board. 2015. iTaukei Landowners. Available at: https://www.tltb.com.fj/itaukei-landowners/ (accessed 2 October 2015).

Kanemasu, Y. 2013. Social construction of touristic imagery: Case of Fiji. *Annals of Tourism Research* 43: 456–81.

Nabobo-Baba, U. 2006. *Knowing and Learning: An Indigenous Fijian Approach*. Suva, Fiji: Institute of Pacific Studies.

Overton, J. 1993. Farms, suburbs, or retirement homes? The transformation of village Fiji. *The Contemporary Pacific* 5: 45–64.

Pigliasco, G. 2010. We branded ourselves long ago: Intangible cultural property and commodification of Fijian firewalking. *Oceania* 80(2): 253–73.

Polanyi, K. 2001 [1944]. *The Great Transformation: The Political and Economic Origins of Our Times*. Boston, MA: Beacon Press.

Presterudstuen, G.H. 2014. Masculinity in the marketplace: Geographies of post-colonial gender work in modern Fiji. In P. Hopkins and A. Gorman-Murray (eds) *Masculinity and Place*. London: Ashgate, pp. 401–14.

Ravuvu, A.D. 1987. *The Fijian Ethos*. Suva, Fiji: Institute of Pacific Studies.

Rutz, H.J. 1987. Capitalizing on culture: Moral ironies in urban Fiji. *Comparative Studies in Society and History* 29(3): 533–57.

—— 1995. Occupying the headwaters of 'tradition'. In R. Foster (ed.) *Nation Making in Melanesia*. Ann Arbor: University of Michigan Press, pp. 71–94.

Scheyvens, R. and M. Russel. 2012. Tourism, land tenure and poverty alleviation in Fiji. *Tourism Geographies* 14(1): 1–25.

Sharma, S. 1999. The control and protection of Native lands in Fiji. *Journal of South Pacific Law* 3. Available at: https://www.usp.ac.fj/index.php?id=13153 (accessed 12 October 2015).

Thomas, N. 1992. Substantivization and anthropological discourse: The transformation of practices into institutions in neotraditional Pacific societies. In J.G. Carrier (ed.) *History and Tradition in Melanesian Anthropology*. Berkeley: University of California Press, pp. 64–86.

—— 1997. *In Oceania: Visions, Artifacts, Histories*. Durham, NC: Duke University Press.

Thornton, A. 2009. Garden of Eden? The impact of resettlement on squatters' 'agri-hoods' in Fiji. *Development in Practice* 19(7): 884–94.

Tomlinson, M. 2004. Memes and metaculture: The politics of discourse circulation in Fiji. *Australian Journal of Anthropology* 15(2): 185–97.

Toren, C. 1988. Making the present, revealing the past: The mutability and continuity of tradition as process. *Man* (n.s.) 23: 696–717.

Turner, T. 2008. Marxian value theory: An anthropological perspective. *Anthropological Theory* 8(1): 43–56.

Tuwere, I.S. 1992. *Making Sense of Vanua (Land) in the Fijian Context: A Theological Exploration*. PhD thesis, Melbourne College of Divinity.

Ward, R.G. 1995. Land, law and custom: Diverging realities in Fiji. In R.G. Ward and E. Kingdon (eds) *Land, Custom and Practice in the South Pacific*. Cambridge: Cambridge University Press, pp. 198–249.

Williksen-Bakker, S. 2002. Fijian business, a bone of contention: Was it one of the factors leading to the political crisis in 2000? *Australian Journal of Anthropology* 13(1): 72–87.

5

Natural Value

Rent-capture and the Commodification of a Waterfall in *Gran Sabana*, Venezuela

Luis Fernando Angosto-Ferrández

In this chapter I examine the transformation of waterfalls into rent-capturing commodities in the Venezuelan *Gran Sabana* (Great Savannah) and discuss the source of exchange-value in this transformation. I argue that the emergence of this type of rent-capturing commodity, in which members of the Pemon indigenous people are actively participating, is related to a form of collective labour that I denominate cultural labour. This type of labour is discursively presented as associated with the collective creational powers of one's group ancestors in relation to a commodified thing, and also with the way in which the forms of life of one's own group (presented through the idioms of culture and tradition) contribute to the conservation of such thing. I will argue that this type of commodification can be interpreted as a response to the negative impacts of historical processes of dispossession, but also that it is essentially a dynamic of capitalist expansion.

An ethnographic vignette will be used to introduce my research questions and theoretical explanations. The chapter's structure will then follow a sequence unfolding in three main sections: the first contextualises the discussion by situating my field site in geosocial terms; the second establishes a theoretical frame to analyse the process of waterfalls being turned into rent-capturing commodities; the final section discusses the potential for developing the concept of modern accumulation to explain such a process and explore its consequences.[1]

An Awakening Swim

In October 2011, I took a trip to the Pemon community of Tuauken, in the Venezuelan Gran Sabana, as an opportunity to visit Sekaikömeru waterfalls.[2]

I was travelling with Francisco, born and raised in that community but living for years in Ciudad Bolívar, where I met him. He had never before visited these falls, despite their relative proximity to Tuauken (some two hours walking). Though I had lived in the community for nearly a year (in 2004) and returned there annually since 2006, I had not even heard about these falls until 2008, when, during one of my visits they were mentioned in casual conversations about work projects. From then onwards it became common for me to hear about Sekaikömeru and other waterfalls in the vicinity I had never heard of. Waterfalls had become more prominent in the conversational mappings of the local territory, and there was an interest in showing them to tourists.

Sitting by the riverside after a refreshing dip at Sekaikömeru, I told Francisco that the place was well worth the detour of over one hour that we were adding to our journey, and also that I could see why people in the community had thought of setting up a tourist camp there. Francisco agreed that Sekaikömeru was more beautiful a spot than the rapids of Kamoiran – one of the most popular tourist attractions in the area.

When we resumed our walk the waterfalls still lingered in our conversation. Francisco recalled that the idea of setting up a tourist camp in Sekaikömeru had originally been suggested by his brother Tomás, who still lives in Tuauken. However, the hut that we had found by the waterfall's top, a declared first step for the establishment of a basic tourist camp, had been erected by Alberto (another member of the community and, while kin, not part of the extended family of which Tomás's household is a part). The camp was still an unfulfilled project then, and it remains so to this date, but in the community everyone took it for granted that Alberto's family would take over if it were to be finally realised.

That particular first swim at Sekaikömeru was awakening for me. The region's waterfalls and the tourist camps around some of them appeared to me in a new light. Nowadays, these camps provide accommodation, toilets and sometimes meals, and are generally run by Pemon families as private ventures. Some of them have been at work in Gran Sabana for decades, but of recent years there has been a noticeable mushrooming. Fences preventing unregulated access are now to be found around several of these spots, and fees are charged for entrance. This is a very recent novelty.

While I had till then taken these ventures as expression of the increasing engagement of the Pemon population in the tourist industry, and more generally in market activities, after that swim I also started to gain insight into the double socio-cultural move that the foundation of any of these tourist camps involves: on the one hand, the *discovery* of (exchange-) value in units of Nature that were not previously objectified by locals as possessing it;[3] on the other hand, the appearance of some form of ownership claims over units of a territory in which individual property rights were non-existent and collective ones gave room to degrees of fuzziness. The project around Sekaikömeru illustrated that question: the (potential) enclosure and establishment of permanent private property rights around this waterfall was dependent on a first move that could have been taken by several inhabitants of the community in whose territory the waterfall is located.

So what caused that (exchange-)value to suddenly crystallise in and around a waterfall that did not previously have it for the local population? And what was the creational source of that value? How had this value been produced, if one could say that there had been a productive process involved at all? What determined the entitlement to set up a permanent camp around one of these waterfalls, and what type of ownership claims supported these new ventures? To what extent did these activities impact on conceptions of property among the Pemon? These questions developed in relation to a variety of episodes and concerns that I registered during fieldwork in the region. In this chapter I will be able to address several of these questions by discussing the process of commodification of units of Nature that transversally connects them.

A description of the geosocial space in which this process has been taking place will provide some clues to understanding such process and its implications for the lives of people in indigenous communities.

The Gran Sabana

The so-called Gran Sabana, geologically situated in the Guyanese Plateau, is a vast region in Venezuela's south-east. Its landscape presents a mosaic of savannah, forest, mountains and hills, all crossed by myriad watercourses. It is ancestral territory of the Pemon people,[4] and at present also the receptacle of a complex of social interests articulated by a variety of actors within and without the region.

In Venezuela, Gran Sabana is commonly identified with the municipal unit to which it lends its name, in Bolívar state. This is the largest federal unit in the country (240,528 sq. km), spreading over one-quarter of the national territory. This region borders with Guyana to the east and Brazil to the south, and has a very low population density (less than one person per square kilometre). These factors mark it as an area of prime importance for national security.[5]

In addition to frontier security concerns, one of the key military posts in the area, the Marikuya fort in Luepa, has gained new strategic salience after becoming one of the two land support bases for the Simón Bolívar satellite, launched on a wave of official publicity in 2008 and a beacon of national sovereignty since.

Most of this region is covered by Canaima National Park, created in 1962 over 3 million hectares and in 1994 declared Natural Patrimony of Humanity by UNESCO. In the western fringes of this region flows the Caroní River, at the core of a basin of crucial importance for the country: its waters feed the dams that generate 80 per cent of the country's electricity. Understandably, the preservation of good environmental conditions in and around the basin region is considered a strategic goal for the country too. An estimated 87 per cent of the basin area is covered under varieties of the so-called Regimes of Special Administration (Áreas Bajo Régimen de Administración Especial [ABRAE]), which aim to regulate the uses that can be given to the territory and resources (Martens Ramírez 2011: 143–44). For decades such preservation goals have been at odds with aspects of traditional production and management of the territory involving practices such as the controlled burning of savannah and forest or hunting, but are also in direct opposition to activities such as mining that are essential pillars of the region's economy.

Medium-sized mine workings are to be found in several locations of the Gran Sabana's vicinity, and small-scale mining of gold and diamonds has taken place in and around this region uninterruptedly since the nineteenth century. Though the aggregate input of small-scale mining into the national economy remains relatively low (an estimated 1.7 per cent of the total national mining production), it is extensive in geographical scope and important in the generation of regional employment and revenue (Milano 2014).[6] Mining sites are in areas with continuing presence of indigenous communities, some of whom are nowadays totally dependent on this economic activity. Yet mining is increasingly a source of conflict. In addition to environmental degradation and the string of accidents and health-related issues that mining generates, there have been violent clashes. These range from contests among rival bands of miners trying to exert de facto control over rights to extraction to confrontations between local miners and members of the National Guard in indigenous communities where the latter are alleged to have established extortive regulations over producers (Angosto-Ferrández 2015: 225–29).

Another way in which economic activity and its links with space are generating remarkable pressures derives from the municipal capital, Santa Elena de Uairén, which holds ever-larger shares of population and economic activity. In addition to being a centre for services and public administration jobs, its economic salience is increased by its status as a frontier town. It is the door to and from Brazil, the largest market in Latin America. In 1999 the town was declared a free port, and over the past decade it has repeatedly been labelled in politicians' declarations and policy documents as an 'engine' for regional development.

Santa Elena is of course the main point for provision of commercial supplies for the inhabitants of indigenous communities and mining centres in the vicinity, but at present also for Brazilians on the other side of the border. With a very favourable exchange rate and the added appeal of the heavily subsidised gasoline prices in Venezuela, Brazilinas living in the town of La Línea/Pacaraima, just across the border, frequently shop and refill in Santa Elena. Some even travel from the city of Boa Vista, nearly three hours away by car, to do part of their household shopping. Smuggling gasoline constitutes a lucrative business in itself, and it is widely recognised as the source of corruption in the area.

In a context of scarcity of goods and rampant inflation in Venezuela (estimated to be above 150 per cent in 2015), the situation for people who live on a salary in a border town like Santa Elena becomes even more complicated than elsewhere. Distribution is not fluid in normal circumstances, with the eight-hour drive that separates the town from the main cities in northern Bolívar being an obstacle for some products – a telling indication is that newspapers only arrive in town in the afternoon and in small quantities, on occasion not making it there at all. But in a period of economic crisis, access to goods and prices worsens exponentially. The inflation in town is increased by the willingness of Brazilians and miners to pay high prices, and of some sellers to speculate. In March 2015, a friend from a Pemon community neighbouring Santa Elena, who teaches in the local school, put it to me jokingly when recalling his shopping visits to town: he regularly quarrels with shopkeepers, asking if the prices marked on the products are those for 'the Brasileros, for the miners or for the Indians'.

The growth of Santa Elena has come up against physical limits, with a lack of housing for newcomers becoming a problem and the indigenous communities surrounding the town actively organising in order to prevent land invasions – in some recent cases using firearms and sticks. This organised defence of land clashes with the interests and perspectives of a variety of actors who arrive in the place in search of jobs, business or better life opportunities. A woman from Ciudad Bolívar, who arrived in Santa Elena in 2011, gave me an illustrative comment about this. She was working in a department of the Ministry of Agriculture and, given the lack of other suitable accommodation, she was living in the same house that serves as the department's office four years after her arrival in town: 'With so much land in this area and one does not have a house!' In an indirect reference to the organised opposition to dispossession among members of the indigenous communities in the area (and which includes but is not limited to participation in institutional politics), she added: 'But you know, the Indians rule here!'

Despite its other appeals, this region remains most renowned, both within and outside Venezuela, as a tourist destination. Among other natural prodigies, it harbours the so-called Angel's Falls (Kerepakupai Meru), the highest waterfall in the planet, and scenic table-top mountains (*tepuys*) such as Roraima, the destination of trekking tours that attract people from around the world. These are two icons among a large range of attractions that, particularly at peak vacation periods in Venezuela (around Christmas, Easter and July and August), bring tens of thousands of visitors to the area.

Up until recently, tourism as a permanent economic activity was only prominent in a few Pemon communities – those located near the most accessible and/or iconic natural attractions in the region. But over the past ten years there has been a very noticeable expansion and diversification of this activity, with adventure tourism and trekking tours moving into new areas and involving new actors. There is growing participation of Pemon people as direct service providers and business owners. This industry provides a viable economic activity for a part of the local population, but is also generating conflicts stemming from different perspectives on relations to the environment and property rights, as we shall see below.

These broad brushstrokes delineate the contours of a complex geosocial landscape. Many competing views regarding land use converge in the region, including conflicting forms of territorial regulation and property claims. Private land titles (whether collective or individual) are an exception in this region, whose use nevertheless remains regulated by a variety of often contradictory sets of regulations, ranging from National Parks to the so-called 'Region of Frontier Security' areas. Pemon communities and the so-called sectors (*sectores*) in which they are organised are currently involved in processes of territory demarcation and collective titling under the constitutional rights granted to indigenous peoples in the Bolivarian constitution of 1999 – with uneven successes (Angosto-Ferrández 2015: 107–13).[7] And all this constitutes the general context in which the transformation of waterfalls into commodities is taking place. A look at the economic foundations of the Pemon community in which Sekaikömeru is located will contribute to further contextualise the processes conditioning (and being affected by) such transformation.

A (Type of) Pemon Community

Sekaikömeru is near Tuaken, a Pemon (Arekuna) community in Gran Sabana. Some 4–5 hours walking along savannah trails, or around two hours by four-wheel drive transportation via a rough unpaved road, separate this community from the Troncal 10 – the only paved road crossing this region. These relatively small distances have been sufficient to maintain the community at the fringes of the capitalist frontier, up to date.

Its local census registers nearly 200 inhabitants, and the community is sustained by a relatively autonomous semi-subsistence economy. In analytical terms, this is a community with *market participation*: most of its members have periodical and generally voluntary involvement with the market. In those same terms, there are other communities in the region with *market dependence*: their members have to participate in the market, having lost access to subsistence goods outside it (Wood, 2002; Byres, 2006). This analytical distinction finds expression in narratives of collective identification circulating among communities situated on different sides of the market boundary. Such narratives present diverging notions of what it means to be indigenous, with communities situated on the 'market participation' side generating narratives in which autonomy from the market and reliance on one's own production for subsistence become associated with a positively invested notion of indigeneity; in communities situated on the other side, narratives can be found associating direct engagement with the market and modernisation with positively invested notions of indigeneity (Angosto-Ferrández 2013). On both sides of the divide, however, one finds today strong evidence that the Pemon population is seeking avenues to create new economic activity, or to consolidate existing activity that enables them to remain rooted in their locality, strengthening threatened ownership over sectors of their territory and avoiding migration as the only avenue to access monetary income. It is worth noting that personal accounts of those who have gone through labour migrations have more the character of an ordeal than of an appealing choice. For example, two men I regularly talk with during my visits to the region worked, respectively, in a bakery (*panadería*) in Ciudad Bolívar and in a mining town on the edges of Gran Sabana. Both of them recall their experiences as times of personal crises and degradation. They recall that often they had to 'endure hunger' (*aguantar hambre*) after drinking their money, and speak of the period with expressions idiomatically associated with poor physical and spiritual health ('*me puse flaco*', '*me gustaba pelear*'). Both of them returned to Gran Sabana eventually, 'to live peacefully' (*a vivir tranquilo*), as they say. The one working in the mines often repeats that, at some point, he was severely ill and was 'rescued' by his father, who travelled to the mines and brought him back to Tuaken.

In this community, nuclear families remain the basic units of production and consumption, and all of them keep at least a garden that, through the system of rotating slash and burn, and with minimal technification, produces the basis of the diet. The production is dedicated to self-consumption and distribution through ordinary intra-community exchanges or, more extraordinarily, communal meals. Occasionally surplus production of cassava bread is sold to people in neighbouring communities with market dependence.

The three schoolteachers receive the only permanent salaries in the community, through the public education system. Recently, some government social programmes have been the source of small and temporary stipends to local facilitators. An example has been *Misión Ribas*, one of the Bolivarian government programmes in the education sector implemented during the past decade – this *Misión* in particular provides a channel to complete the equivalent of secondary education.

In peak tourist seasons, many people, and on occasion entire families, move in temporarily with relatives in the neighbouring community of Riwo-Riwo, where a famous waterfall attracts thousands of visitors. In those periods cash is obtained through temporary jobs and the selling of artisanal production which relies on local resources – except for materials such as the plastic strings used for necklaces or the instruments for carving and puncturing. In the community or its near proximity there are no other sources of regular monetary income.

Despite a couple of attempts at setting up a shop, no one in the community monopolises the existing small-scale intra-community commerce of products such as hooks, matches, soap, salt and batteries –

and, more recently, rice, pasta, corn flour, oil or snacks. The availability of these products is never guaranteed, and it is common to find that buyer and seller exchange roles. Anyone making a trip outside the community and with some cash available could buy produce and become an occasional seller.

Other basic subsistence activities include fishing. This is carried out with hooks in the rivers and small water courses of the vicinity, and occasionally with artisanal traps or *barbasco* (in Pemon: *ada*). Ever more marginally, hunting with shotgun provides some meat (at present, basically from a type of *paca*). The nowadays taken for granted scarcity of prey has been accompanied by that of ammunition for the shotguns. In 2015, amid the general economic crisis, ammunition was scarce and sold at astronomic prices in towns like Santa Elena.

Hens that freely range around the family houses are consumed on special occasions or during the prolonged absence of other meat, and a few families possess cattle. These cattle had never been herded nor fed on cultivated pastures, but in the past five years an extended family has embarked on systematic cattle-raising, building a pen and supervising their cattle almost daily. On occasion they buy health supplements (e.g. salts, vaccines). They have the support of a relative living in the community of Maurak and working in a farm-school. The family's herds are growing in number and raising cattle for commercial purposes is an explicit part of the venture.

All these activities have been maintained in a social sphere in which conceptions of landownership fit into a model that, for heuristic purposes, can be classified as communal. Different types of collective rights are recognised in a community like Tuauken, ranging from those corresponding to regionally identified groups to those of local communities and families. However, permanent individual property rights upon demarcated land were not conceptualised, and in fact the boundaries of the land over which a family is recognised to exercise preferential rights are not rigidly defined. Among other factors, this relates to the fact that strongly sanctioned rights, such as those stemming from usufruct of the land that is being cultivated, never fully translated into permanence, given the rotational nature of the slash-and-burn system (gardens generally have a productive period of around three years). This ecological factor and associated patterns of settlement mobility in the Gran Sabana environment were congruent with conceptions of ownership over land not linked to rigidly fixed boundaries – these boundaries exist, but are dependent on process and social manoeuvre, and not cartographically demarcated. At any rate, formalised legal titles backing indigenous land rights are largely non-existent, though demarcation and titling claims are being processed at present. In this context, and with the threat of dispossession that, from many angles (mining, the military, growing pressure in Santa Elena), casts its shadow over this region, a transformation in the ways property rights are conceived is accompanying transformation in what is produced, and how it is produced. Against this background, let us discuss what transformations the plan for a tourist camp at Sekaikömeru might entail.

Where Does Value Come From?

Lest one naturalise the processes of commodification or conceptually detach them from the analysis of their causes and implications, the reasons why, at particular historical conjunctures, people actively embark on such processes deserve some scrutiny. The transformation of a thing into a commodity might indeed be an expression of change in 'the social life' of that thing, and perhaps only temporary – as Kopytoff (1986) and Appadurai (2003 [1994]) would have it. Yet primarily it is expression of change in the social life of the people around it.

Social relations are always modified by such transformation, and most saliently when people decide to make a commodity out of something that previously was not – and that might even have been part of some form of commons. In those cases, the constitutive components of that thing do not necessarily change, at least apparently, and the commodification move might be initiated without the mediation of labour power as a generative element in the transformation – let us think of the case of the waterfalls. In these cases, two questions can be fruitfully explored in order to shed light on the causes and consequences of the commodifying process: why does it happen (and why then), and how does it that happen? Marxian contributions to the definition of commodities and to the theorisation of value are useful tools for answering both questions.

Any answer to the first question will have to be accompanied by a logical (if sometimes overlooked) complement: this type of commodification becomes an index of incorporation (the degree of which can vary) into a system of relations in which commodities are recognised as units of wealth, and as concrete forms in which things with use-value are exchanged and circulated. Capitalism is currently such a system, and it can be said to expand or consolidate every time that a thing is transformed (always involving some form of conscious human decision) into a commodity. The reasons why concrete people embark on this process can be ethnographically explored, of course, as well as the consequences that such commodification have for sets of social relations and culturally mediated meanings. Yet even before such exploration one can safely surmise that social relations will be affected, particularly when commodification processes imply (and require) the creation of new forms of (private) property rights. These rights have a social character, for they always regulate people's relations with each other – as they affect and are affected by things (Nedelsky 2008).

In order to answer the second question, resorting to the Marxian theory of value as a starting point is probably even more illuminating. Commodities have an exchange-value, and clarifying where that value springs from might become revealing of concrete social conditions. To analyse the type of commodification I address here, I suggest that, initially, there must be a 'discovery' of exchange-value in/onto a thing and, subsequently, a '(re) production' of that value. In what follows I propose an explanation of how that occurs, but some additional discussion about what a commodity is will be necessary. Let me address this discussion by engaging Appadurai's influential work on commodities (1986, 2003 [1994]).

For Appadurai, understanding what a commodity is requires 'focusing on its total trajectory from production, through exchange/distribution, to consumption' (2003 [1994]: 82). Despite this appealing holistic proposal, his work has a tendency to slide towards an emphasis on the dynamics of exchange – at the expense of those of production. Appadurai considers that, rather than defining what a commodity is, it is more fruitful to discern how the exchange of commmodities differs from other forms of exchange – such as barter and gift exchange. In his view, all things have a 'commodity potential' and 'commodity candidacy'; commodities are thus just things in a particular situation at a particular moment of their social life. The commodity candidacy is dependent, Appadurai suggests, on conceptual constraints: 'the standards and criteria (symbolic, classificatory and moral) that define the exchangeability of things in any particular social and historical context' (2003 [1994]: 83). However, sidestepping the clarification of what a commodity is prevents any possibility of enquiring where value comes from (how it is produced). And this in turn strengthens the fetishism of commodities, for the mists it casts over the analysis of social relations within capitalism. So let us come back to conceptual definitions.

A conventional definition of commodity presents it as something that combines the following characteristics: it satisfies human necessities of some type, results from some process of human labour and is the depository of some exchange-value that does not depend on its natural properties but on the social relations implied in the idea of the market. The second of these characteristics is the one I am interested in discussing for the type of commodification addressed here: one in which there is no apparent human labour involved. Has Sekaikömeru been produced by Tomás or by Alberto? If so, how? An overview of theories of value in relation to Nature will help us clarify these questions.

Nature, Value and Rent-Capturing Commodities

An avenue to approach the analysis of the commodification of spaces of Nature is provided by the so-called Ecosystem Services (ES) conceptualising frame, through which setting a price on Nature becomes justified in order to conserve its services. In this volume, Fiona McCormack (chapter 8) critically engages this frame, sharing in the analysis of those who understand ES as an ideological frame that facilitates (capitalist) market expansion. For the case I address here, I will complement that perspective with others that, in analysing the emergence of commodities, have placed emphasis on the sphere of production.

Fernando Coronil (1997, 2001) was among those who have underscored the importance of theorising nature as a constitutive element of capitalist wealth – as something that was at its core from inception, and not only as a sphere into which capitalism can expand. Complementing Marxian theories of value, Coronil highlighted the importance that the commodification of what he denominated 'rent-capturing' or 'nature intensive' commodities, such as oil, had for the emergence and development of capitalism. He distinguished this type of commodity from those whose exchange-value directly rest on labour power.

Following this avenue to analyse the commodification of Sekaikömeru, a starting point is to situate this waterfall as part of what Marx conceptualised as 'land', which included agricultural land but also units of Nature such as mines, rivers or waterfalls – all 'powers of nature', as Coronil reminds us (1997: 47). Marx presented land as a material ingredient of any productive process: a non-produced condition of such process. Since he situated labour as the source of value, land obviously could not have such a thing – it could have price, but never value. That distinction explains why land, within that theoretical frame, is said to generate 'rent', which in turn was conceptualised as a form of value appropriation – value necessarily created elsewhere. This characteristic of land situated it as a competitor with capital in the appropriation of value – let us remember that capital, as Marx demonstrated, also does not itself produce value without the mediation of labour. The very existence of rent is therefore made dependent on two factors: on the one hand, the existence of surplus; on the other, the existence of property rights over land.

Against that backdrop, Coronil made a stimulating contribution by proposing a distinction between societies in which the commodification of Nature is the main source of revenues and societies in which the commodification of labour is such source. Though Coronil hastened to underscore that the commodification of Nature and that of labour were mutually dependent (Coronil 1997: 32), he nevertheless suggested that in the first of those two types of societies rent-capture becomes an important organising principle of economic life. With that proposal in mind, it is significant that in many postcolonial environments (and not only in Venezuela) one finds at present people who are transforming units of Nature into 'rent-capturing' commodities – and not only capital holders and their political agents, but also people belonging to groups whose social identities are partly defined by a history of exposure to dispossession and exploitation.

What we are now witnessing is that this creation of rent-capturing commodities is made through forms of propertisation and value generation that discursively present a direct negation of a central postulate of neoclassical macroeconomics: that natural resources do not have a cost of production. That is, people embark on the commodification of objectified units of Nature through a process in which their exchangeability becomes inextricably linked to demonstrating that 'land' (i.e. 'every power of nature') has a cost of production. Yet this appears as a particular type of production: one that rests on what I will denominate cultural labour.

De-Fetishising Commodities: Remembrance and Cultural Labour

As articulated by the actors involved in this form of commodification, cultural labour is associated with the collective *creational* powers of one's group ancestors in relation to the commodified thing, and/or with the emphasis on how the forms of life of one's own group (presented through the idioms of culture and tradition) contribute to the conservation of that particular thing. This type of labour can only be uncovered discursively, by revealing, as it were, the cultural identity of the commodity. For example, by revealing its intimate connection with the collective territory of which one is a part, with one's culture, with one's ancestors. Faced with the very real and historically experienced threat of dispossession and proletarianisation, revealing the existence of this type of cultural labour behind a commodity becomes a reinforcement of one's legitimate links with the 'producers' of such commodity. From an etic perspective, this type of commodification is then based on a de-fetishising move.

The fetishism of commodities, according to Marx, translated into the elimination from public awareness of the fact that abstract labour power is inscribed in commodities. Through this mechanism, an object (a commodity) ends up appearing as the representation and source of traits and powers that human labour inscribed in it. In Marx's view this was one of a number of deceitful beliefs that contribute to the shaping of social reality, distorting the actual groundings of the creation of value and its distribution in capitalist societies.

This type of commodification requires de-fetishisation, for it partly consists of discursively bringing into collective awareness that there is cultural labour inscribed in the newly uncovered (but always age-old) commodity. History, Culture and Identity thus become indispensable ingredients in these processes of commodification and propertisation. The producers of the commodity immediately become conservers of the commodified thing, revealing the cultural labour on which it rests and maintaining it as a de-fetishised object to be conserved.

This can theoretically explain what one finds in Gran Sabana around waterfalls, but also in many other parts of the world in which, for instance, units of Nature are being commodified by people belonging to groups whose social identities are partly defined by a history of dispossession and exploitation, generally in the periphery or semi-periphery of the world system. In consuming this type of commodity (for example, in the form of 'a visit'), one often finds an uncovering of the cultural labour that would have produced it. This can possibly be verbal (as in stories provided by guides), written (as in the signs to be found around the commodity), performative (as in a welcoming dance), or a combination of such signs that facilitate the revealing of that cultural labour (as well as the propertisation of the commodity). In Gran Sabana, for instance, this is identifiable in the narratives of creation that are currently articulated in some tourist literature and by some camp owners: the location of the fall within the Pemon aetiological myths can be brought out. But also in narratives of conservation: fences around a fall are justified as necessary to protect (to conserve) that unit of Nature from the degradation to which it is exposed by unregulated visitors.

Two types of remembrance can be distinguished in the creation of this type of commodity out of something that previously was not. One is remembrance of one's cultural past in the presentation of the commodity at the moment of exchange; it is the remembrance of a particular collective cultural history. The other is a more general remembrance, working as an antidote against the forgetting that Marx associated with the emergence of capitalism and with his concept of alienation: this is remembrance of the past of dispossession on which capitalism rests, often hidden from public awareness (cf. Eiss 2008: 89). A discursive uncovering of this forgotten history is often to be found when approaching the type of commodity discussed here – recollections of the violent impacts of colonialism upon the population of a colonised territory, for instance.

From Primitive to Modern Accumulation

Marx considered that it was indispensable to explain the emergence of capitalistic production, approached as a historically situated mode of production, in a way that could overcome the mystifying proposals of contemporary classical economists (ideas about the role of individual industriousness, savings and sacrifice, etc.). In his terms, there was a riddle to unravel: 'the accumulation of capital pre-supposes surplus value; surplus value pre-supposes capitalistic production; capitalistic production pre-supposes the pre-existence of considerable masses of capital and of labour power in the hands of the producers of commodities' (Marx 2008: 363). The concept of primitive accumulation contributed to unravel it: 'an accumulation not the result of the capitalist mode of production, but its starting point' (Marx 2008: 363). For him, primitive accumulation named those forms of (violent) expropriation that transformed land and means of production into capital and immediate producers into wage labourers.

This concept has been reoriented in a range of current analyses of capitalism, implying that 'primitive accumulation' would not be a historically completed process. From this angle primitive accumulation is considered to be a continuing process and not an early and overcome stage of the development of capitalism (Perelman 2000).

Stimulating redefinitions of the concept have associated it with 'the act of enclosure of a commons, whether that be the enclosure of land, bodies, social structures, or ideas', but also with 'the creation of capital for the first time through the commodification of things that previously lay outside the realm of capitalism' (Kelly 2011). This type of definition facilitates the analysis of late capitalism, where commodification seems to pervade human practice all over the world – as well as to generate opposing reactions all over the world too (examples of these reactions in the global north are provided by David Boarder Giles and Fern Thompsett (chs 9 and 10 in this volume). However, such definitions are less useful when it comes to explaining some of the particular characteristics of current capitalist expansion. Today, partly in response to histories of dispossession and proletarianisation, and also in the face of the apparent lack of political alternatives, new actors are incorporating themselves in the cycles of accumulation. They include people belonging to historically subaltern groups whose social identities have previously been partly defined by exploitation within capitalism, who now constitute a distinctive type of historical subject within the process of accumulation. Added to this peculiarity are the forms through which the active incorporation of these subjects into the global economy takes place (for instance, through the type of commodification that I have been analysing). In combination, these factors shape a process that deserves a distinctive conceptualisation: modern accumulation.

Modern accumulation is to be understood as a concept with structural rather than temporal connotations – I obviously do not mean 'modern' as opposed to 'primitive' in temporal-historical terms. This type of accumulation involves forms of value appropriation that transform the 'producers' into 'conservers' of commodified things, actively incorporating peripheral subjects into the world economy from a more advantageous position than that by which they had been historically constrained. It contributes to avoiding forms of proletarianisation associated with the vanishing of independent sources of subsistence that turns producers into wage labourers, and, which in peripheral areas of the world economy, often translated into forced migrations of the freed labour forces – when displacement had not been immediately forced in literal ways by the direct use of violence, in some variant of what Harvey (2005) conceptualised as accumulation by dispossession. The history (and present) of capitalism is therefore behind the creation of these new subjects of (modern) accumulation.

Polanyi made an important point when arguing that, among his contemporaries, the understanding of dispossession and destructuration of colonised populations was failing to develop a complementary understanding of the fact that that dispossession had previously occurred also among 'white' populations of the eighteenth century (2007: 261, 271, 292). Those populations had been largely unarmed (militarily, as it were, but also legally and conceptually) to respond to dispossession. But at present the people who continue to be threatened with it, as well as the descendants of some of the dispossessed, are evidently seeking alternatives. One of them is expressed in the direct confrontations against dispossession generated out of land invasions and extractivist projects. Another consists of an active incorporation into capitalism from positions of relative advantage by seeking, for instance, to secure ownership over 'land' ('every power of nature') and create rent-capturing commodities. This latter form can be read under the frame of modern accumulation processes. While effectively expanding the capitalist frontier, as did the so-called primitive accumulation, those processes enable (some) members of subaltern groups to gain advantages.

A Final Note

In analysing the commodification of a waterfall in this chapter I drew attention to the structural conditions that put growing socioeconomic pressures upon Pemon territory and stimulate the reactive process of modern accumulation. I also explained theoretically the process that underpins this. However, I did not elaborate on another, parallel and fundamental question: what conceptions of property rights – and thus social relations – these forms of commodification entail. This question relates to the potential effects of modern accumulation (as a form of capitalist expansion), some of which have already materialised. One of the effects of this process is that it is leading to the emergence of new forms of private property among the Pemon and within its ancestral territory, obviously affecting social relations. In this regard, modern accumulation is a concept that can facilitate the analysis and understanding of a particular type of cross-cultural current of capitalist expansion that we can witness today. But it also invites reflection on new mechanisms of class formation. One of those forms is the constitution of new classes of landowners in competition with capitalists for the appropriation of value. At present it is impossible to maintain teleological preconceptions about the character of 'cultures' and 'cultural groups' in relation to their position in the face of capitalism and capitalist social relations (cf. Li 2010), and, going against lingering conventional wisdom, some members of indigenous peoples are constituting themselves as one of the new classes of landowners in parts of the world, normally with the legitimate support of rights won through historical struggles against exploitation and dispossession. The other, but partly related form, rests on the constitution of class-based cleavages within some of the groups nowadays embarked on the process of what I have defined as modern accumulation. There are no waterfalls for all, as it were. In this sense, it is evident that the creation of new forms of property and rent-capturing commodities hints at the establishment of new classes structuring groups such as the Pemon.

Notes

1. I have presented versions of this chapter in panels of conferences in which I have received very helpful feedback (AILASA 2014, ASAANZ/AAS 2014 and AIBR 2015) from panel members and members of the audience. I am indebted to all of them. I am also very grateful to Geir H. Presterudstuen for insightful suggestions on a previous version of this chapter.
2. I am using pseudonyms for this particular location and the people appearing in these ethnographic notes.
3. The type of production of value that is involved here is obviously different from the one resting on labour, and it requires some distinctive name and conceptualisation. In order to facilitate it I choose the verb 'discovering'.
4. Pemon communities are scattered throughout the region and in adjacent areas of eastern Guyana and northern Brazil. There are three main subgroups in Venezuela of this Carib-speaking people: Arekuna, Kamarakoto and Taurepan. The Makushi, dwelling to the south of the nowadays Venezuelan Pemon, and with a long history of intermarriage and commercial exchange with the latter, self-denominate as Pemon too.
5. The frontier with Guyana is particularly sensitive. Venezuela does not officially recognise the territory east of the Esequibo River as Guyanese, and in fact claims sovereignty over it – the international Arbitration in 1899 that declared that territory as belonging to the then colonial British Guiana has been officially considered null and void by Venezuela since 1962 (Márquez 2002). The year 2015 was a very tense one in Venezuela–Guyana bilateral relations. In Venezuela, that year was marked by an important economic crisis that, in turn, underpinned the first institutionally significant electoral defeat of the governing Bolivarian bloc since the late Hugo Chávez gained the presidency in 1998. It was also precisely in 2015 that US company Exxon announced an oil discovery in disputed coastal territory, and an escalation of tensions ensued whose appeasement involved a meeting of the Venezuelan and Guyanese heads of state (Nicolás Maduro and David Granger, respectively) in the UN Assembly quarters in New York.
6. Data about the gold reserves in the Guyana mining region (which also includes other parts of Bolívar, Amazonas and Delta Amacuro states) varies substantially

according to different public sources (Milano 2014: 219), but the reserves are considered to be a very important asset for the national economy.

7. These sectors were a creation of the regional indigenous federation (Federación Indígena del Estado Bolívar) for organisational purposes. In some cases, the process of demarcation and titling has revealed contested views among the type of collective subject that should be recognised as a depository of rights: 'the community', 'the sector' or even 'the people'.

References

Angosto-Ferrández, L.F. 2013. Mundo perdido, paraíso encontrado: Lugar, identidad y producción en la Gran Sabana, Venezuela. *Revista Colombiana de Antropología* 49(1): 11–43.

—— 2015. *Venezuela Reframed: Bolivarianism, Indigenous Peoples and Socialisms of the Twenty-first Century*. London: Zed Books.

Appadurai, A. (ed.) 1986. *The Social Life of Things: Commodities in Cultural Perspective*. Cambridge: Cambridge University Press.

—— 2003 [1994]. Commodities and the politics of value. In S.M. Pearce (ed.) *Interpreting Objects and Collections*. London: Routledge, pp. 76–91.

Byres, T.J. 2006. Differentiation of the peasantry under feudalism and the transition to capitalism: In defence of Rodney Hilton. *Journal of Agrarian Change* 6(1): 17–68.

Coronil, F. 1997. *The Magical State: Nature, Money, and Modernity in Venezuela*. Chicago: University of Chicago Press.

—— 2001. Toward a critique of globalcentrism: Speculations on capitalism's nature. In J. Comaroff and J. Comaroff (eds) *Millennial Capitalism and the Culture of Neoliberalism*. Durham, NC: Duke University Press.

Eiss, P.K. 2008. Beyond the object: Of rabbits, rutabagas and history. *Anthropological Theory* 8(1): 79–97.

Harvey, D. 2005. *The New Imperialism*. Oxford: Oxford University Press.

Kelly, A. 2011. Conservation practice as primitive accumulation. *Journal of Peasant Studies* 38(4): 683–701.

Kopytoff, I. 1986. The cultural biography of things. In A. Appadurai (ed.) *The Social Life of Things*. Cambridge: Cambridge University Press, pp. 64–91.

Li, T.M. 2010. Indigeneity, capitalism, and the management of dispossession. *Current Anthropology* 51(3): 385–414.

Márquez, O.J. 2002. *La venezolanidad del Esequibo*. Caracas: Gráficas Franco.

Martens Ramírez, R. 2011. La demarcación del hábitat y tierras de comunidades y pueblos indígenas del estado Bolívar, entre el desarrollo nacional y la identidad cultural. *Boletín Antropológico* 29(82): 132–62.

Marx, K. 2008. *Capital: A New Abridgement*. Oxford: Oxford University Press.

Milano, S. 2014. Venezuela. In C. Heck and J. Tranca (eds) *La realidad de la minería ilegal en los países amazónicos*. Lima: Sociedad Peruana de Derecho Ambiental (SPDA), Negrapata.

Nedelsky, J. 2008. Reconceiving rights and constitutionalism. *Journal of Human Rights* 7(2): 139–73.

Perelman, M. 2000. *The Invention of Capitalism: Classical Political Economy and the Secret History of Primitive Accumulation*. Durham, NC: Duke University Press.

Polanyi, K. 2007. *La Gran Transformación: crítica del liberalismo económico*. Madrid: La Piqueta.

Wood, E.M. 2002. The question of market dependence. *Journal of Agrarian Change* 2(1): 50–87.

6

Capitalist Ventures or Solidarity Networks? Self-employment in Post-Soviet Cuba

Marina Gold

In the 1990s, following the collapse of the Soviet Union, Cuba was plunged into a severe social and economic crisis known as the Special Period in Times of Peace. Self-employment and private ventures re-emerged and proliferated in the socialist island. Observers of Cuban politics saw this as foreshadowing the end of socialism and the collapse of the revolution. However, in 2015, and in spite of the recent political rapprochement between Cuba and the USA, the Caribbean island still proclaims itself socialist. The purpose of this chapter is to consider the value of private property within a socialist context, at a time when capitalist trends increasingly penetrate Cuba and become somewhat transformed in that context. Is self-employment, or *cuentapropismo*, a symptom of the collapse of socialism in Cuba? What kinds of social relations coalesce around *cuentapropista* activities, such as rental houses? Are they only to be understood as petty capitalists, or is there a socialist ethos informing how people understand value in Cuba? I will first consider the Marxist notion of value, and relate it to the emergence of capitalism in Cuba. After tracing a brief history of house ownership throughout the revolution, I explore how Cubans understand the value of house ownership, and the activities that take shape within these ventures. I conclude with an analysis of the relationship between self-employment and the concept of revolution in Cuba.

Labour and Property

The value of capital relies on the capacity to capture and alienate someone's labour. However, Marx understood that speaking about value was not simply about labour. As Angosto-Ferrández suggests in the Introduction to this volume, Marx was interested 'in broader and deeper questions about the so-called modern society'. In his analysis of the emergence of capital, Marx considered the transition from a feudal economy to a capitalist one. This transition indicated not only the transformation of class relations, but also the transformation of relations between labour and property. The abolition of serfdom freed individuals to own their labour power, in order to then sell it as a commodity (Marx 1999: 117). Subsistence farmers who had previously worked feudal land were 'obliged to offer for sale as a commodity that very labour power, which exists only in his living self' (Marx 1999: 119). This transformation is central to the process of the formation of capital. The capitalist mode of production 'totally separates land as an instrument of production from landed property and landowner', who is so disconnected from the land that he may not even be in the same country (Marx 1996 [1894]: 441). This was the situation of landownership in Cuba before 1959: absentee North American landlords managing their sugar plantations through capitalist farmers who paid ground-rent to the landowner.

The Cuban Revolution of 1959 aimed to subvert exploitative relationships between labour and property characteristic of the neocolonial, US-supported republic. From 1960 the revolutionary government passed successive legislation that first saw the confiscation of foreign-owned businesses, then large farms, and eventually of all large businesses. While people could retain ownership over their houses, all industrial capital and land was to be the property of the state. It was at this stage that many Cubans decided to leave for Miami. The property confiscated from these upper-class Cubans and North American citizens provided a large pool of resources for the state to redistribute. Many mansions were turned into communal housing or schools for rural Cubans during the Literacy Campaign.[1] Small-scale enterprises, like hairdressers, were allowed to operate privately, and people maintained ownership over their houses to the extent that they were able to pass them on through inheritance, but were not allowed to sell them. Those who did not own their houses before the revolution were allocated one by the state, paying a token rent for 20 years (Mesa-Lago 2013: 6). Houses were exchanged between people, but could not be sold for money, and people could not generate rent from them. Houses, therefore, were de-commodified and removed from the market.

Following the collapse of the Soviet Union, Cuba lost its only significant trading partner and its main source of food and energy, leading to the war-like austerity measures of the Special Period (from 1990 to approximately 1997). Out of necessity, Cuba opened itself up to tourism, resulting in radical transformations of the kind experienced in other post-Soviet locations (see for example Heyat 2002). One of the first measures adopted by Fidel Castro was the decriminalisation of the US dollar and the creation of private and semi-private enterprises. In the mid 1990s, farmers were given land in usufruct to grow vegetables and fruit, and were allowed to sell their produce in agricultural markets. A plethora of *cuentapropista* activities emerged surrounding the tourist industry: 1950s cars used to transport passengers (*almendrones*), private restaurants (*paladares*), craft shops and rental accommodation for tourists (*casas particulares*).

Against this backdrop, in 2011, for the first time since 1960, Cubans were able to buy and sell houses. There were limits: people could own only two properties, one dwelling as a permanent residence and one other as a vacation home (Anillo 2012: 206). Decree-Law No. 288 of 2011 also eliminated the need to obtain an authorisation from the Municipal Housing Authority before transferring a house. The state was no longer involved in the transference of property except through taxation. Until 2011, property had no exchange-value. The value of a house in Cuba was determined by its use-value, outside of market logics. Since 2011 this has changed. Given that house ownership existed in Cuba throughout the 56 years of revolution it is not the case, as in post-Soviet Kazakhstan, of the completely new emergence of private property relations (see Alexander 2004). However, property has increasingly become incorporated into the market, heavily influenced by US Cubans frantically buying houses on the island, pumping up prices. Crucially, while market mechanisms and the Cuban diaspora increasingly influence the sale and purchase of property on the island, the value of houses in Cuba can be understood by considering it not just as it is revealed in the process of exchange, but, more importantly, through the role of value in the process of cultural continuity and change. While on the one hand the increased price of houses reveals the penetration of the market into the socialist island, the mechanisms through which people make sense of this transformation requires conceptualising value not only in economic terms, but also in relation to Cuba's geo-political past and present. In order to understand home ownership for Cubans, it is not enough to consider the increase in exchange-value of houses. The ontological dynamics of value within the revolution are as important in understanding Cubans' conceptualisation of value.

Property in Cuba is a highly political category, because it condenses the Marxist struggle that initially motivated the Cuban Revolution. Struggles over property conceptions perpetuate the quintessential anti-colonial struggle underpinning the Cuban Revolution as *émigré* Cubans are buying property, reclaiming their space within the nation and annulling the victories of a revolution that once aimed to eliminate exploitative labour relations. For *émigré* Cubans, buying houses represents a political victory over a regime that once excluded them. For Cubans on the island, property represents a new battle in the name of national liberation against neocolonial powers. However, more concretely, property also becomes a way of articulating social relations. Through the various *cuentapropista* activities that occur within rental houses, owners are able to amass a broad network of relations that can then be activated in times of need. The use-value of rental houses is their capacity to coalesce different activities (plumbers, delivery people, information networks, government relations, etc.), which will grant the owner access to the possibility of future social relations, as I will exemplify below. Rental properties act as redistribution depots at neighbourhood level, reallocating resources extracted from tourists, which require the accumulation of solidarity networks in favour of the property owner. Rental property becomes a repository of labour power. I hope to contribute to this book's objective of analysing the ways in which different dimensions of value (economic and cultural) are mutually constitutive and become intertwined through concrete human practice that can both reproduce and contest capitalism.

The Emergence of Self-Employment

An abbreviation of the expression '*trabajo por cuenta propia*' (to work on one's own account), *cuentapropista* labour is different from state employment and from the cooperative.[2] Between 1959 and 1961 the revolutionary government nationalised the private and cooperative sectors. In 1960 the sale, rental and construction of houses by individuals was prohibited and, while smaller private ventures continued to exist, by 1968 the 'Revolutionary Offensive' had reduced the private sector to a minimum, circumscribing it within the tolerated black market (Ritter 1998: 67). By 1971, however, the inefficiencies of the Soviet model and Guevara's 'moral incentives' became apparent, and the private sector was allowed to resurface. Regulations were eased so that state enterprises were made more autonomous under the Systema de Dirección y Planificación de la Economía (Economic Management and Planning System – SDPE). Voluntary labour was eliminated, wage scales, work quotas and material incentives were reintroduced, and by 1978 Decree-Law 14 reintroduced self-employment. The first activities to be privatised were hairdressers, taxis, photographers, plumbers, electricians, carpenters, mechanics and certain professionals such as physicians, dentists and architects (Henken 2004: 217). However, private ventures were seen in a negative light until Raúl Castro's new policies were introduced in 2011. Since 1989 mixed capital enterprises have emerged, particularly around the tourist industry, giving rise to a semi-private sector where the Cuban state owned and administered part of foreign companies investing in Cuba. Property reforms increased after 2008, when Raúl Castro assumed office.

In 2011 regulations concerning self-employment were further relaxed. One of the most radical reforms emerging from the Sixth Party Congress in 2011 was the legalisation of the sale of private houses. Today, the state has relaxed controls over the building industry, and construction materials have been 'liberalised' (made available on the market). Cubans living in Cuba, as well as resident foreigners, can purchase houses. These can be inherited and passed on to the families of *émigré* Cubans (Mesa-Lago 2013: 7). The prohibition against non-residents is indirectly targeted at preventing Cubans in the USA from invading this real estate market. However, as I shall discuss below, in practice most of the funds to purchase and renovate houses come from *émigré* Cubans.

This brief overview of house ownership and means of production since 1960 highlights dynamics that have been noted for other post-Soviet locations (see Humphrey 1999; Lampland 1995): first, that increasing penetration of the market in Cuba does not encounter an isolated socialist planned economy. Official and informal forms of private property and activities have long had their own place in Cuba, producing a much more complex encounter. Second, the movements of capital are often erratic, as is evident in the contracting and expanding private sector in Cuba. Third, private spaces and entrepreneurial activities are to a certain extent the domain of the individual, yet the benefits of engaging in these activities are not only dependent on individual skill and hard work. They are rather tied to the individual's capacity to liaise with broader social networks: as a provider of employment contributing to the national good, as reliant on social networks to obtain resources, and as representatives of a revolutionary effort to keep the economy afloat at times of crisis. It is the activities that happen around and through objects that explain value, notes Graeber

(2001: 49), and next I shall detail the activities that happen around *casas particulares* and the business of renting out a room in order to explore the solidarity networks that become the object of accumulation of the business of rental properties.

Casas Particulares: *The Business of Renting Out a Room*

In December 2013 there were 444,109 people[3] working as '*cuentapropistas*' throughout the island (*CubaDebate* 2013a, 2013b), mostly within the food industry, the transport of passengers, the rental of properties and the provision of household services. Most *cuentapropistas* started their activities in the mid to late 1990s, either to supplement their government job income or to help their family after retirement. Today this has changed and *cuentapropistas* are becoming younger, as university students turn to the private sector in an expression of dissatisfaction with state employment.

The practice of renting a room to tourists was initially an expression of what Cubans call *invento* (invention); an extra-official though not necessarily illegal mechanism through which Cubans find alternative forms of income. *Invento* also refers to networks of social relations that aid Cubans in obtaining scarce goods (like flour), guaranteeing access to services (such as jumping the queue for a doctors' appointment) or navigating bureaucratic processes (in obtaining licences to run a self-employed business) (see Armengol 2013). The rental of rooms to tourists was a result of the inventiveness of Cubans' mechanisms to syphon tourists and their hard currency out of the officially controlled state hotels. This phenomenon was also fuelled by tourists' curiosity regarding what they deemed to be the more authentic side of Communist Cuba. Rather than prohibiting this practice, the state soon regulated it, so that Cubans were able to obtain licences to offer rooms for rent to tourists. Licences were expensive and had to be paid in hard currency (CUC – *Cubano Convertible* – Cuban Convertible)[4] instead of CUP (*Peso Cubano* – Cuban Peso). Nonetheless, renting a room to tourists was a profitable enough venture, and in many cases the initial cost of refurbishing and licensing a house came from *émigré* relatives in Miami or Spain.

A licence can cost between CUC150 to CUC400 a month, depending on the type of house, the services offered (whether it has an independent bathroom and kitchen, an independent entrance, a patio, etc.), and the location. This licence has to be paid monthly, regardless of whether the house is rented out. Renting a room can cost between CUC25 and CUC50 a day, which is significantly cheaper than official hotel rates of around CUC100 a day. If the tourist rents the room for longer periods, the cost of the room will go down. I rented four different houses, and paid in one CUC1,000 a month, and in the others CUC800 a month. In the house I rented the longest, located in Playa, where I paid CUC800 a month, the landlady paid a monthly licence of CUC300 as well as a monthly CUC40 inscription fee every time she had to renew the rental contract. She also paid an income tax of 60 per cent. Her earnings were of CUC460 a month, out of which she had to pay 60 per cent in taxes (CUC276), leaving her with a profit of CUC184 a month. Assuming, by current house prices, that her property was worth CUC30,000, she would have had to rent the house for 14 years to make that amount. Nevertheless, a monthly profit of CUC184 is a marked improvement from the 30 pesos earned in a state job, but still not comparable to the possible CUC1,000 made monthly as a chef in a *paladar* (Brenner et al. 2015: 375). Out of the CUC184 my landlady would have had to pay a portion of that towards the government inspection that ensured the house was run according to the terms of the licence. She would also have paid a cleaning lady, around CUC20 a month, to clean for her guests (but this cost is sometimes passed on to the tourist). If the tourist required it, landladies also provided breakfast and meal services, for which they charged extra to cover the cost of groceries. This set of socioeconomic relations and financial obligations may begin to reveal the complexity of the human practices that coalesce around the rental of a room in the city of Havana.

Rental properties, heavily reliant on the tourist market, are among the most successful *cuentapropista* ventures, and they interconnect with other *cuentapropista* activities as they require maintenance (plumbers, cleaners, builders, chefs) and provision of other services, such as chauffeur, tour guide, middlemen to bring in tourists, delivery of goods, etc. Landladies are also expected to redirect their tourist visitors to other *cuentapropista* establishments, including local restaurants, movie rental, taxi services and newspaper delivery. Retired women usually run these ventures. The typical situation sees a retired mother and her daughter (both home owners) move into one of the properties. This was the case with one of my landladies, Ivelis, and her mother Benita. Benita was granted a licence to rent out her property. Meanwhile Ivelis maintained her government job, which granted her a small but steady income and, most importantly, contacts within administrative offices where she had to register guests, her mother's income and other bureaucratic requirements attached to the private venture. Her job also offered office equipment such as a printer, photocopier and internet.

Ivelis' husband also had a state job and only contributed to the rental activity when he was needed to procure goods or favours from his position in a state company, or his car was needed to get spare parts for the house. In order to rent out their house, Ivelis, her husband and their 13-year-old son had to move in with Benita, Ivelis' mother, generating tensions in their relationship. However, thanks to their income, Ivelis' son could get private guitar lessons, her husband could fix up the car, and Benita could visit her other son living in Miami, who had sent the initial funds to fix up the house for rental. Having a relative overseas determines whether a person can apply for a licence to rent to tourists in CUC as opposed to renting in Cuban pesos to Cubans. The initial investment can also come from savings that a family earned from working in an international mission, or from living overseas for a short period (Feinberg 2013).

The Accumulation of Solidarity

Rental properties depend on other *cuentapropistas* for their success. Many landladies hire a person to clean the property. The licence title for this activity is 'domestic worker' (*trabajador doméstico*) and it costs 30 Cuban pesos a month. The cleaner in Ivelis' house, Olga, was paid CUC5 a week, but worked in both the rental property and at Benita's house. Olga did not determine how much she got paid, she was offered that amount and CUC25 a month is more than she was making through her government job taking care of elderly people. *Cuentapropista* activities rely on carpenters, builders, plumbers, mechanics and other trades.

Alba, another one of my landladies during my fieldwork between 2009 and 2011, had a trustworthy handyman. He did not work solely for Alba, but Alba could rely on him to come when she needed him. He would never overcharge and Alba could pay him as much as she could afford. He liked working for Alba, however, because she always estimated a high price for his repairs. Alba also referred him to other *cuentapropistas*, increasing the number of his clients. Armengol (2013) tells of a similar relationship between Lourdes, a woman who rents her house to tourists, and Paco the plumber/handyman, as their relationship extends beyond the parameters of the rental property. Paco sometimes borrowed money from Lourdes, and her husband, a state-appointed defence attorney, once provided Paco with some legal assistance in a matter concerning his brother. Like

Lourdes, Alba also maintained good relations with her neighbours as she considered them essential for a successful business: if she kept the neighbours happy they would not gossip, or report her to the Poder Popular (local level of government) which would require an inspection that cost money to '*salvar*' (save = bribe) the inspector. Alba referred me to local residents if I wanted to buy eggs or other groceries that were missing from the markets, and connected me with the newspaper deliveryman. She employed local residents to clean the property and participated actively in the CDR[5] (Committees for the Defence of the Revolution) meetings in order to ensure that the neighbourhood watch was duly conducted, as a safe neighbourhood was not only good for business but also strengthened her bonds with the neighbours. In this way, engaging in a self-employed venture requires a landlady to ably manage social networks as well as to maintain active involvement in local-level political activities in order to ensure the business encounters the least amount of opposition.

Cuentapropistas like Alba are seen positively within the neighbourhood, as they are not considered to be exploitative and greedy. Others, like Ivelis and Benita, are not so popular. People in the neighbourhood said Ivelis was a good capitalist. Alba made a smaller margin of profit than Ivelis. This was clear not because they revealed their income – *cuentapropistas* are very reluctant to share their figures – but rather in the lifestyle that both landladies displayed and the reinvestments they made. Ivelis constantly refurbished both her own and her mother's house with new tiles, paint, furniture and electrical appliances such as air conditioning. Her son was dressed in branded clothes and they were seen out in *paladares*. These are not objective indicators of income differentials or personal qualities, but rather subjective observations made by neighbours to distinguish the 'good neighbour' from the 'greedy capitalist'. Ivelis participated in CDR meetings, but always in defence of her own interests, and she exploited those working for her. Alba's houses were well kept but more modest, without the shiny tiles and air conditioning, an important marker of income or resourcefulness. She did not own a car and she was always more plainly dressed (her mother was a seamstress and made all her clothes). Her participation in CDRs revealed the larger concerns of a 'good citizen' (clean streets, well-lighted sidewalks, fair prices at the local farmers' market), and she established a trusting relationship with other *cuentapropistas*. While the emergence of *cuentapropismo* is inevitably understood as a sign of a market economy, there are degrees to which people can participate in this economy without becoming ruthless capitalists. Success is measured as the balance between running a profitable business without losing sight of revolutionary commitment.

The hierarchical valorisation of entrepreneurship and its resultant profit is not unique to Cuba. Many former Eastern bloc countries adopted market relations by incorporating them into previously existing moral codes and social networks. Kaneff (2002) demonstrates the different moral connotations of participating in the market in rural Bulgaria, which vary according to the participants' engagement in the Soviet system. Younger women who had been state employees regarded the market with suspicion and shame, whereas their mothers, who had been relegated to household activities, found pride in engaging in a 'productive' activity outside the house. Similarly, Pine's (2002) research among the Górale of Poland demonstrates that the provenance of money is valorised to reflect Górale beliefs about the primacy of the household and their hostility to the Soviet state. Money that was produced through economic migration or entrepreneurial practices was seen as positive, whereas that which was obtained through state employment was devalued.

Cuba is different from Eastern Europe in that it is not a post-socialist state, and it was not subjected to the IMF/World Bank Structural Adjustment Policies (Anderson 2012), allowing the Cuban government to maintain a larger degree of autonomy. As opposed to Eastern European countries, where people may have deplored the penetration of the market while their governments engaged with it unreservedly, in Cuba the autonomy of the Cuban political system is still a priority for the government and, to a large extent (although manifested in more contradictory ways), for the people. While many Cubans avidly seek to engage with the market, they do so with varying degrees of apprehension.

Cuentapropistas' moral judgements of each other in relation to their commitment to the social and civic project of the revolution give meaning to the emergence of private property and the rental activities surrounding it. It is worth recalling Marx's argument that 'in an economy the relations between material things are really an expression of social relations between people' (Firth 1984: 34), so that property embeds social relations represented and mediated by things. In many instances, the very social networks established by engaging with the private sector grant people power within their local neighbourhood. And vice versa, not fostering the correct social networks can mean becoming cut off from the local community, which can cost dearly in both political and monetary terms. The difference between Alba's careful nurturing of her neighbours and

Ivelis' more obviously self-interested intentions meant that Alba received fewer surprise inspections, and that, in order to avoid these, Ivelis had to pay a high price to bribe someone in ONAT (Organización Nacional de Administración Tributaria – National Tax Administration Organization) to notify her of any unplanned visits.[6] The perceived success of *cuentapropistas* is closely connected to how well they uphold their social networks.

Cuentapropistas are a product of the economic circumstance of the Special Period, resulting from the proliferation of market mechanisms. However, as Cuban economist Pérez Villanueva (2004) has argued, it is important to distinguish between markets and capitalism. Markets are a mechanism, and 'capitalism used markets in accordance with the logic of its ideology' (Catá Backer 2012: 217). This does not preclude the existence of socialist markets. Within this context, rental properties act as 'redistribution depots', where the main resource is the tourist. The importance of owning a house lies in the possibilities it provides for tapping into this resource, in order to redistribute it among a broad network of social relations, accumulating solidarity networks that can be translated into access to goods and service. If the landlady is savvy she can use the tourist as the source of redistribution. However, in order to run the activity successfully, the landlady needs to trust her *socios*[7] (business partners) and this is only achieved by generating long-lasting links through trade, barter and gift exchange. The more *socios* one has, the more 'resources' one can harness to resolve things. In order to run a successful business, it is essential to establish a strong solidarity network. The solidarity resulting from the need to resort to social networks in order to set up a private enterprise is simultaneously one of the main achievements of the business. Solidarity, therefore, becomes an object of accumulation (Armengol 2013: 209).

Those who operate culinary ventures face their biggest challenge when it comes to obtaining the necessary materials to prepare meals. Until recently there was no wholesale provider of goods, so *cuentapropistas* had to buy their raw materials from state-run hard currency stores or private farmers' markets. However, this does not always provide the full range of products needed. Knowing people working in state distribution companies or state-run hotels provides a source of resources such as flour, tea, meat, potatoes, oil and other scarce goods.

Another expression of the *cuentapropista* network is the support they provide each other in terms of leisure activities. Since *cuentapropistas* are left out of the state system of subsidised holidays, when *cuentapropistas* take holidays they do so using other *cuentapropistas*' services: rental houses in

Varadero, Viñales or Trinidad, for example, where they arrive in a *cuentapropista* rental car. These are the services their guests use, but by using these services themselves, they are further reinforcing their networks. *Cuentapropistas* will charge Cubans less than foreigners, even when they rent their property in CUCs. There is a sense that 'exploiting' (their term) foreigners is accepted because they apparently have endless supplies of money, but it is not the right thing to do to a fellow Cuban. This points to the highly moralised nature of the market surrounding *cuentapropistas*. Cubans are careful not to become exploitative in relation to their own people, but feel justified in exploiting foreigners who come to consume their island. This points to a distinction made by Cubans: while they are not naïve enough to overlook the clear penetration of capitalist relations into their socialist island, they are also aware of not wanting to lose sight of the solidarity owed to their *compañeros* (comrades). How can Cubans become entrepreneurs and continue functioning within the socialist project of the revolution?

Revolutionary Values and the Value of Property

In Cuba the term 'revolution' connotes more than a state ideology, or a propaganda slogan. For Cubans, revolution is also practice, as people define their revolutionary commitment by engaging in social activities with friends, by getting involved in the neighbourhood watch or by growing their own food (Gold 2015). Revolution is also a nationalist discourse, although not one that ennobles a soldier or battle, but rather the notion of struggle: against prior Cuban leaders such as Batista, against the USA and, more vaguely, imperialism, and against the apocalyptic possibilities of environmental disasters (Gold 2014). Revolution is also a system of values that determines what it means to be (a good) Cuban. This system of values is not fixed and has radically changed throughout the last 55 years. Certain aspects, however, have remained relatively stable: above all the commitment to, and struggle in the name of, national sovereignty. This ideology of struggle has proven quite flexible, incorporating changes emerging throughout different crises in the history of the Cuban nation, and extending retrospectively to incorporate Cuba's colonial past. This connotation of 'revolution' as a national struggle is paramount in understanding the value of private ventures. As a form of conclusion, I will now explore the relationship between 'revolution' as a system of values (the social values of *cuentapropistas*) and the value of *cuentapropista* activities in Cuba.

In the post-soviet era, Cuba has often been characterised as a place 'in transition'. That Cuba has been forced to radically adapt to a changed global scenario is unquestionable. The nature of these transformations since the 1990s, however, is still open to debate. Emerging during the Special Period as spontaneous responses to shortages, private and semi-private ventures have often been conceptualised as sites of civil society, independent from the state, and the motors of change towards a more democratic future. In this view, Cuba is conceived as following Eastern European countries towards incorporation in a global market economy. Within this context of change, *cuentapropistas* initially represented an affront to the values of the revolution: the pre-eminence of the social over the individual, the aversion to capitalist accumulation, and the repudiation of class differences. Yet, as Austin-Broos (2003: 3) argues, 'never a solitary act, valuing involves others', so that social values are essential for the integration and permanence of the social body (Dumont 1992: 240). *Cuentapropistas* were initially valued against *el pueblo* (the people), which was seen as a more pure expression of the spirit of the revolution. However, more recently they have been positioned against more diffuse 'others', such as the bureaucracy, neo-colonialism, or inefficiency. Instead of viewing private and semi-private ventures as oppositional to the state, these represent the proliferation of state regulatory authority penetrating the spaces of private property, by granting these ventures the status of revolutionary. *Cuentapropistas* represent part of the state's commitment to keep the revolution sovereign from USA intervention and from the penetration of Miami Cubans.

In the 1990s and the first decade of the twenty-first century *cuentapropistas* were viewed with suspicion, antagonism, shame and a measure of envy from those holding state jobs. During my fieldwork I was able to appreciate the shift in attitude taking place between 2008 and 2014. In 2008, Raúl Castro began promoting the resurgence of private businesses; by 2010, the issue of private ventures was becoming a daily topic in work centre meetings; in 2011, the Proyecto de Lineamientos was approved and the list of approved private enterprise activities expanded to 178;[8] by 2014, even the children of high-ranking government officials operated their own *cuentapropista* activities.

Another radical change implemented in 2011 was the possibility of individuals hiring contracted labour, until then prohibited (Henken 2013:390). Individuals or households could now obtain licences in more than one occupation, which allowed them to legalise the activities they had formally carried out illicitly under a food service licence (Henken 2013: 391). The creation of more licences and the increase of the list of accepted activities for self-employment represents a double movement between a shift towards capitalism, or a liberalisation of the economy and, simultaneously, an expression of the extension of the state's regulatory power over these activities. At a time when the main revolutionary concern has shifted from education to economic efficiency, those contributing to streamlining economic processes and offloading financial burdens from the state are construed as vanguard revolutionaries.

One of the first means through which the state attempted to incorporate *cuentapropista* activities, beyond legislative mechanisms, has been through their unionisation. While they started out as individually coordinated activities, *cuentapropistas* were encouraged to join existing national unions most related to their activities or closest to their place of residence. So, for example, in 2004 vendors in the Malecón tourist market voted to join a national union of Light Industry (Phillips 2006:118). Unionisation allows the state to control and benefit from *cuentapropista* activities, and it grants *cuentapropistas* a level of legitimacy within the political arena, as many things within Cuban politics happen at the level of the work centre. In 2013, *cuentapropistas* marched in the Labour Day parade as a group bearing banners that read: 'united for a prosperous and sustainable socialism'.

Furthermore, Marxist analysis on the importance of the producer-proprietor has been revived, an example of which appeared in the officially sanctioned social science journal *Temas* in 2008. This argued that the realisation of a socialist man is mostly centred on the 'socio-economic realisation of himself as a producer-proprietor', prioritising the economic activity of people over 'other elements, social, cultural, psychological, sociological and political' (Alemán Santana et al. 2008: 41). Armando Nova González (2011), a Cuban economist, professor at the Centre for Studies on the Cuban Economy (Centro de Estudios de la Economía Cubana – CEEC), published an analysis of the nature of property in the Cuban economy in light of the publication of the Lineamientos project. Referring to the importance of the recent reduction of state property he recalls the warning of José Martí, Cuba's 'national Apostle', warning against a paternalistic state and the type of complacent workers it generates. Rather than being slaves of capitalists, Martí warned, people would become slaves of the bureaucracy (Martí, cited in Nova González 2011: 3).

Fitting with Martí's appraisal and the Marxist valorisation of producer-proprietors, Raúl Castro's first objectives after he assumed the presidency in 2008 included streamlining the cumbersome bureaucracy that plagued government processes and reinvigorating the role of small and medium enterprises (PYMES – *Pequeñas y Medianas Empresas*). Through decentralisation Raúl intends to reduce the government's role in the economy and increase productivity without relinquishing the socialist system (Pujol 2011: 4). *Cuentapropistas* are no longer discussed in the official newspapers, such as *Granma*, as suspicious and exploitative as was still the case in 2010 (see for example Borges Mujica 2010; Betancourt Nápoles 2010). Articles discussing *cuentapropistas* today are limited to how the economy is implementing measures to incorporate them (Borrego Díaz 2014; *CubaDebate* 2011, 2014).

Credit programmes have been established through Cuban banks, such as the Banco Popular de Ahorro (BPA – Popular Savings Bank) and the Banco de Crédito y Comercio (Bandec – Credit and Commerce Bank) in order to lend money to *cuentapropistas*. University courses and degrees in management have been set up to provide people with the necessary skills to become self-employed. The state has allowed Cuban entrepreneurs to officially tap into the tourist industry, so that owners of rental properties can offer their services directly to a foreign tourist company and get paid from overseas by their client into a Cuban bank account.

Rental properties, therefore, become articulators of social relations in the neighbourhood. They create *socios*, provide employment for local residents, reinvigorate CDR activities and serve as a link between Cubans and their *émigré* relatives and other foreigners. These positive relations articulated through rental property have a downside: the economic and social burden of *sociolismo*, too much involvement of neighbours in people's personal life, the scrutiny of CDR members and local Poder Popular representatives of people's daily activities, the often conflicting relations with *émigré* relatives, who provide the funds and thus sometimes act as 'absentee landlords'. Solidarity networks, while both a blessing and a curse, are nonetheless highly regarded, as they are central to formal and informal social, political and economic activities.

Private ownership over houses is also a powerful source of income, not because of the price of a house, but through rent. Moreover, rental properties require the accumulation of social relations in order to successfully run a rental business. However, *cuentapropistas* often complain about the increased responsibility and longer working hours that accompany self-employment, even as they appreciate the increased freedom and higher profit they enjoy. Therefore, the usefulness of property is not so much as a commodity but as a means of rent capture. The utility of the house is always a potential one that is given by the buyer's capacity to fix it and use it for self-employment, resulting in the accumulation of solidarity networks that can at any time be translated into service provision.

In spite of the recent policy changes in Cuba that favoured an increase of the private sector, the meaning of property is still defined by its relation to the project of revolution. The privatisation of small-scale businesses has been incorporated into the revolutionary project as an expression of people's struggles to keep the Cuban economy autonomous from foreign intervention. *Cuentapropismo* is not an exclusively private space, as people engage in both public employment and private activities, if not directly then through family members, and rely on state resources and social networks to run their private businesses. The involvement with the unions, CDRs and Poder Popular demonstrate that *cuentapropistas* do not exist in a purely private realm, and the more successful ventures thrive because they better articulate the concerns of the neighbourhood. *Cuentapropistas* have been recently heralded as examples of revolutionary struggle and expressions of the commitment of the people to maintain their national sovereignty.

Notes

1. The Literacy Campaign was carried out in 1961. It was a large-scale mobilisation of the population, where every Cuban who could read and write was sent to the country to teach the rural population. Villagers were also brought into the city and housed in the mansions expropriated from North Americans and Cubans who left for Miami.
2. Cooperative ownership in Cuba emerged in 1990, when previously large-scale state farms were divided into cooperatives (UBPCs – *Unidades Básicas de Producción Cooperativa* – Basic Units of Cooperative Production). These were intended to manage land more efficiently at a time when the state was unable to do so, mostly due to a dramatic fall in petrol supply following the collapse of the Soviet Union. These were not completely autonomous enterprises, as state entities still maintained control over production and distribution. Since 2011, cooperative ownership has become one of the state's most prevalent strategies for the decentralisation of the economy.
3. Cuba has a population of 11,227,270. In May 2015 the number of self-employed Cubans had risen to 504,613, which represents 8 per cent of employment and

generates 5 per cent of the GDP, according to the Cuban Oficina Nacional de Estadísticas (ONE [National Statistics Office] 2013).

4. This was one of two currencies operating in Cuba. The Convertible Peso is fixed at US$1, and is therefore considered hard currency. Since 2013 there have been attempts to unify both currencies.
5. CDRs are neighbourhood-based organisations initially created as a response to bombings by Cubans in Miami in September 1960. They have been instrumental in mobilising the population in different social and political activities since then: the Literacy Campaign in 1961, massive polio vaccination campaigns, the fumigation of households against dengue, and the neighbourhood watch, among others.
6. ONAT is the government office that manages the taxing of all Cuban enterprises, issues licences for self-employed ventures and regulates the limits of these activities.
7. *Sociolismo*, is a pun on the word 'socialism', to refer to the informal provision network operating in Cuba since the Special Period. Fernández (2000: 110) describes *sociolismo* as 'the system of access to goods and social standing based on who you know and who you love, on *amiguismo* and cronyism', which can help Cubans obtain jobs or scarce goods. It can also help people overcome the obstacles needed to obtain a rental licence. The networks created through *sociolismo* extend beyond a person's intimate circles, and can reach as far out as other towns and provinces (Fernández 2000: 110).
8. Proyecto de Lineamientos de la Política Económica y Social – Aligning Project for Economic and Social Policy. This was the result of the VI Party Congress, held in 2011, which had as its main objective the reassessment of Cuba's economic policies. A working document was drafted before the Party Congress, and in 2009 and 2010 it was circulated and discussed throughout different work centres, in order to elicit participation of the people in the process of reshaping the Cuban economy. In 2011 a set of guidelines was drafted into a pamphlet that was widely distributed throughout Cuba.

References

Alemán Santana, S., O. Saroza Monteagudo and J. Pérez Méndez. 2008. El proceso de realización de productor-propietario socialista en Cuba. *Temas* 54 (Abril–Junio): 37–47.

Alexander, C. 2004. Value, relations, and changing bodies: Privatization and property rights in Kazakhstan. In K. Verdery and C. Humphrey (eds) *Property in Question: Value Transformation in the Global Economy*. Oxford: Berg, pp. 251–74.

Anderson, T. 2012. Independent structural adjustment: Cuban and neo-liberal models compared. *Journal of Iberian and Latin American Research* 9(1): 49–72.

Anillo, R. 2012. Cuban real estate framework laws. In ASCE (Association for the Study of the Cuban Economy) (ed.) *Cuba in Transition*, vol. 22: *Papers and Proceedings of the Twenty-second Annual Meeting*, Miami, pp. 202–7.

Armengol, R.I. 2013. Competitive solidarity and the political economy of the *invento*. In ASCE (Association for the Study of the Cuban Economy) (ed.) *Cuba in Transition*, vol. 23: *Papers and Proceedings of the Twenty-third Annual Meeting*, Miami, pp. 205–15.

Austin-Broos, D. 2003. Globalisation and the genesis of values. *Australian Journal of Anthropology* 14(1): 1–18.

Betancourt Nápoles, R. 2010. Todas las ideas son validas, pero siempre Socialismo. *Granma*, 5 February, p. 10.

Borges Mujica, D. 2010. No creo en la privatización. *Granma*, 8 January, p. 11.

Borrego Díaz, J.A. 2014. Banca espirituana espera por los cuentapropistas. *Granma*, 7 August. Available at: http://www.granma.cu/cuba/2014-08-07/banca-espirituana-espera-por-los-cuentapropistas

Brenner, P., M.R. Jiménez, J.M. Kirk and W.M. Leogrande. 2015. Social change. In P. Brenner, M.R. Jiménez, J.M. Kirk and W.M. Leogrande (eds), *A Contemporary Cuba Reader: The Revolution Under Raúl Castro*, 2nd edn. Lanham, MD: Rowman and Littlefield, pp. 373–80.

Catá Backer, L. 2012. The proletarian corporation: Organizing Cuban economic enterprises in the wake of the *lineamientos* – property rights between corporations, cooperatives and globalization. In ASCE (Association for the Study of the Cuban Economy) (ed.) *Cuba in Transition*, vol. 22: *Papers and Proceedings of the Twenty-second Annual Meeting*, Miami, pp. 212–36.

CubaDebate. 2011. Más de 83000 cubanos solicitaron licencias para Trabajo por Cuenta Propia. *CubaDebate* (electronic newspaper). Available at: www.cubadebate.cu/noticias/2011/01/07/mas-de-83-000-cubanos-solicitaron-licencias-para-trabajo-por-cuenta-propia/#.Vxc6lHErLcs (accessed 3 February 2011).

CubaDebate. 2013a. Autorizan diez nuevas modalidades de trabajo por cuenta propia y reactivan licencias para otras ocho. *CubaDebate* (electronic newspaper). Available at: www.cubadebate.cu/noticias/2013/09/26/autorizan-diez-nuevas-modalidades-de-trabajo-por-cuenta-propia-y-reactivan-licencias-para-otras-ocho/#.U9hN34CSzxZ (accessed 30 July 2014).

CubaDebate. 2013b. Cuba cuenta con casi 445 mil cuentapropistas. *CubaDebate* (electronic newspaper). Available at: www.cubadebate.cu/noticias/2013/12/20/cuba-cuenta-con-casi-445-mil-cuentapropistas/#.U9hkTICSzxY (accessed 30 July 2014).

CubaDebate. 2014. Cuba cuenta con casi 445 mil cuentapropistas. *CubaDebate* (electronic newspaper). Available at: http://www.cubadebate.cu/noticias/2013/12/20/cuba-cuenta-con-casi-445-mil-cuentapropistas/#.Vxc8fHErLcs (accessed 30 July 2014).

Dumont, L. 1992. *Essays on Individualism: Modern Ideology in Anthropological Perspective*. London: University of Chicago Press.

Feinberg, R.E. 2013. *Soft Landing in Cuba? Emerging Entrepreneurs and Middle Classes*. Washington, DC: The Brookings Institution.

Fernández, D.J. 2000. *Cuba and the Politics of Passion*. Austin: University of Texas Press.

Firth, R. 1984. The sceptical anthropologist? Social anthropology and Marxist views on society. In M. Bloch (ed.) *Marxist Analyses and Social Anthropology*. London: Routledge Taylor & Francis Group, pp. 29–60.

Gold, M. 2014. Peasant, patriot, environmentalist: Sustainable development discourse in Havana. *Bulletin of Latin American Research* 33(4): 405–18.

Gold, M. 2015. *People and State in Socialist Cuba: Ideas and Practices of Revolution*. New York: Palgrave Macmillan.

Graeber, D. 2001. *Towards and Anthropological Theory of Value: The False Coin of Our Own Dreams*. New York: Palgrave.

Henken, T.A. 2004. Between ideology and pragmatism: The revolution and the private sector before the Special Period, 1959–1990. In ASCE (Association for the Study of the Cuban Economy) (ed.) *Cuba in Transition*, vol. 14: *Papers and Proceedings of the Fourteenth Annual Meeting*, Miami, pp. 212–23.

Henken, T.A. 2013. The rebirth of the Cuban *Paladar*: Is the third time the charm? In ASCE (Association for the Study of the Cuban Economy) (ed.) *Cuba in Transition*, vol. 23: *Papers and Proceedings of the Twenty-third Annual Meeting*, Miami, pp. 389–402.

Heyat, F. 2002. Women and the culture of entrepreneurship in Soviet and post-Soviet Azerbaijan. In C. Humphrey and R. Mandel (eds) *Markets and Moralities: Ethnographies of Post-Socialism*. Oxford: Berg, pp. 1–18.

Humphrey, C. 1999. Russian protection rackets and the appropriation of law and order. In J.M. Heymn (ed.) *States and Illegal Practices*. Oxford: Berg.

Kaneff, D. 2002. The shame and pride of market activity: Morality, identity and trading in postsocialist rural Bulgaria. In C. Humphrey and R. Mandel (eds) *Markets and Moralities: Ethnographies of Postsocialism*. Oxford: Berg, pp. 33–52.

Lampland, M. 1995. *The Object of Labour: Commodification in Socialist Hungary*. Chicago: University of Chicago Press.

Marx, K. 1996 [1894]. *Capital: A Critique of Political Economy*, vol. 3 New York: International Publishers. Available at: Marx.org

Marx, K. 1999. *Capital: A Critique of Political Economy*, vol. 1. Available at: www.marxists.org/archive/marx/works/download/pdf/Capital-Volume-I.pdf

Mesa-Lago, C. 2013. Panorama de las reformas econónmico-sociales y sus effectos en Cuba. In ASCE (Association for the Study of the Cuban Economy) (ed.) *Cuba in Transition*, vol. 23: *Papers and Proceedings of the Twenty-third Annual Meeting*, Miami, pp. 1–15.

Nova González, A. 2011. La propiedad en la economía cubana. Available at: http://www.lahaine.org/mundo.php/la-propiedad-en-la-economia-cubana (accessed 2 May 2016).

ONE (Oficina Nacional de Estadísticas). 2013. *2013 Anuario Estadístico de Cuba*. Available at: http://www.one.cu/

Pérez Villanueva, O.E. 2004. The Cuban economy today and its future challenges. In J.I. Domínguez, O.E. Pérez Villanueva and L. Barberia (eds) *The Cuban Economy at the Start of the Twenty-first Century*. Cambridge, MA: Harvard University Press, pp. 49–90.

Phillips, E. 2006. *Cuentapropismo* in a socialist state. In M. Font (ed.) *Cuba: In Transition? Pathways to Renewal, Long-term Development and Global Reintegration*. New York: Bildner Center for Western Hemisphere Studies, pp. 107–24.

Pine, F. 2002. Dealing with money: Zlotys, dollars and other currencies in the Polish Highlands. In C. Humphrey and R. Mandel (eds) *Markets and Moralities: Ethnographies of Postsocialism*. Oxford: Berg, pp. 75–100.

Pujol, J.P. 2011. Main problems faced by the Cuban economy and what the government is doing to try to solve them. In ASCE (Association for the Study of the Cuban Economy) (ed.) *Cuba in Transition*, vol. 21: *Papers and Proceedings of the Twenty-first Annual Meeting*, Miami, pp. 1–17.

Ritter, A.R.M. 1998. Entrepreneurship, microenterprise, and public policy in Cuba: Promotion, containment or asphyxiation? *Journal of Interamerican Studies and World Affairs* 40(2): 63–94.

PART II

Tribulating Values in the 'Global North'

7
The Relative Value of Penguins

Moira White

Introduction

Ernest Shackleton's Imperial Trans-Antarctic Expedition (ITAE) embarked in 1914 with the aim of traversing the Antarctic Continent from the shores of the Weddell Sea, at latitude 78 degrees south for nearly 3,000 km 'past the Pole', to the Ross Sea coast; as he described it, 'the greatest Polar journey ever attempted' (Shackleton 1999: 19).[1] Two ships were involved. The main party, carried in the *Endurance* and consisting of 28 men including Shackleton, were to start the overland trek from the Weddell Sea coast. The second and supporting ship, the SY *Aurora*, carried the other members (Captain Aeneas Macintosh and 27 men) to the Ross Sea end of the planned route. From there they were to place food and fuel depots for the Weddell Sea party to use in the final stages of their trek. That task completed, a return in March 1916 was anticipated.

The expedition also had a number of scientific objectives. Shackleton wrote that they would undertake 'scientific work on a scale and over an area never before attempted by any one Polar expedition' (Shackleton 1999 [1919]: 20). Study and collection of fauna was planned as well as a programme of geographical, geological, hydrographic and meteorological work. The *Aurora* was fitted with tanks to bring back seals, penguins and fish (*New Zealand Herald* 1 January 1914: 7).[2] One of the anticipated outcomes was to obtain comprehensive film footage of Emperor penguins. The expedition carried equipment to take photographs in the hope that it would obtain 'a series of unique films depicting every stage of penguin life' (*Otago Daily Times* 20 November 1914: 8).

As we now know, both parties met with unexpected and severe misfortunes. The fate of the *Endurance* and Shackleton's extraordinary achievement in saving the lives of the Weddell Sea party are well known. Having abandoned the *Endurance* before it sank, crushed by pack ice, her

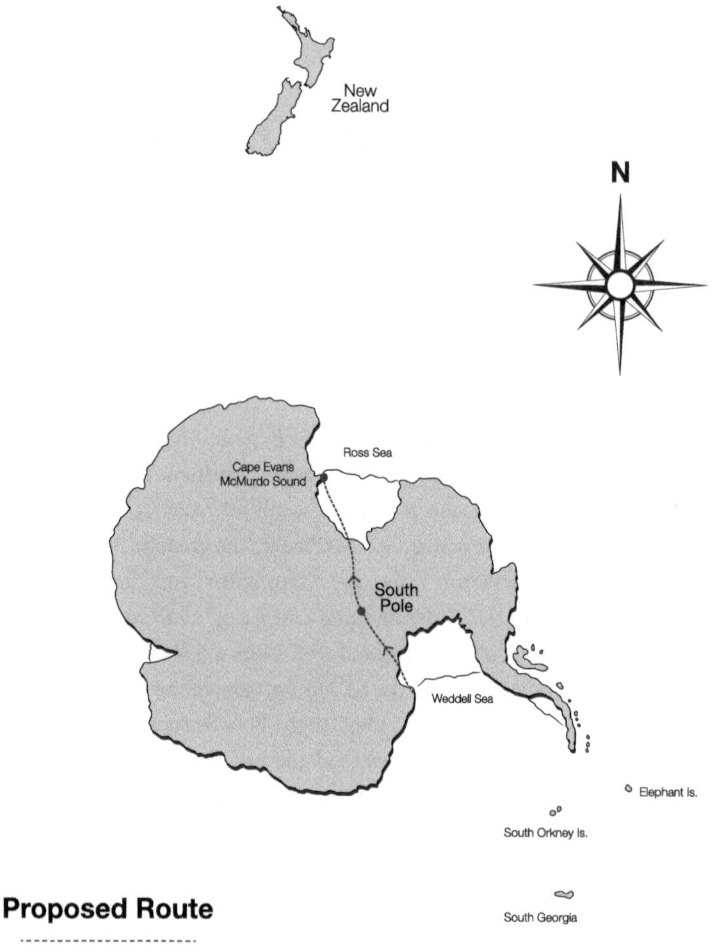

Figure 7.1 Imperial Trans-Antarctic Expedition

crew lived on the ice floe for months and then rowed to Elephant Island in three small lifeboats. From there Shackleton and four colleagues sailed 800 miles to a whaling station on South Georgia to arrange the rescue of those left on Elephant Island. Actors Kenneth Branagh and Liam Neeson have both played Shackleton in the films *Shackleton* (2002) and *The Endurance* (2000) respectively, and books include *South*, Shackleton's own account (1999 [1919]), Hurley (2001) and more recent critical texts (for example, Alexander 1998, and Jarvis 2013). The fate of the *Aurora* and her crew had received less public and scholarly attention until recent years (Tyler-Lewis 2006; McElrea and Harrowfield 2004). Her anchor cables tore loose in bad weather in McMurdo Sound in May 1915, with the depot-laying teams ashore and only a small crew aboard. She drifted at sea trapped in pack ice for months but eventually was able to reach Port Chalmers, Dunedin, in April 1916.

Shackleton's ambition of a Trans-Antarctic crossing was not realised and most of the expedition's scientific work was not completed. Antarctic historian David Harrowfield (2015) has noted that the work which did eventuate – and is often overlooked – comprised primarily meteorological observations but also included some glaciological observations, tidal recordings, and the collection of zoological and other specimens. Faunal specimens were frozen in the hold of the *Aurora* when she arrived in Dunedin. Their specific provenance and context meant they constituted a finite group of material that possessed considerable value to a number of people, but they were a category of material not usually thought of as a commodity with an exchange value. Their eventual allocation in the face of competing interest from scientific institutions, crew members, and political and financial supporters of the expedition is the subject of this chapter.

The Aurora

The *Aurora* had been Douglas Mawson's Antarctic expedition ship in 1911–13. She was purchased by Shackleton, and prepared in Australia for use by the ITAE. On that voyage she 'carried materials for a hut, full equipment for landing and sledging parties, stores and clothing of all kinds required, and an ample supply of sledges. There were also dog-teams and one of the motor-tractors' (Shackleton 1999 [1919]: 168).

Captain Aeneas Lionel Acton Mackintosh (1879 –1916), previously assistant secretary to the Imperial Merchant Service Guild (Stancombe 2004), had been a member of the Shackleton-led 1907–9 British Antarctic Expedition and was in charge of the ITAE Ross Sea support party. The *Aurora* sailed south under his command, and reached McMurdo Sound in January 1915. Mackintosh was ashore with the depot-laying teams when she broke free from her mooring in Cape Evans Bay in a gale on the evening of 6 May 1915 (Church 1997: 34). He had left Lieutenant Joseph Russell Stenhouse, appointed as the *Aurora*'s first officer, in overall command of the ship with a small crew. Stenhouse was in charge through the ensuing period of drifting and then her slow voyage to New Zealand. When they arrived at Port Chalmers, Shackleton's fate and that of all the men on the *Endurance* was still unknown.

The situation of the men left on the Ross Sea ice was of the utmost concern, and arrangements for the repair and revictualling of the *Aurora* ready for a rescue expedition began immediately as an urgent matter at a national level. However, the preservation of the specimens she carried was also necessary, and a pressing task. Stenhouse contacted the Otago Museum's Curator, William Blaxland Benham, for help. Benham was already known to Shackleton, who had written to him from the *Nimrod* expedition in 1907 about the possible collection of seal and penguin skins for the Otago Museum (Shackleton 1907). They may have been in contact again prior to the 1914 expedition. Benham later noted that soon after the *Aurora* had berthed on her return from the Ross Sea:

> I was waited on by a representative of the acting-commander with the purpose of obtaining the assistance of a taxidermist who should preserve the birdskins and sealskins which had been brought to New Zealand [...] Mr Gibson's services were lent to Lieutenant Stenhouse, and some weeks were spent by him on the 'Aurora' in putting these specimens in order, and thus preventing their decay, for they had only been frozen, and had not been treated with preservatives. (Benham 1917: 3)

A distinguished zoologist, English-born William Benham was Curator of the Otago Museum from 1898 until 1937. He arrived in New Zealand with a significant publication record (Benson 1951) and continued his research in Dunedin, together with teaching duties at Otago University and his museum obligations. It was during his tenure at the museum that he published reports on the Oligochaeta and Polychaeta collected on Douglas Mawson's Antarctic expedition (Benham 1921, 1922; Otago Museum 1915: 7), and on the Polychaeta collected by the members of Scott's *Terra Nova* Antarctic Expedition (Benham 1927).[3] In the time of his curatorship the Otago Museum acquired material from Scott's National Antarctic Expedition (Otago Museum 1915: 4); mineral and rock samples from Shackleton's 1907–9 expedition (*Otago Daily Times* 8 December 1909:6); and faunal specimens from the ITAE.

Shackleton, the ITAE, and the material that had been brought back from Antarctica were all of great interest to the people of Otago, and to the wider New Zealand public. The *Aurora* was towed to Dunedin's Rattray Street wharf for an open weekend attracting 'throngs of visitors [...] fascinated by the glamour of romance which clings around the vessel' (*The Dominion* 20 April 1916: 4). A display of items in a nearby cargo shed, including artefacts and natural science specimens, raised more than £106 for the Red Cross over two days.[4]

The seals, penguins and a number of artefacts and artworks associated with the ITAE were soon available for the public to see again at Otago's annual Agricultural and Pastoral Society Winter Show, held in Brydone Hall in Dunedin's warehouse precinct, also in aid of the Red Cross. Visitors could view 'Captain Scott's tent and sledge, ski-sticks, ice axes, and shovels, samples of clothing, stuffed birds, photographs, coloured sketches of huge ice ridges, and of the Emperor and Adelie penguins, and seal life' (*Otago Daily Times* 15 May 1916: 7).

Of the weeks that the museum's taxidermist expended on the *Aurora* specimens, Benham recorded: 'In return for the work thus performed, [the] Expedition presented to the Museum a number of penguins and seals' (Benham 1917: 3). In addition to these, a further group of Emperor and Adelie penguins was temporarily deposited at the museum by Stenhouse. He asked Benham to arrange their delivery to a list of people he had given to Gibson – relations and other social and/or professional acquaintances (Stenhouse 1917). Independently, however, Shackleton also had offered faunal specimens to a number of people. At some time before Shackleton left New Zealand for the United States of America in 1917, it was recognised that although they included an overlapping set of obligations and friends, altogether the promises he and Stenhouse had made were likely to add up to more than the number of available penguins. The situation was complicated and, as with many other matters, was passed to Leonard Tripp, Shackleton's Cambridge-educated attorney and friend in Wellington, to resolve.

The final decisions were made bearing in mind legal ownership; friendship; the scientific outcomes of the expedition; reputation; financial assistance; political relationships; souvenirs; personal feelings; the importance of keeping promises; perhaps the value accorded to harmony; and possibly the complicated situation regarding the personal politics of the Ross Sea party rescue.

Otago Museum

Two separate groups of faunal specimens were delivered to the Otago Museum soon after the *Aurora* arrived in Dunedin. One was uncontentious; the other led to an extended discussion. The first was described by William Benham in the museum's annual report. He recorded that 'due to the kindness of Lieutenant Stenhouse' (Benham 1917: 9) the Otago

Museum had received 'five Antarctic seals, three Emperor penguins, six Adelie penguins, two Giant petrels, two Snowy Antarctic doves, and one Antarctic skua, on behalf of the Expedition'.[5] In making the offer, Stenhouse signed as 'Commander "Aurora"' (Stenhouse 1916).

Many of these specimens were destined for display in a large case in the museum's Hocken Wing, planned to show life in the Antarctic. Benham noted that the museum's taxidermist, Gibson, had spent some weeks in preparing the specimens for display and that early in the following year he would paint a background 'in illustration of the Antarctic regions' (Benham 1917: 5). In the next annual report, Benham described the installation of the Antarctic specimens as one of the two principal pieces of work for the museum in 1917, saying:

> the scene represents at the back mountains and a glacier, and the rest of the case is occupied by the rocky shore, covered by ice, sloping down to the frozen sea in the foreground [...] A Crab-eating Seal [...] is rising through a hole in the ice [...] At the back are three of the large Emperor Penguins [...] and scattered about on the rocks are several of the little Adelie Penguins in a variety of attitudes [...] Standing on one of the rocks is a Skua Gull [...] The case is very effective, and provides visitors with much interest. (Benham 1918: 1–2)

Shackleton and Stenhouse were in agreement about the donation of these specimens, Shackleton explicitly endorsing Stenhouse's action.

Stenhouse's Promises

In addition to the material he had offered as donations, Stenhouse also left at the museum a number of Emperor penguins, Adelie penguins, a bird described as a 'Dove (?)' and some other material including jars of bottled wet specimens, for safe keeping until the formal completion of the expedition (Stenhouse 1916). The specimens he asked Benham to distribute on his behalf came from this group of material. Final decisions about the recipients took time and trouble to resolve.

On 20 March 1917, Leonard Tripp sent a telegram to Benham asking about Stenhouse's instructions (Tripp 1917a). Benham's handwritten note on the telegram form, which might have been the text of his reply, remarked that 'Stenhouse requested we distribute birds to his various friends.'

An annotated memorandum from Benham offers us a guide to some of the people Stenhouse must have named. It is headed 'Specimens sent out to the following addresses' with the following list:

> 2 Adelies to Mr A. E. Mabin (Wellington) [POST][6]
> 2 Adelies Mr Stenhouse Wreaks End House, England [POST][7]
> 1 Emperor to Andrew Stenhouse, St Kilda, Melbourne [PS this emperor sent to Invercargill Museum per your order][8]

The next section was headed 'These people I will see. Personally', and allocated two Adelie penguins each to a Mr Lapsley, an Acton Adams and a Miss Stock.[9] Under this was written 'PERSONAL INTERVIEW'.

In a letter to Shackleton later that month, Tripp (1917b) summarised his own understanding of Stenhouse's list. He did not mention Mr Lapsley, but did note that two Adelie penguins had been promised to a Mr Hanlon, two to a Mr Tabley, and that one Adelie penguin was to be given to the taxidermist, Mr Gibson.

Shackleton's Promises

Shackleton's list is harder to ascertain. In prefacing *South* he wrote:

> to the people of New Zealand and the Dominion Government I tender my most grateful thanks for their continued help [...] Mr James Allen (acting Premier), the late Mr McNab (Minister of Marine), Mr Leonard Tripp, Mr Mabin, and Mr Toogood, and many others have laid me under a debt of gratitude that can never be repaid. (Shackleton 2014: xxi)

We know, however, that he did attempt to repay at least some of these people and that he did so, in part, by means of the faunal specimens brought back on the *Aurora*.

From Leonard Tripp's archived correspondence we can gain indications of some of the individuals or general categories of people to whom Shackleton offered a penguin. He sent Tripp a telegram marked urgent: 'Tell Benham I instructed one Emperor ten Adelies be sent you in addition gift Invercargill Museum this is imperative Benham must arrange' (Shackleton 1917).

Tripp posted the telegram on to Benham and wrote the same day explaining these were decisions made by Shackleton before he left New

Zealand, and that the gift to the Invercargill Museum was to fulfil a request to him from the late Dr Robert McNab (Tripp 1917c).

McNab was Minister of Marine when Shackleton met him and he played an important role in resolving various difficulties surrounding the Ross Sea relief voyage.[10]

The specimens Stenhouse deposited at the museum seem not to constitute all the penguins available but might have included an important number of Adelies. Tripp told Benham:

> When Sir Ernest arrived in New Zealand certain people helped him very substantially financially, and he wrote to them from the ice and promised each of them a penguin skin. It may be that I have sufficient skins here for them. Luckily Sir Ernest was able to sell his boat, and these gentlemen have all been paid back the moneys they advanced [...]
>
> I have no doubt that Sir Ernest will naturally want to carry out Stenhouse's promises as well. (Tripp 1917c)

One might speculate whether the gesture was a suggestion that originated with Tripp, if the astute advice he offered Shackleton on a range of other matters is a guide.

Tripp at Work

Money was undeniably tight. Once back in New Zealand, clothing, unused coal and items of equipment were sold, and speaking engagements were undertaken to pay off the expedition's debts, to raise money for the Red Cross and/or to establish a fund to help Captain Mackintosh's widow. The 'moneys advanced' to which Tripp refers were needed primarily to cover the wages of the men who sailed on the *Endurance* (McElrea and Harrowfield 2004: 258). Tripp organised the fundraising, but its success was tied strongly to Shackleton's personal predicament.

The offers to 'certain people' were obviously appreciated. For example, William McAlpine Duncan wrote from Wanganui: 'Many thanks for your promise to forward me a souvenir of your expedition. It will be very interesting to have this rare specimen of Antarctic bird life, and I am looking forward with pleasure to its arrival' (Duncan 1917).[11]

Soon after, Tripp told Shackleton (then in New York), 'I have got a list of the Emperors here, and, as far as I can make out, there are over twenty birds here. Joyce thinks there are 25. If that is so there will be plenty' (Tripp 1917b).[12]

Tripp wrote to Benham again the following month, still not fully decided:

> It is quite clear that no one will be able to get two Adelies even supposing that Shackleton agrees to Stenhouse's gifts being carried out. I would take the responsibility now of asking you to send to Stenhouse in accordance with the address one Emperor and one Adelie: also send two Adelies to Invercargill and tell the authorities there that I will let them know later on if I am able to get an Emperor for them.
>
> I have seen Mr Mabin here and he says that of course he quite understands the position and that the birds are Shackleton's and his wishes must be carried out. He said that if necessary he will forego his Adelie but I told him that I would endeavour to get him one but that he certainly cannot have two. (Tripp 1917d)[13]

Seals were perhaps not in such demand as penguins. There may have been fewer available. It may be simply that penguins were considered more attractive or exotic by the public, equated to a greater extent with Antarctica, or more likely to fit a domestic accommodation. In 1910 New Zealanders had access to images from Shackleton's previous *Nimrod* expedition at their local theatres and the newspaper accounts mentioned both Adelie and Emperor penguins in some detail (*Wanganui Herald* 5 February 1910:6; *Hawera & Normanby Star* 12 February 1910: 5). Shackleton was referenced in a 1912 article which said penguins were 'the most amusing creatures in existence' (*Auckland Star* 16 March 1912: 13).[14] Ponting mentioned their 'quaint' courting and was quoted as saying that 'Adelie penguins are [...] the funniest creatures you ever saw' (*Marlborough Express* 30 April 1912: 6).[15] Possibly also the distinction between Antarctic seals and those that could be seen in New Zealand was not considered substantial. None of the correspondence directly addresses the point. Shackleton gave one to Leonard Tripp, however, and in 1975 its head was mounted as the Shackleton Tripp Seal Trophy, usually awarded to the winner of a cricket match between Chapman-Tripp staff and teams from the New Zealand Law Society.

Stenhouse wrote to Benham from England after the First World War to ask what had happened:

> When I was in Dunedin with the 'Aurora' (I.T.A.E.) I left a number of Emperor and Adelie penguin skins with the Museum taxidermist, Mr

> Gibson; I also left the address of friends to whom I wished the birds to be sent after mounting.
>
> I have just arrived in England from N. Russia after a year's absence & having heard nothing from Mr Gibson, am anxious to hear what has happened in this matter. (Stenhouse 1919)

Benham must have forwarded the enquiry to Tripp, who wrote: 'Apparently I have overlooked the disposition of skins in your possession [...] I think you had better follow out Stenhouse's wishes and I will tell Shackleton that I have agreed to that course being adopted' (Tripp 1920).

Stenhouse wrote again in the new year, indicating that a resolution had been reached:

> I have seen Sir Ernest and he has promised to cable to Mr Tripp to, as far as now possible, carry out my wishes. I hope everything will be all right as I must keep my word. We are all keen to get away to the IceLands again. (Stenhouse 1920)

With the passage of time, resolution of the expedition's finances, and additional psychological distance, the matter might have seemed less acute than it had appeared three or so years earlier, and allowed for more personal generosity. Perhaps Stenhouse had also come to be seen by Shackleton as one of the parties for whom generosity was desirable.

Cooler Reflections

The subject of the conversations between Tripp, Shackleton, Stenhouse and Benham is the allocation of a sought-after group of Antarctic wildlife, collected under the auspices of the ITAE. While the economic factors contributing to the cost of obtaining these items can be enumerated, I suggest that their desirability in subsequent social contexts demonstrates a form of value creation (cf. Graeber 2001) consequent primarily on their association with the celebrated, charismatic figure of Sir Ernest Shackleton. That two individuals both believed they had the authority to make commitments about who would receive these items adds to the complexity of the situation. It offers us an opportunity to assess the obligations that were considered by the different voices arguing their eventual disposition, and also to consider which theoretical perspectives might offer insight into various aspects of the process. In order to make decisions about beneficiaries, agreement about ownership was required and an ordering of obligations.

Stenhouse was a strong supporter of Shackleton.[16] When he left the natural science specimens at the Otago Museum in 1916 he probably believed that he was the most senior member of the expedition alive, and in a position to make decisions of that nature. It seems highly likely that he felt it was appropriate to ask the museum to send the deposited specimens to his list of contacts.

Shackleton was the owner of the *Aurora* and the terms of the expedition seem to have made all material related to it his property. There is a possibility that the circumstances under which the penguins were caught could have led to confusion over their standing. If they were collected as zoological specimens in accordance with the scientific objectives of the expedition then the situation seems clear. If they were unconsumed items caught for food while the *Aurora* drifted, their standing might have appeared ambiguous. In either case, Tripp seems adamant that the birds were Shackleton's to dispose of as he thought best. For both Stenhouse and Shackleton, however, having offered a gift, the importance of honouring the promise added consequence to the outcome of the distribution.

In considering the strength with which Shackleton argued his rights in this matter, one might also consider whether the tense and at times unpleasant discussions surrounding his right to lead, or even participate in, the Ross Sea relief expedition could have hardened his attitude to any possible perception that the full rights he felt due to him as the owner of the *Aurora* and leader of the expedition were being infringed.[17]

Values

Notwithstanding the scientific aims of the expedition, most of the seals and penguins caught by the crew of the *Aurora* seem to have been taken as food to ensure the survival of the crew. For example, Lionel Hooke wrote in his diary for 1 October 1915: 'Three Adelie hove in sight from nw & were added to larder';[18] and on 19 December: 'Meat will soon become a serious item [...] no seals have been seen for days. We have a few penguins but they don't go very far' (Hooke 1914–16). At this point they have a straightforward use-value. Penguin meat is comparable to seal or other meat from the perspective of quantity and nutrition. It is reasonable to suggest that those on the *Aurora* when she arrived in Port Chalmers might have been consumed if the voyage to New Zealand had taken longer. Yet on docking their value was immediately transformed. They underwent a dramatic and almost instantaneous reduction in use-value as food, given the ready availability of other and much more desirable foodstuffs. Shortly thereafter, they also gained use-value in a number of alternative contexts.

Both Stenhouse and Shackleton understood that in New Zealand penguins could be of interest to a range of people: the museum staff, the general public, family members and friends, associates and supporters. The numbers attending the *Aurora* open days and associated displays indicates their popularity with the wider community. The failure of the expedition to achieve its original aims does not seem to have had any impact on the desirability of the specimens. To different individuals – recipients or consumers in one way or another – they had a scientific, educational, topical or public interest worth. Beyond that, their connection to the expedition and its participants indicated some measure of personal association with a famous international event and a charming peer of the realm by their recipients. While they cannot be described as fetishised objects to the extent that they were seen to take on the qualities of Shackleton and his colleagues themselves, their value was increased by direct association with the actions and public image of heroic Antarctic exploration. As a local newspaper said of Shackleton: 'He is the fashion – and a mighty fine fashion, too, if one may be permitted to say so' (*Free Lance* 16 February 1917: 16).

Were the ITAE penguins a 'natural resource' or the product of human effort? Although both Emperors and Adelies were gathered unmodified, so to speak, in their natural habitat, their natural habitat was a long and dangerous journey away from the population centres of New Zealand, Australia and England. Physically transporting these animals from Antarctic waters to the land masses of a different latitude helped make them exceptional. Time and human effort were needed to catch each specimen. Preservation on the journey to Dunedin depended on the ice taken aboard the *Aurora* by her crew to slow decomposition (Hooke 1914–16: 1 December 1915). The mounted penguins that were offered as gifts represented hours of work by a taxidermist.[19] Without that labour they would not have survived long enough to have a future value. Exponentially more resources were required for the ITAE crew members to be in a location where they could be captured. If replacement-value sums were to be calculated then one can make a case for the price paid for the *Aurora*; wages for her crew; fuel, equipment and provisions, to be taken into account. These costs were met by fundraising for the expedition. So the penguins that were eventually offered by Stenhouse and Shackleton were not really a natural resource, and yet a part of their appeal was that they symbolised exactly that: an untouched natural continent; an uninhabited wilderness.

To bridge the gap between the disparate values of the penguins on their arrival in Port Chalmers, and in the various gift and gift-exchange situations in which they featured shortly after, Graeber's (2005) query about what would happen if one tried 'to create a theory of value starting from the assumption that what is ultimately being evaluated are not things, but actions' offers insight. If we consider that what was being evaluated was not only a penguin, but an object that represented some part of the history of Antarctic exploration and the heroic characterisation of the men who undertook it, the actions of the crews of both the *Endurance* and the *Aurora*, Shackleton's efforts in saving the members of the Weddell Sea party, the feat of seamanship involved in getting the *Aurora* to Port Chalmers, and the organisation and success of the Ross Sea party rescue, might we not come closer to understanding the value bestowed on the ITAE penguins?

The Growth of a Market

One might view the situation regarding the penguins on the *Aurora* as a precursor to the vigorous twenty-first-century market for memorabilia associated with the heroic age of Antarctic exploration.[20] In 2002, Bonhams sold a copy of the ITAE prospectus with an accompanying letter for £4,000 in a Polar sale (Bonhams 2012). In a 2007 Christie's Exploration and Travel sale, a two-page 1901 letter from Shackleton to Cyril Longhurst, secretary to the British National Antarctic Expedition, realised £4,375 (Christie's 2007). First edition Antarctic histories have become a feature of specialist book sales; Sotheby's advertised a group of Shackleton-related rare books 100 years after he set out on the ITAE.[21] Although the current situation marks a new stage in the engagement between the public and this type of object, it shares some characteristics with Shackleton's and Tripp's network of exchanged favours. Items associated with the best-known explorers – even unexceptional items – tend to realise the highest prices today. It would seem they offer a contemporary urban collector a safe link to the excitement of travel, the remote, harsh Antarctic landscape, and the resilience of the men who suffered the privations of venturing there a century ago. In 1917 an ITAE penguin would have encapsulated the same resonances but also been of-the-moment, newsworthy and have evidenced a personal connection to the expedition members.

The Give and Take

The age-old appeal of a memento; the interest in a talking point; the respect shown by offering something unusual with social currency, are well understood. The museum aside, both Stenhouse's and Shackleton's gifts were probably appreciated by recipients for comparable reasons. Similarly they were probably generated with analogous motivations – recognition of past debts and future hopes. The difference between the two might reflect a difference in worldview and the contexts in which they identified themselves. Overall, however, the tenor of Stenhouse's gifts appears to be of a personal nature – his father; his uncle; the museum taxidermist, Gibson, with whom he seems to have been on friendly terms; other people who may have supported him in some way during this difficult time. The intent of Shackleton's gifts seems to operate in a different type of network: to have included more establishment figures; to be more strategic in nature. It rewarded those who had helped the expedition and may have been in a position to help in the future, and it enabled Shackleton's reputation as a man who kept his word to flourish.

Near the top of his list was Robert McNab's request for the museum in Invercargill. The President of the Southland Museum acknowledged receipt of 'the birds presented to the Invercargill Museum by Sir Ernest Shackleton' on 5 April 1917. One Emperor and four Adelie penguins from the ITAE are currently documented in the museum's collection.[22] Fulfilling his request may have had an added weight given his death so soon after his interventions on Shackleton's behalf, but it was also a tactful diplomatic gesture.

Tripp had his own sense of the priority for allocation of the penguins:

> I must see that the men who lent you the money get their birds first, because they are all expecting them, and they appreciate the fact of your having written from the ice; and Magnus has not the claim that these other men have. (Tripp 1917b)

Tyler-Lewis (2006: 249) alluded to Tripp's skills and achievements in her acclaimed account of the Ross Sea Party: 'The modest attorney was an impeccable organizer and prudent manager. When funds became available, he duly paid back every pound donated in 1917 with interest, and for the most beneficent, enclosed a stuffed emperor penguin.' In such negotiations it might be helpful to view the allocation of the *Aurora* penguins from the perspective of Gregory's (1994) identification of the need for a qualitative concept of value when considering gift transactions. Although the penguins were spoken of as gifts, not commodities, and they were not sold as such, they did have a realisable value. The ITAE penguins were effectively part of gift exchanges that included both practical and less well-defined returns: skilled labour; encouraging public interest in Antarctic exploration; increasing support for Antarctic science; 'easing' and rewarding the process of seeking financial assistance (and perhaps making it more likely that these could be available in the future); making the sort of social and political connections that might be of use in mounting further explorations; ensuring one's good name; personal honour. There is an explicit statement from Stenhouse of what was expected in return for the specimens given to the Otago Museum. For others, the accumulation of gratitude, generosity shown in repayment; enabling other people to keep their obligations; generation of goodwill; overt recognition of assistance and connection are part of the relationship-building on which social and political networks depend.

Conclusion

Penguins per se were not rare in 1916. Diary entries make it clear that penguins and seals were frequently killed and eaten by ITAE members, both those left on the ice, and those on board the *Aurora*. Ninnis recorded that he killed 289 (Shaughnessy 1990: 277);[23] Hooke's diary mentions many hunts; and when the *Aurora* arrived in Dunedin jokes were made and much sympathy was evinced for the seal and penguin meat diet the men had endured (*Oamaru Mail* 5 April 1916: 6). However, the penguins on the *Aurora* when she berthed at Port Chalmers in April 1916 very quickly acquired an altered import. While their value as food items immediately plummeted, at almost the same time they can be argued to have transitioned from natural to cultural objects. Their change in social and physical location, and the widespread interest in objects associated with Sir Ernest Shackleton and Antarctic exploration altered their social worth and allowed them an imprecise, flexible but widely recognised value in a variety of contexts.

Hundreds, possibly thousands of people paid small sums of money to see the faunal specimens and other material associated with the expedition on public display. They were fashionable and exotic. The Otago Museum was eager to acquire faunal specimens that could be used for a planned display aimed at public education about the Antarctic regions. Both the

Otago and Invercargill museums sought to add scientific specimens to their collections.[24] Shackleton's admirers and supporters of the expedition valued the recognition of their help and goodwill that the gift of a penguin might demonstrate. Some were offered within a more familial set of connections.

From indications in lists given to the Otago Museum, notes from Stenhouse and Shackleton, and Leonard Tripp's correspondence, we can demonstrate a range of social contexts in which their values were articulated. It has been suggested that the penguins functioned as return for assistance with processing skins and taxidermy, gifts to relatives (we do not know if that motivation was affection or something else), personal souvenirs, a means of public education about Antarctica; to honour third-party requests, as marks of gratitude to financial backers of the expedition (not, in the event, as a substitute for repayment); and possibly a more nebulous reward for 'loyalty'.

This chapter examines the singular situation surrounding a group of items that were difficult to access but not in-and-of-themselves rare when they were 'natural' objects. In the journey from Antarctica to New Zealand, however, and with the labour involved in their preservation, the value they held changed from a very practical one (as essential food items) to a situation where they embodied a range of more complex social transactions, as they became part of a network of exchanged favours, finance and support. The prestige of association with the expedition overall and Shackleton personally, scientific authority, the romance of adventure, the influence demonstrated by the capacity to bestow a gift connected to such popular current events, all became entwined with possession of the wildlife specimens on the *Aurora*. The expedition's tight (or inadequate) funding, added to the ways in which they became a part of asking for favours, and a return for assistance of one kind or another. Chance timing, limited communication and unpredictable weather conditions led to at-least-theoretical competition for this finite group of objects, which in turn led to an articulation of the obligations and cultural norms with which they became associated.

Notes

1. A number of people assisted by making archival material available, or drawing it to my attention. My thanks to Chapman Tripp, Wellington, in particular to Anne Wood, Information & Research Librarian. Thanks to the staff of the Hocken Collections Te Uare Taoka o Hākena, Dunedin, the Alexander

Turnbull Library, Wellington and the Mitchell Library, Sydney. Thanks to Craig Scott, Head of Design, Otago Museum for the map.

2. All newspapers were accessed at the Papers Past website, available at http://paperspast.natlib.govt.nz/cgi-bin/paperspast. The website is copyright of the National Library of New Zealand Te Puna Mātauranga o Aotearoa.
3. Both Oligochaeta and Polychaeta are species of segmented worms.
4. A sum with a purchasing power calculated to be roughly equivalent to NZ $14,000 today.
5. In 1916 indigenous New Zealand penguins, petrels and skuas were seabirds protected under the Animals Protection Amendment Act, 1910 (*Timaru Herald* 25 April 1916: 4).
6. Arthur Emerson Mabin (c. 1867–1944) was a supporter of the expedition and seems to have had a personal friendship with many of its members. He received a personal mention in the foreword of *South*, when Shackleton published it in 1919. He worked for the Wellington export and import company Levin & Co. Ltd for many years, joining it as a wool clerk, but manager of the company when he retired.
7. This Mr Stenhouse is Lieutenant Joseph Stenhouse's father.
8. Andrew Stenhouse (1836–1918) was a successful businessman and a relative; Tripp described him as Stenhouse's uncle. He was born in Scotland, moved to Australia, spent some time in New Zealand, and then shifted back to Australia.
9. Tripp says Mrs Acton-Adams. That might indicate the wife of William Acton Blakeway Adams (1843–1924), a significant landholder in Canterbury and Marlborough, who returned to London later in his life but if so, the reason for the gift is unknown. Benham's handwriting means the second letter here is unclear, but the name appears as Stock in Tripp's correspondence. Andrew Stenhouse was in partnership with a William Stocks in New Zealand for a time but that is probably too long a bow to draw.
10. Born in Invercargill, McNab (1864–1917) worked in Southland in a number of legal and public service roles before entering Parliament (representing the seat of Mataura, initially) in the 1890s and early years of the twentieth century (Traue 2000).
11. From Tripp's notes it appears that Duncan lent £200 and that this sum was repaid.
12. Ernest Joyce, another *Aurora* crew member, appointed 'in charge of dogs'.
13. Mabin, mentioned by both Shackleton and Stenhouse, was obviously a good friend but perhaps did not lend such large sums as others.
14. Although the same article described seals as 'the most remarkable animals of the Antarctic region'.
15. Herbert George Ponting (1870–1935) was the photographer on Scott's *Terra Nova* expedition.
16. And that loyalty eventually meant that he was unable to participate in the Ross Sea rescue expedition.

17. The *Aurora* sailed under Admiralty orders in the Antarctic Relief Expedition, although, as the *Otago Daily Times* put it, 'when she went south she was part of the expedition, and was still so when she arrived at Port Chalmers' (6 October 2016: 2). It asked openly if Shackleton could establish a claim to her and if anyone could prevent him.
18. The *Aurora*'s wireless operator.
19. Whether the taxidermy costs came from personal or Expedition funds is not always clear.
20. The first exclusively polar sale (at Christie's) was in 2001 (Baynes 2002: [2]).
21. See: http://www.theguardian.com/books/2014/aug/08/ernest-shackleton-expedition-book-auction-sothebys), accessed 04 November 2015.
22. Pers. comm Tracey Wedge, Collection Manager, Southland Museum and Art Gallery Niho o te Taniwha, 6 November 2014.
23. This is Aubrey Howard Ninnis, another *Aurora* crew member, who Tripp said at this time had recently stayed with him in Wellington for a week and helped with the post-Expedition tasks.
24. Not all this material was placed on display. In Dunedin at least some of the penguins are still study skins.

References

Alexander, C. 1998. *The Endurance: Shackleton's Legendary Antarctic Expedition*. London: Bloomsbury.

Baynes, L. 2002. The issues associated with a market for Antarctic artefacts. Available at: http://www.anta.canterbury.ac.nz/documents/GCAS_4/Baynes_V_Lit.Review.pdf (accessed 7 August 2015).

Benham, W.B. 1917. *Annual Report for the Otago Museum for the Year 1916*. Dunedin: Otago Daily Times and Witness Newspapers Co. Ltd.

—— 1918. *Annual Report for the Otago Museum for the year 1917*. Dunedin: Otago Daily Times and Witness Newspapers Co. Ltd.

—— 1921. Polychaeta: Scientific reports (Australasian Antarctic Expedition 1911–1914). *Series C, Zoology and Botany* vol. 6, pt 3. Sydney: Govt. Printer.

—— 1922. Report on the Oligochaeta of Macquarie Island: Scientific reports (Australasian Antarctic Expedition 1911–1914). *Series C, Zoology and Botany* vol. 6, pt 4. Sydney: Acting Government Printer.

—— 1927. Polychaeta. British Antarctic 'Terra Nova' Expedition Natural History Reports. *Zoology* vol. 7, no. 2: 47–182. London: Printed by Order of the Trustees of the British Museum.

Benson, W.N. 1951. William Blaxland Benham. 1860–1950. *Obituary Notices of Fellows of the Royal Society* 7(20): 293–301.

Bonhams. 2012. Auction 19552: Polar Sale: Scott and Amundsen Centenary. Available at: https://www.bonhams.com/auctions/19552/lot/210/ (accessed 5 August 2015).

Christie's. 2007. Sale 7470 – Exploration and Travel. Available at: http://www.christies.com/lotfinder/books-manuscripts/sir-ernest-henry-shackleton-4966497-details.aspx (accessed 17 March 2015).

Church, I. 1997. *Last Port to Antarctica*. Dunedin: Otago Heritage Books.

Duncan, W. 1917. Letter to E. Shackleton, 19 February. Alexander Turnbull Library MS-Copy-Micro-0630, Wellington.

Graeber, D. 2001. *Toward an Anthropological Theory of Value: The False Coin of Our Own Dreams*. London: Palgrave Macmillan.

—— 2005. Value: Anthropological theories of value. In J. Carrier (ed.) *A Handbook of Economic Anthropology*. Cheltenham: Edward Elgar, pp. 439–54.

Gregory, C.A. 1994. Exchange and reciprocity. In *Companion Encyclopedia of Anthropology (33). Humanity, Culture and Social Life*. London: Routledge.

Harrowfield, D.L. 2015. 'For the sake of science and country': The Ross Sea party 1914–1917. *Polar Record* 51: 343–65.

Hooke, L.A.G. (1914–16) 'Log book written on board S.Y. *Aurora* whilst employed as wireless operator for the Imperial Trans-Antarctic Expedition', 15 December 1914–24 January 2016. MLMSS 7110 / Item 1 from the collection of the State Library NSW.

Hurley, F. 2001. *South with Endurance: Shackleton's Antarctic Expedition 1914–1917: The Photographs of Frank Hurley*. London: Bloomsbury.

Jarvis, T. 2013. *Shackleton's Epic: Recreating the World's Greatest Journey of Survival*. Sydney: ABC Books.

McElrea, R. and D.L. Harrowfield. 2004. *Polar Castaways: The Ross Sea Party (1914–17) of Sir Ernest Shackleton*. Christchurch, New Zealand: Canterbury University Press.

Otago Museum. 1915. *Otago Museum Annual Report for 1914*. Dunedin: The Otago Daily Times and Witness Newspapers Co. Ltd.

Shackleton, E.H. 1907. Letter to W. Benham. Hocken Collections Te UareTaoka o Hākena MS-0762, Dunedin.

—— 1917. Telegram to Tripp dated 21 March. Hocken Collections Te UareTaoka o Hākena MS-0762, Dunedin.

—— 1999 [1919]. *South: The story of Shackleton's Last Expedition, 1914–1917*. London: Pimlico.

—— 2014. *South: The Last Antarctic Expedition of Shackleton and the Endurance*. London: Bloomsbury.

Shaughnessy, P.D. 1990. Bird and mammal life recorded during the Antarctic drift of SY *Aurora*, 1915–16. *Polar Record* 26: 277–88.

Stancombe, R. 2004. Articles by Aeneas Mackintosh. Available at: http://www.spri.cam.ac.uk/library/archives/shackleton/authors/mackintosh.html (accessed 9 March 2015).

Stenhouse, J. 1916. Letter to Benham dated 13 June. Hocken Collections Te UareTaoka o Hākena MS-0762, Dunedin.

—— 1917. Letter to Benham dated 5 January. Hocken Collections Te UareTaoka o Hākena MS-0762, Dunedin.

—— 1919. Letter to Benham dated 30 November. Hocken Collections Te UareTaoka o Hākena MS-0762, Dunedin.

—— (1920) Letter to Benham dated 6 April. Hocken Collections Te UareTaoka o Hākena MS-0762, Dunedin.

Traue, J.E. 2000. McNab, Robert. *Dictionary of New Zealand Biography*, vol. 3, *1901–1920*, 2nd edn. Auckland, New Zealand: Auckland University Press and Department of Internal Affairs.

Tripp, L. 1917a. Telegram to W. Benham dated 20 March. Dunedin: Hocken Collections Te UareTaoka o Hākena MS-0762.

—— 1917b. Letter to E. Shackleton dated 29 March. Wellington: Alexander Turnbull Library MS-Copy-Micro-0630.

—— 1917c. Letter to W. Benham dated 21 March. Dunedin: Hocken Collections Te Uare Taoka o Hākena MS-0762.

—— 1917d. Letter to W. Benham dated 13 April. Dunedin: Hocken Collections Te Uare Taoka o Hākena MS-0762.

—— 1920. Letter to W. Benham dated 13 January. Dunedin: Hocken Collections Te Uare Taoka o Hākena MS-0762.

Tyler-Lewis, K. 2006. *The Lost Men: The Harrowing Saga of Shackleton's Ross Sea Party*. New York: Viking.

8

Quota Systems
Repositioning Value in New Zealand, Icelandic and Irish Fisheries

Fiona McCormack

In this chapter I use fisheries quota systems to examine the entanglement of neoliberalisation with new ways to manage the environment through ecosystems services. My argument is not about fisheries per se, nor the comparative biological sustainability of different fisheries management regimes. In many ways it is not even about fish in the sea. My interest lies in highlighting the creativity involved in the emergence of virtual fish and the attendant relegation of nature, and labour, as inconsequential in generating wealth.

Three main strands inform my thinking about value: First, the privatisation and marketisation of fishing rights is a highly constructed political process. There is no natural connection between property creation and marketisation. Second, a shift from positioning value in production to value in the marketplace incurs the emergence of future value. The marketisation of nature is accompanied by an intense focus on the future and a rejection of historical context and awareness (Büscher et al. 2012). Such a future fetish is apparent in the increasing attention paid to virtual fish, those that come alive in exchanges and in electronic marketplaces, and upon which extraordinary sums of money can be made (McGuire 2014). Third, the structural exploitations resulting from neoliberalising the environment are locally contested, and the reorientation of that systemic force can be read as a double movement. Ethnographically, I draw on long-term fieldwork in New Zealand and more recent fieldwork in Ireland and Iceland. As field sites the three countries are historically and culturally distinctive, yet, in terms of the pivotal role of the sea, and a perceived peripherality of their economy and society, they are markedly similar: they collectively demonstrate the tensions and contradictions that arise at the nexus of global and local economies, social orders and struggles over environmental governance.

The marketisation of marine environments has drawn attention away from productive activities, holistically perceived: from catching fish in nearby waters, and the transformation of the labour and knowledge tied up in small-scale production; from the spatial and temporal dislocation of fish; from the fact that, in New Zealand, 60 per cent of the offshore quota is caught by foreign chartered vessels (often under conditions described as horrific and inhumane if not 'slave labour'),[1] much of which is processed in China and then further exported or shipped back to New Zealand for sale (Pinkerton 2014). A focus on value in the market obscures the increasing litigation surrounding the quota system, and the criminalisation of fishermen, including indigenous producers, who risk selling fish without quota – fishing practices, which in another place or time, would be considered subsistence production (McCormack 2015). Focusing on the sphere of market exchange also draws attention away from consumption; contrary to popular sentiment it is highly unlikely that fish purchased from a quintessential fish-and-chip shop in New Zealand's coastal communities will have been caught by local fishermen, or that it will have been landed and processed nearby. Importantly, it draws attention away from a critical evaluation of the principles that govern the distribution of wages, profit and rent.

I use the term 'neoliberal' in two ways: to describe a particular philosophy, programme and practice that has emerged in the last few decades, and as a form of critique, an oppositional badge (Castree 2010; McCormack 2011, 2012). One of the significant things about studying neoliberalisation anthropologically is to foreground how it plays out in different contexts, how it is an impure process. This is apparent in the different degree to which property, in this case fishing rights, has been privatised and made transferable in New Zealand, Iceland and Ireland. It is also apparent in the tempering of neoliberalisation by local economies (Castree 2010; Mansfield 2007).

The chapter is laid out as follows: I first discuss the processes involved in concretising fishing rights as property. I then investigate quota transferability in the context of marketisation and financialisation. In the third section I draw on ethnographic research in Dún na nGall (Donegal), Ireland, and use anthropological approaches to 'nostalgia' to explore local discourses of loss and forms of dissent.[2]

Privatisation

As a property rights regime for natural resources, quota systems provide a rich historical record of the outcome of struggle; a litany of winners and losers and of the social accommodation implied by the economic and political contention over a nation's direction (Kennedy 2011). They are associated with the rise of the discourse of sustainability in local and global political agendas, and the enmeshment of this with neoliberal institutional reforms designed to save nature by commodifying it (McAfee and Shapiro 2010). Quota systems are rooted in Hardin's (1968) 'Tragedy of the Commons' thesis,[3] that is the assumption that privatisation is the solution to the alleged inevitable tragedy flowing from common ownership: thus it is postulated that private owners of resources will behave efficiently, be future-oriented and sustainable users, and that rights will accumulate naturally to those who best exhibit these characteristics.

The operation of quota systems can be divided into two main processes: configuring biological sustainability through assessments of the Total Allowable Catch (TAC), on the one hand, and generating wealth through the creation of property – that is, quota – on the other. The TAC is an administrative tool for ascertaining the amount of fish that can be harvested from a given Quota Management Area (QMA).[4] In New Zealand, for instance, there are ten QMAs, and under the TAC in each area a certain quantity of fish stock is set aside for Māori customary take, recreational users and commercial operators. The latter is called the Total Allowable Commercial Catch (TACC) and is set in tonnage.

The conversion of fishing rights into property requires deliberate government intervention – quota is created by policy and legislation and is initially gifted to qualified users, typically those with a recorded catch history above a particular quantity and/or amount of capital investment. These criteria evidently favour large-scale and full-time producers. This gifting is everywhere contentious. In Iceland the initial distribution of fishing rights in 1984 is at variance with the later wording of the 1990 Fisheries Management Act, and also with the Icelandic Constitution (Einarsson 2011). The official version of the Act reflects the constitutional vesting of Icelandic fish stocks in the common ownership of the Icelandic people, and is a celebration of equality, fairness and common good. Einarsson claims that there is a discrepancy between the declarations of the purpose of the Act and its implementation so sharp that, in practice, Icelandic quota bears all the characteristics of an exclusive property right. Struggles over fish as commonly owned, or as exclusive property, was the subject of an Icelandic human rights claim to the United Nations (Einarsson 2011b).

Quotas can become individualised and made transferable: thus, New Zealand's Individual Transferable Quota (ITQ) and Iceland's Individual Fishing Quota (IFQ). Of the three systems under study, New Zealand has the strongest version of private property rights, an achievement that requires continuous innovative tinkering given the somewhat intangible nature of the 'thing' subject to commodification: the future right to catch a certain quantity of fish species from a certain geographically defined stock. The Quota Management System (QMS) was introduced in New Zealand in 1986 and during the first few years the strength of the actual property right involved was uncertain. Over this period, the government intervened in the quota market, buying or selling quota when it wanted to alter the TAC. Additionally, ITQs were not readily accepted as loan collateral by banks,[5] hence the status of ITQs as financial assets was insecure. This changed in 1990 when ITQs were denominated as a percentage of the TAC rather than a specific tonnage. Adjustment thereafter required no government intervention, simply the automatic *pro rata* adjustment of all ITQ holdings at the beginning of each season to match the TAC (Yandle 2008).[6]

Three other developments were crucial in solidifying this property right. First, the use of ITQs in 1992 to fully and finally settle Māori Treaty claims to commercial fisheries, a repatriation which had major symbolic and economic implications and reinforced the growing perception of quota as a tangible thing of value. Second, in 1994, and again in 1999, aspects of management were devolved from government to quota owners, now relabelled stakeholder groups, a strategy in neoliberal governance associated with strengthening the perception of quota holders as owners as opposed to resource renters. Third, in 2001 (under the auspices of 1996 administrative reforms geared towards encouraging loan financing) Annual Catch Entitlements (ACEs) were introduced. ACE refers to the tonnage of fish that the quota owner is able to harvest in the year. In terms of strengthening the property aspect of quota, it provided a clear distinction between short-term harvesting rights, and rights concerned with the perpetual ownership of the resource.

Concerning marketisation, it created a second market in fisheries quota. Under the new conditions there is a market in which ITQs can be bought, sold and inherited – what is traded in the exchange is the right to receive ACE in perpetuity – and another market in trading individual ACEs – this is the market in which the quota holder leases out yearly fishing rights to generate income. The ACE trading market has grown, particularly in the inshore fisheries, as quotas have been aggregated, via market trading, into fewer and fewer 'more efficient' users' hands, whose preference is to rent out yearly fishing rights.[7] Over time, the market price of quota has risen considerably. For instance, the average price of *pāua* (abalone) quota increased by more than 50 per cent in the first six months of trading – from NZ$11,000 to NZ$17,999 per metric tonne – and by 2003 the average price reached NZ$300,000 per metric tonne, 27 times the price at the start of *pāua* quota trading in 1988. *Pāua* quota holders currently describe their property right as akin to having won the lotto.[8] Preliminary estimates put the 2014/15 *pāua* quota at $824,000 per tonne.

In Iceland, the consolidation of private fishing rights is perceived to give the lie to the supposed free-market orientation of the ITQ system. A fisheries expert commented: 'Adam Smith would be disappointed. It's simply not capitalist enough.' Einarsson observes:

> There exists an elaborate and pervasive vocabulary of feudal metaphors in Icelandic culture, with 'sea lords' (quota holders) and serfs or tenants (those forced to rent or buy catch shares) reflecting a social discourse of increasing stratifications and inequality within the fisheries and the nation as a whole. (2011a: 117)

Such a discourse conflicts with the traditional national ideology of an egalitarian and classless society, with considerable social mobility and relatively little economic inequality.

In terms of the configuration of property, there is a major distinction between the Irish quota system and its New Zealand and Icelandic counterparts. In Ireland, quota is neither formally privatised nor is it transferable. Quota 'ownership' is filtered through a hierarchy of levels – from the European Union (EU), to the national government, to vessel owners, which has implications for the perceived character of the property as well as for marketisation.

Irish quota operates under the European Common Fisheries Policy, whereby each of Europe's 49 designated fishing areas is yearly assigned a TAC. The TAC is then divided among the member states according to formulae determined by socioeconomic criteria. Member states are then allocated quotas for each commercial species. The waters to be fished include the entirety of the EU member states' 200 mile limit, except in specified waters. States have responsibility for policing national waters and internal quota allocation policies (for example, through licences, limited entry or IFQs). In Ireland, quota is attached to fishing vessels and the method of allocation allegedly favours larger operators.[9] It is the Irish state which quintessentially 'owns' the national quota. Yet this is a tenuous claim given the centralised European management structure; the historic propensity towards TAC – and thus national quota – reductions;[10] the perceived political biases in the European annual TAC setting process; and the allegations of inequity in the national distribution of the quota.

Property struggles are most commonly expressed in terms of class and nationalist ideologies. For instance, the inshore sector (boats less than 12 meters fishing within 6nm of the shore), which comprises 80 per cent of the Irish fleet, is pitted against the large-scale sector as poverty is to wealth: 'there is a quota for the rich and a quota for the poor', explained a fisherman from Árainn Mhór. The Scottish, Spanish and French fleets are thought to overly fish what are perceived to be Irish waters, and 'control by Europe' of fisheries is identified as threatening Irish sovereignty: 'Michael Collins must be turning in his grave at what we have done to an independent Ireland', the same fisherman commented. Recent changes to the European Common Fisheries Policy regulations mean that further privatisation and marketisation, though strongly contested by inshore fishermen organisations and the Irish government,[11] is on the table: Transferable Fishing Concessions, essentially an ITQ, although rejected in the most recent EU Common Fisheries reforms, are increasingly promoted as the way to do fisheries management.

Transferability: Value Creation, Labour vs. Ownership

In ecosystem services, transferability describes one of a bundle of rights that accompany the creation of private property rights, that is, the right to transfer goods from one entity or asset holder to another and the regulation of this right through a market-based instrument. This right directly capacitates an economistic valuation of 'natural capital': since individual quota are freely tradable it is deemed possible to calculate the commercial value of the fish resource from the market price of quota, where the price of quota reflects the commercial value of the fish stock in conjunction with the resource rent.

In Iceland and New Zealand, where quota is individualised and freely transferable, more wealth can be generated from trading virtual fish than chasing fish in the sea. To exemplify: SNA1 refers to snapper off the east coast of the north island in Quota Management Area One (QMA1), and is New Zealand's most valuable inshore finfish fishery. Over the last few years the TAC in SNA1 has been set at 7,550 tonnes. Of this, 4,950 tonnes is set aside for the commercial take (TACC). The combined market price of quota rights in the 2011/12 fishing year was NZ$186 million. On a smaller scale, the average quota price per tonne for SNA1 in that year was NZ$47,049. This is the asset value which can then be used as collateral in banks. The average ACE value (the earnings quota owners receive when trading their annual catch rights) was NZ$4,130 per tonne. The average port price (the price that fishers receive) was NZ$5,770; thus, after paying for the trading arrangement, fishermen receive NZ$1,640 for their effort per tonne of fish sold.

The ratio of the price of quota to the price of fish is approximately 8:1 (NZ$47, 049: NZ$5,770).[12] The differential evaluation of ownership and labour is illustrated by the inequality in outcomes: The owner obtains 2.5 times as much from leasing quota for one year (NZ$4,130) than the fisher gets from harvesting (NZ$1,640). However, this underestimates the degree of inequality since the accountancy conceals the totality of links between property rights, marketisation and new ways of accumulating value under ecosystem services. For instance, the crew, vessel, maintenance and compliance costs that the skipper has to meet are obscured, as is the fact that quota owners are also likely to be Licensed Fish Receivers (LFRs), that is, fishermen likely lease ACE from the same body that they sell their fish to.

The tension between labour and ownership is reflected in the distinction between production and quota trading. Production, including the vertical integration of companies and the sale of fish, is a historic process and arguably a real, or at least visible market, whether free or not. The quota trading system is a virtual market in which the participants buy and sell 'fish' without ever having any need to have fish to sell (sellers) or ever wishing to own fish (buyers). Fish, in this instance, may be considered an exercise in Polanyian fictitious commodity production. Quota trading, however, may be a radically different type of fiction: while there is a limit to the amount of fish that can be harvested, quota trading does not appear to have any such boundaries.

Transferability encompasses a much broader social field than that represented by a narrow economistic interpretation of market valuation. For instance, it is associated with market power, the emergence of new types of labour, and the conversion of fishing rights into financial assets. The tendency of quota systems to consolidate quota shares embeds a political structure that limits substantive participation in management decisions to those who hold quota. Thus, for instance, stakeholder groups in New Zealand, gradually silencing the voices of more and more groups of people who consider themselves participants in fisheries – fishermen who lease fishing rights, fish processors, fishing families, boat builders, net makers, pot makers and so on. Such a silencing has structural implications – the rendering of livelihoods and communities as obsolete and/or the movement of people into even more exploitative relationships with capital.

Transferability has created new forms of labour. In New Zealand the latter include services surrounding quota and ACE maintenance, the management of share registers, the registration of ACE transfers, the registration of caveats and mortgages over quota shares, the recording of catch effort returns and vessel registration. Such services, among other statutory requirements, are undertaken by FishServe, a privately owned company.[13] Quota trading occurs via brokers and bilateral trading agreements. Most small and medium-sized quota holders make their transactions via brokers, whereas larger companies often employ specialist personnel to engage in bilateral trading with other large companies (Lock and Leslie 2007). Various online systems have emerged in conjunction with these exchanges. Among the many instances are FishStock, which provides an online auction system for dealing with the buying and selling of ACEs; FishTech Ltd, which offers an ACE 'balancing service' which purports to optimise the value of ACE distribution; and FinestKind, a company which sells seafood, sources quota and acts as a broker. The devolution of regulatory and market responsibilities to private entities has reconstructed the government's role to that of policing and compliance, the ultimate guardian of private fishing rights (McCormack 2013).

The potential for ecosystem services to incorporate the functions of nature as exchange value is not a radical event. Rather, Gallagher and DiNovelli-Lang (2014) persuasively trace the origins of this movement to the evolution of twentieth-century ecology and its ongoing relation to classical and later neoclassical economics. Similarly, neither is financialisation a new phenomenon, rather it should be understood as a recurrent phase in capitalist development (Arrighi 1994). Yet what is perhaps new is the entanglement of neoliberalism, ecosystem services and financialisation. Many scholars argue that this most recent phase of financialisation, traceable to the rise of neoliberalism in the 1970s, has distinctive characteristics. Kotz (2011), for instance, contends that the financial sector displays specific qualities under neoliberalism. In the current era the financial sector does not stand in a relation of dominance vis-à-vis the non-financial sector (as it did in the 1920s, before the 1929 economic collapse), rather the financial sector is now independent of it. It is this seeming independence that helps explicate the discontinuities between quota holders, leasing arrangements and fishermen.

The Magic of Finance

Transferability makes possible the transformation of fishing rights into financial assets. Finance is distinct from traditional banking in that traditional banks sell money in their possession whereas financial firms sell something they do not have. This virtual quality underlies the thrust in the financial sector to be innovative. It is in the context of this requisite hyper-creativity that Sassen conceives of finance as a capability – 'though one with variable valence' (2014: 118) – which first creates an economy and then seeks to expand to a point where it securitises just about everything in it. Securitisation involves the relocation of a good, a building or a debt, into a financial circuit where it becomes mobile and can be bought and sold over and over in local and global markets. In the past few decades the financial sector, which has long been peopled by mathematically trained physicists, has invented very complex instruments to securitise arcane instances of familiar items – for example, used car loans and fishing rights. Once an input is securitised, financial engineering can keep on building long chains of increasingly speculative instruments that all rest on the alleged stability of that first step. In this sense Sassen warns: 'The power of finance, and what makes it dangerous, is its capacity to build up its own value even as households, economies and governments lose value' (2012: 118). It is precisely this magical aspect of finance that underpinned the Icelandic financial crash of 2008, an event linked to the evolution of transferable fishing rights as financial assets (Benediktsson and Karlsdóttir 2011; Einarsson 2011a; Flaaten 2010). By recreating fishing rights as transferable property a spectacular investment frontier was opened. This enabled finance to seemingly disembed value from nature and labour and resituate it in an unencumbered, utopic future.

Fishing rights were the foundation of the pre-crash Icelandic economic renaissance, an era in which the country was transformed from one of modest means to one of the world's wealthiest nations. In the process of throwing off the shackles of a colonial past, a revitalisation of Viking imagery occurred and attached itself to the new fearless, adventure-seeking business entrepreneurs (Loftsdóttir 2010). In 1990, when quota was made transferable and thus alienable, new conditions of accumulation by dispossession were created and fortunes were made by a handful of increasingly consolidated quota holders. In 1997, when it became legal to use quota as collateral for loans, fishing firms began to accumulate enormous debts through the mortgaging of fishing rights. This marked the point where the rift between work and value creation became substantiated: wealth could be attained simply by owning and exchanging quota and no longer required direct engagement in fishing.

In the late 1990s, the three main Icelandic banks began a process of privatisation that coincided with a growth in investment companies. A number of large quota holders became owners of the new banks, a move alleged to have involved corruption and partisanship (Benediktsson and Karlsdóttir 2011). The new owners of privatised banks and investment companies engaged in frenetic, speculative, overseas investment adventures (football teams, pension funds and so on), much of which rested on the alleged stability of quota as a first step. Thus quota became activated as capital and was financialised to create credit expansion and its corollary indebtedness. Icelandic economist Ragnar Arnason enthused 'ITQ wealth is living capital [...] with the help of the financial system, ITQs have been used to generate financial capital to be used in other industries' (2008: 32). The level of indebtedness, which doubled between 1997 and 2007, is here seen as a sign of the strength of the system. The historic hierarchy of the expansive power of credit and the restrictive capacity of debt is in this instance challenged: it is debt that becomes the crucial constituent of financial markets, a phenomenon that suggests that debt itself has productive qualities (see Roitman 2005).

The new dispensation to use fishing rights as collateral meant that the market price of firms and the prices of stocks and markets escalated rapidly. Such collateral also enabled banks to convince foreign investors that they had strong assets and equity, and therefore credibility. The market price of fishing rights became increasingly inflated. In 2000 the price of cod equivalent was 800 Icelandic krona per kilo[14] – far more than any fisherman could consider as a reasonable investment given the disparity between the price of actual fish landed and the price of quota. By 2008 the price was 4,400 krona per kilo, creating a brick wall for new entrants. The profit to be made from the sale of virtual fish, at this stage, amounted to approximately 80 years of fishing revenues (McGuire 2014). The total value of the Icelandic national quota in 2008 reached a ridiculous 2,000 billion

Icelandic krona, 50 times the entire annual profit of the fishing industry (Einarsson 2011a), a disparity which is reflective of the capacity of finance to innovate, to securitise and to alienate what was once perceived as a natural, common and constitutional right to a natural resource.

Quota debt also spread to the small-scale sector, with devastating consequences. As large quota holders with newly acquired wealth abandoned coastal villages for the pull of Reykjavik and a perceived modernity, small-scale fishers and smaller firms, with the encouragement of banks, took out loans to purchase the quota before it disappeared entirely from the local fishery. It is important to consider the way in which the debt/credit relationship may be thrust on debtors by zealous creditors. Strathern (1992) notes that debtors are not necessarily needy; rather, new needs are created to promote the necessity for taking on new debts. In the case of quota, this implies acknowledging the key role ecosystem service reforms play in global and national environmental governance. In this context, Icelandic banks merely acted on the need already incentivised by the introduction of transferable property in fishing rights. Banks, keen to optimise quota transactions, began offering seemingly generous loans in foreign currency for investments in quota shares. This, in turn, raised the price of quota, the banks' collateral equity and the virtual fish asset base in the balance sheet of the banks (Einarsson 2011a: 147). After the financial crash, the quota-cum-collateral, or virtual fish, was in the control of the banks (newly salvaged by state funds) and their foreign creditors. The difficulty in discharging these quota debts, especially those denominated in foreign currencies, has been compounded by the collapse in the value of the Icelandic krona and is, for many small-scale operators, extremely difficult, if not an unachievable fantasy.

After the 2008 collapse the fishing industry owed about 465 billion krona, roughly twelve times the industry's annual profits. Ragnar Arnason's praise of the natural ability of living capital to stimulate the economy is now considered an exercise in speculative gambling; an immoral risk-taking that mortgaged the entire industry, including future generations of fishermen, without any significant improvements in boats, processing facilities or fishing technologies (McGuire 2014).

While a discussion of the changing moral positioning of the credit/debt pairing in the Icelandic crash is beyond the scope of this chapter, it is interesting to note the link between the evolution of ITQ and debates over the morality/immorality/amorality of the dyad itself (see Peebles 2010). Debt is conceived of as both destructive and productive, as creator and dissolver of social borders and hierarchies. This dual capacity is contingent not only on how people strategically position themselves, but also, and in particular, on the entrenchment of pre-existing inequalities during the financial crisis. As a result of the crisis, small-scale, quota-holding fishermen frequently became trapped in a vicious cycle of debt, whereas large firms and corporate quota holders were able to deflect their supposed obligations (Einarsson 2011a: 147). Verdery's (2003) work concerning the socialisation of debt is helpful here – she points to the tragic ways in which collective debt is foisted on individuals while corporations accrue previously collective credit onto themselves.

Nostalgia and Local Discourse

> The sea is our identity, our road, our livelihood. Sometimes it takes people, but you take the fishermen off an island, that's it. The life and soul of the island has gone. (Fisherman, from Árainn Mhór island, Ireland)

Litanies of loss permeate all three research sites. Conceptualising these memories as a form of pragmatic nostalgia focuses attention on the intersection of the individual, the social and the economic. Anthropologists have long made a connection between a heightened nostalgia and accelerated social transformation, and more recently research in Eastern Europe, has established a link between nostalgia, the adoption of neoliberal markets and social remembrance of a communal past (Hann 2015; Todorova and Gille 2010). While nostalgia seems to imply sentimentalism, historical fabrication and a politically regressive subject, the opposite is also the case. Nostalgic laments may be a moral critique of present inequalities and may provide a charter for social change (Parla 2009). Nostalgia may be creative, may empower agency, may be used as a weapon of the weak, and may have a critical role to play in the field of power and resistance (Angé and Berliner 2015; Berdahl 1999). Hann (2015) insists that any treatment of nostalgia must take into account the larger socio-political context and must provide a lens through which to interpret contemporary politicisation. Nostalgia, in this instance, can be likened to Polanyi's 'double movement', the creative tension between systemic forces and counter-cyclical human practice (see Angosto-Ferrández's Introduction to this volume). Employing this conceptualisation, I will discuss the crucial role of nostalgia in kindling resistance, using the situation in Ireland as an exemplar. However, in order to understand the heightened discontent of the last few decades, it is important to acknowledge the effect of collective memories of marginality over a much longer period.

In Ireland the fishing industry is divided into pelagic, offshore (or whitefish) and inshore segments. Although the combined economic value of the first two fisheries exceeds that of the inshore sector, there is a broad understanding of the crucial socioeconomic role fishing plays in coastal communities.[15] Indeed, the Irish fishery is culturally imagined as inshore: that is, as populated by small owner-operator vessels, with labour supplied by family members, and as comprised of fishermen who fish part-time and on a seasonal basis, and whose livelihood is supplemented by subsistence farming, seaweed and shellfish gathering and turf (peat) digging. This imagery is also supported by statistics: of the 1,400 vessels in the Irish fleet, 1,000 operate in the inshore sector, mostly on a part-time and seasonal basis, most of which now fish non-quota species. In Ireland the quota system has not yet enveloped fisheries to the extent it has in New Zealand and Iceland, and other ways to manage commercial fisheries exist, such as gear and net restrictions and licences such as, those that govern the Irish brown crab fishery, and, until recently, the wild salmon fishery.

Fishing is a particularly embedded way of life in coastal communities of Donegal: more people are employed in fisheries there and seafood consumption rates are higher than in any other county in the Republic of Ireland. Donegal, however, is also the most socioeconomically disadvantaged region, and this is especially the case in its coastal communities. Often referred to as the 'forgotten county', Donegal consciousness is imbued with sentiments of peripherality, remoteness, poverty, backwardness and contradictory loyalties over its historic permeability to the movement of people and ideologies from the troubled North ('The North' is a colloquialism for Northern Ireland). Although employment in fisheries is declining, it remains enormously significant given the lack of alternative cash-earning opportunities and a history of high unemployment rates. Maintaining a viable fishing industry is emotionally charged as any decline is associated with the physical loss of kin. Emigration is an historic wound in Donegal, a place often characterised as an 'emigrant nursery', an employment 'black spot' (MacLaughlin 1994). The recent struggle of many small fishing-dependent communities is experienced locally as an economic and cultural assault and further evidence of the region's marginality.[16] The weight of this loss is crystallised on the *Gaeltacht* (Gaelic/Irish speaking) island of Árainn

Mhór, the largest inhabited island off Donegal,[17] situated in the culturally distinctive *Na Rosann* parish.

In Árainn Mhór fishing is a historically crucial cash and subsistence activity, supplemented by agriculture (though this is a tenuous pursuit given the lack of suitable land) and turf cutting. The main species fished were salmon, herring and lobster, though also pollock and dogfish, each of which had its own season. Burtonport, situated three miles away on the mainland, served as the port of landing, a place for socialising, and or the marketing of island-caught fish. Deep social ties, arising from fishing activities, exist between islanders and mainlanders.

Population decline in both Árainn Mhór and Burtonport from the 1980s is associated with a radical change in fisheries: the implementation of the 1983 European Common Fisheries Policy and the reorganisation of fisheries management as a quota regime. This encompassed the herring, pollock and dogfish fisheries, and had a spatial dimension: the dislocation of commercial fishing rights away from small ports and fishing communities. In Donegal, fishing rights shifted to Killybegs (*Na Cealla Beaga*), to large fishing companies and, it is thought, to Spanish, Scottish and French fleets. This dispossession was compounded by a 2007 nationwide ban on drift-netting of wild salmon at sea, a move perceived to favour the interests of a powerful coalition of anglers, the tourist board and conservationists, though also larger commercial, mostly Norwegian-owned, salmon farms.[18] These changes affected numerous fisheries in Árainn Mhór leaving only lobster and the more recently targeted crab. Such changes have implications for sustainability: they have transformed a multi-species, multi-gear, fishing tradition based on seasonal harvesting into a single-species, single-gear, year-round fishing effort. An oversupply of markets and reduced catch per unit of effort has shrunk earnings, and threatened the continuation of fishing as a way of life and source of livelihood. The island has now reached a critical point in terms of the survival of the community: if the population declines any further, social services will be cut. Meanwhile Burtonport, formerly famous for its herring fishery, has become, in the words of some of its inhabitants, a 'ghost town'.

The following extract from an interview with a woman in her mid 50s, and former Burtonport resident, captures how nostalgia reflects economic and social criteria, but also provides a moral commentary on the present:

> I was born and bred in Burtonport; there were seven fish factories then and six pubs, over 100 in the fleet of boats. Entire families were

> involved. My father and brothers fished, and me and my sisters worked in the processing factories. I started at 13 years of age. Burtonport was a booming fishing village then. Boats used to land from Greencastle, all over Ireland and Scotland. Fisheries used to be a great living, you could live comfortably. I enjoyed the work. It was a great laugh. We worked long hours.
>
> It is not because the fish have gone, they haven't. The French and Spanish can fish but we can't. Irish fishermen are being done left, right, and centre, because of the stupidity of our politicians. Going to Burtonport makes me very sad now. We lost all our buses. All our fishermen. The men there were always working, fixing nets and all. Now it is a ghost town. In some places people didn't know anything else but fishing. People feel shoved out, people haven't the freedom.
>
> It's like the farmed salmon, what are they feeding the fish? Look at the colour of them. They are hemmed in, just like us now. With prey you have to give them a chance, poor old bloody salmon. It's not fishing, there is no fun in it, not even for the salmon.

Nostalgic discourse also provides a means through which seemingly powerless people can expresses the social and phenomenological disruptions that accompany economic transformations:

> Back then the sea was another city at night. You could look out and see the light, now you see nothing. My family were all fishermen, not one of them fish any more, where has all that knowledge gone? Most people lived off the sea, I miss that food, the salt water taste, I miss the freshness. *Cèilidh* – it means going to visit people. Music and dancing carried on into the wee hours. People danced on slate floors and sparks would come flying off their shoes, you know, with the nails in them for Irish dancing. I have never had that happiness again.

The cultural identity of being an islander is synonymous with fishing activity and the knowledge necessary not just to be a successful producer but also to survive on and with the sea:

> The sea is the fabric of what and who we are. I end up crying when I talk about it. There is a sadness. What will I do with this knowledge that I was given freely and with generosity? There is nowhere to go with it. I can't pass it onto my children. Knowledge of the weather, the ocean swells, the moon when it is lying on its back. Our grandfathers and fathers gave

> this to us. No one taught us to fish only one species of fish. They taught as to go fishing on a seasonal basis. That is sustainable. That is reading nature. Now we buy our fish from Killybegs. We are living on an island and have to buy our fish from the mainland. When tourists ask whether the fish was caught locally, I am ashamed.
>
> Many people think that island people are stupid, that we don't know anything about the world, but in reality we are highly articulate people. We know that our fisheries have been systematically broken down. We know that the rich are always rewarded. We know that islanders are the peasants of the system. (Árainn Mhór generational fisherman)

Nostalgia may be a weapon of the poor. It is bound up with perceptions of crisis and of uncertainties around the viability of cultural transmission (Berliner 2015). It can provide an alternative to confront social change and in this sense can empower resistance. For island fishermen in Donegal, the mobilising potential of nostalgia has been married to an indigenous rights rhetoric to provide a critique of economic and cultural dispossession, and leverage through which to envision an alternative future. The following excerpt, from a presentation by Árainn Mhór fisherman Jerry Early, given to the Joint Committee on Agriculture, Foods and the Marine Debate at the Tithe an Oireachtais (Irish parliament) in 2012, captures this rhetoric:

> We call for the fair treatment of small island communities and respect for fishermen as custodians of our fisheries and the sea. We ask for the responsibility and right to practise traditional livelihoods that are ecologically sustainable, socially just and culturally diverse, and pass down our traditions, knowledge and skills to future generations … Our islands have characteristics that are intrinsically valuable and play an important role in the mixture that forms Europe's diverse coastal economy. Islands should be maintained not as museum pieces, but as vibrant and critical elements of modern Europe … if islands can gain consideration and return to the traditional way of life … we can foresee the return of the emigrant, the need for more schools, the possibility of small businesses growing … [a] return to self-sufficiency, practising traditional, small-scale fishing and supported by a diversity of livelihoods … The island man has been given a task to keep this way of life alive. We are different, a breed apart. We are part of a whole yet, at times, undeniably alone and separate. Ireland has entrusted its islanders to keep the lights burning, keep the traditions and be at the forefront

> of the culture, the language, the skills, the crafts … island fishermen will happily undertake the responsibilities involved in preserving the traditions held in high esteem throughout Europe and beyond.

Jerry Early and John O'Brien (of Árainn Mhór and Inisbofin islands) are founders of the Donegal Islands Marine Resource Organisations (DIMRO). They now navigate national and international political forums to agitate for special recognition of their fishing traditions and livelihood rights.[19]

The local lament of small-scale producers cannot be understood simply as an irrational inability to modernise, an attempt to cling onto traditional values (as in Runolfsson and Arnason's [1999] satires on Icelandic ITQ opponents). Making sense of these anxieties and uncertainties, of people losing control over their own fate and that of their communities, is to engage with the mechanics of a particularly recent alienation, a particularly recent curtailment of freedom. In the context of such economic transformations, nostalgic memories of a pre-neoliberal era can serve to activate an alternative future trajectory. To argue for a return to a system of commoning (Linebaugh 2012), for an egalitarian distribution of resource rights, is no more romantic than the capitalist utopia of free markets operating in entirely privatised space.

The DIMRO has had successes to date, though these have mostly been in terms of identity politics and a recognition of the legitimacy of their cultural rights claims. Thornier economic and social issues remain unresolved, a situation that is likely to become increasingly fraught given the pressure to recreate quota as newly transferable, a mooted European conservation directive to designate the seascape surrounding Árainn Mhór a nature protected area (under Natura 2000),[20] and the tendency of neoliberal governance to discipline dissent. These contestations hinge on competing, though also overlapping, discourses of value; the enclosure implicated in conserving nature and a shifting of wealth generation to future markets in ITQ systems are not unconnected. Both involve a manipulation of value creation, align with a 'greening of the economy', and are at odds with community understandings of human–nature relationships and the perpetuation of historical livelihoods.

Neoliberalising the Environment: the Fiction of Future Value

In many ways what has happened, and is happening, in fisheries is a particular manifestation of the onshore destruction of industrial and manufacturing capacity in the name of economic progress. But with a new twist. Payment for ecosystem services, of which the QMS in fisheries is an early example, seemingly marries a new spiritual concern for the environment with the ideology of neoclassical economics: that is, the assumption that sustainability will emerge through the incentivised bargaining of those with private property allocations. Other examples of ecosystem services include: cap and trade schemes, carbon markets, emission trading schemes and conservation banking.

Ecosystem services work to make clear the monetary exchange value of nature so that a price can be calculated in order to conserve its services (Büscher et al. 2012: 8). However this is not just about attempts to preserve ecosystems, that is, payment for ecosystem services. It is about finding new arenas for markets to operate in, and thus to expand and remit. And it is about the circulation of capital (Büscher 2012). Arguably, investments and speculation in ecosystem services and biodiversity markets can only be concerned with their own profitability. Regardless of what the personal motivations of an individual investor may be, the market ensures that profit is the ultimate consideration (Büscher et al. 2012: 13). And it is the future, not the past, that is the reference point for further profits.

Taken together, New Zealand, Iceland and Ireland illustrate a spectrum of ITQ modelling as it has evolved over the last three decades – from partial (Ireland) to full privatisation of fishing rights (New Zealand and, to a lesser extent, Iceland); from restrictions on transferability of fishing rights (Ireland) to free transferability (New Zealand and, to a lesser extent, Iceland); from the acceptance of quota as collateral (New Zealand), to productive debt and financial asset (Iceland). These different degrees of implementation represent the chinks in the neoliberal project, the nexus where practice confronts the hypothesised culmination of capitalist evolution.

Neoliberalising the environment can only be an impure process. Its philosophy, programme and practice is everywhere moderated by local biophysical environments as well as the economies, communities and social systems with which these engage. In New Zealand this hybridity is apparent in Māori *runanga* (corporate tribal body) attempts to balance the oft-conflicting demands of customary obligations and market engagement (McCormack 2013); and in growing tensions between corporate leasing activities and the fishing and livelihood rights of coastal *iwi* (Māori tribes) and *hapū* (Māori sub-tribes). In Iceland, it is apparent in recent efforts to pull back from the more extreme alienations of the ITQ system: by attaching quota to communities, and in setting aside some quota for summer coastal handline fishing. And in Ireland, it can be seen in the ongoing resistance of the inshore sector, and the reluctance of the Irish government to implement Transferable Fishing Concessions. Such impurities are grounds for possibilities (Graeber, 2007), for a Polanyian double movement and the reimagining of fisheries economies. Global concerns over food security, increased inequality and the marginalisation of small-scale producers, suggest that moves to marketise nature may be a tenuous undertaking.

Notes

1. Stringer and Simmons' research into foreign charter vessels 'found disturbing cases of human rights abuses ... physical and sexual abuses, as well as the non-payment of wages' (2014: 253).
2. See McCormack (2012) and Auth (2012) for accounts of loss from New Zealand and Icelandic fishermen. The Irish ethnographic material is of greatest interest here as it captures the link between my later conceptualisation of nostalgia and Polanyi's double movement. This is, arguably, a result of quota not yet being fully privatised nor transferable, and thus an opening is perceived to exist for contestations.
3. Hardin's 1968 thesis was preceded by the work of fisheries economists Howard Gordon (1954), Anthony Scott (1955), and Jens Warming (1911).
4. Quota Management Areas are species specific. Most correspond to one or more of the ten Fisheries Management Areas (based on likely stock boundaries and administrative considerations) in New Zealand's 200nm (nautical miles) Exclusive Economic Zone.
5. There was no legal impediment to the use of ITQs as security for bank loans, but the Ministry of Fisheries did not make explicit provision for the registration of liens or caveats against the title to ownership.
6. TACs are ideally set so as to maintain stock at the biomass associated with the maximum sustainable yield (MSY). They are modified to account for natural fluctuations in stock size and/or to correct the effects of historic overfishing. Stocks require ongoing monitoring. In reality, TACs change relatively infrequently. This is partly due to budgetary restrictions. In New Zealand there is sufficient information to characterise stock status for 101 of the 629 stocks in the QMS. TACs are also difficult to establish due to the intertemporal relationship and the multispecies character of most fisheries, involving complicated interactions between different species.
7. The distribution of quota to *iwi* (Māori tribes) is likely implicated in an upsurge of ACE leasing.

8. This is associated with the 'natural' increase in value after incorporation into the quota system, in addition to a lucrative export market to Asia, especially China, following local abalone stock depletions.
9. This is a common sentiment. In the Celtic sea herring fishery, for instance, 89 per cent of the national quota is allocated to boats over 15 metres in length (Le Floc'h et al. 2015). A participant fisherman stated: 'Eighteen per cent of fishermen typically obtain access to 98 per cent of Irish quota, and of this 18 per cent there are eight to ten main contenders.'
10. This increases the value of the quota for the quota holders.
11.

> Ireland strongly opposes any attempt to introduce an ITQ management system at European level and will not support any arrangement that leads – either directly or indirectly – to privatisation of national 'public resource' fish quotas … Ireland states clearly that an enforced ITQ or similar system will result in the concentration of resources into the hands of large corporations which will have no link with the coastal communities dependent on fishing. (Department of Agriculture, Fisheries and Food n.d.: 13)

12. Recent preliminary figures indicate that the price of SNA1 quota is now $72,000 per tonne, and the ratio of the price of quota to the price of fish is 12:1.
13. Since the Fisheries Act 1996 many registry-based QMS services are devolved or contracted to Seafood New Zealand (SNZ, the commercial industry organisation funded by quota owner levies), as an approved government provider. FishServe is the trading name of Commercial Fisheries Services, which is a wholly owned subsidiary of SNZ.
14. Cod equivalent refers to weight. It implies the relative value of different fish species on the market compared to cod.
15. Though this understanding has yet to find clear expression in direct action at the managerial and policy-making level and there is a vocal sense of grievance in the inshore sector.
16. In 2011, 15 towns in Donegal had a dwelling vacancy rate of 35 per cent or higher: all were coastal settlements. There are about 10, 000 vacant properties in coastal Donegal areas (Central Statistics Office 2012).
17. At 8 square miles/22 sq. km it is the second largest island in Ireland. Two-thirds of the island is covered by peat land.
18. Eighteen Árainn Mhór vessels held salmon licences at the time of the ban, half of which were held independent of any other licence, thus effectively proscribing these vessels from fishing (Nautilus Consultants 2007).
19. This politicisation has international traction: the involvement of NGOs such as the indigenous knowledge promoter, the Gaia Foundation; The International Collective in Support of Fishworkers; the European Small Islands Federation; Alyne Delaney, EU fisheries social scientist; Scottish Crofting Federation

member, Iain MacKinnon; and French documentary filmmaker, Loïc Jourdaine.

20. Natura 2000 is a network of nature protection areas in the EU. It incorporates both terrestrial and sea sites, the latter of which are designated as Marine Protected Areas (MPAs) where no commercial fishing can take place.

References

Angé, O. and D. Berliner. 2015. Introduction: Anthropology of nostalgia – anthropology as nostalgia. In O. Angé and D. Berliner (eds) *Anthropology and Nostalgia*. Oxford: Berghahn Books, pp. 1–16.

Arnason, R. 2008. Iceland's ITQ system creates new wealth. *Electronic Journal of Sustainable Development* 1(2): 35–41.

Arrighi, G. 1994. *The Long Twentieth Century: Money, Power and the Origins of Our Times*. London: Verso.

Auth, K. 2012. 'Fishing for common ground', Master's thesis, University of Akureyri, Iceland.

Benediktsson, K. and A. Karlsdóttir. 2011. Iceland: Crisis and regional development – Thanks for all the fish? *European Urban and Regional Studies* 18(2): 228–35.

Berdahl, D. 1999. (N)ostalgie for the present: Memory, longing and East German things. *Ethnos* 64(2): 192–211.

Berliner, D. 2015. Are anthropologists nostalgist? In O. Angé and D. Berliner (eds) *Anthropology and Nostalgia*. London: Berghahn Books, pp.17–34.

Büscher, B. 2012. Payments for ecosystem services as neoliberal conservation: (Reinterpreting) evidence from the Maloti-Drakensberg, South Africa. *Conservation and Society* 10(1): 29–41.

Büscher, B., S. Sullivan, K. Neves, J. Igoe and D. Brockington. 2012. Towards a synthesized critique of neoliberal biodiversity conservation. *Capitalism Nature Socialism* 23(2): 4–30.

Castree, N. 2010. Neoliberalism and the biophysical environment: A synthesis and evaluation of the research. *Environment and Society: Advances in Research* 1: 5–45.

Central Statistics Office. 2012. *Profile 4: The Roof Over Our Heads – Housing in Ireland, 2012*. Dublin: The Stationary Office.

Department of Agriculture, Fisheries and Food. n.d. Ireland's response to the Commission's Green Paper on the reform of the commons fisheries policy. Available at: http://ec.europa.eu/fisheries/reform/docs/ireland_en.pdf

Einarsson, N. 2011a. *Culture, Conflict and Crisis in the Icelandic Fisheries*. Uppsala: Uppsala Universitet.

Einarsson, N. 2011b. Fisheries governance and social discourse in post-crisis Iceland: Responses to the UN Human Rights Committee's views in case 1306/2004. *Yearbook of Polar Law* 3(1): 479–515.

Flaaten, O. 2010. Fisheries rent creation and distribution – the imaginary case of Codland. *Marine Policy* 34(6): 1268–72.

Gallagher, P. and D. DiNovelli-Lang. 2014. Introduction: Nature and knowledge – contemporary ecologies of value. *Environment and Society: Advances in Research* 5(1): 1–6.

Gordon, S. 1954. The economic theory of a common-property resource: The fishery. *Journal of Political Economy* 62(2): 124–42.

Graeber, D. 2007. *Possibilities: Essays on Hierarchy, Rebellion and Desire*. Edinburgh: AK Press.

Hann, C. 2015. Why post-imperial trumps post-socialist: Crying back the national past in Hungary. In O. Angé and D. Berliner (eds) *Anthropology and Nostalgia*. London: Berghahn Books, pp. 96–122.

Hardin, G. 1968. The tragedy of the commons. *Science* 162(3859): 1243–48.

Kennedy, D. 2011. Some caution about property rights as a recipe for economic development. *Accounting, Economics, and Law* 1(1, Art. 3): 1–62.

Kotz, D. 2011. Financialization and neoliberalism. In G. Teeple and S. McBride (eds) *Relations of Global Power: Neoliberal Order and Disorder*. Toronto: University of Toronto Press, pp. 1–18.

Le Floc'h, P., A. Murillas, M. Aranda, F. Daures, M. Fitzpatrick, O. Guyader et al. 2015. The regional management of fisheries in European western waters. *Marine Policy* 51: 375–84.

Linebaugh, P. 2012. Nedd Ludd & Queen Mab: Machine-breaking, Romanticism, and the Several Commons of 1811–1812. Retort Pamphlet Series 001. Oakland, CA: PM Press.

Lock, K. and S. Leslie. 2007. New Zealand's Quota Management System: A history of the first 20 years. Motu working paper 07-02, Motu Economic and Public Policy Research. Wellington: Ministry of Fisheries.

Loftsdóttir, K. 2010. The loss of innocence: The Icelandic financial crisis and colonial past. *Anthropology Today* 26(6): 9–13.

MacLaughlin, J. 1994. *Ireland: The Emigrant Nursery and the World Economy*. Cork: Cork University Press.

Mansfield, B. 2007. Property, markets, and dispossession: The western Alaska community development quota as neoliberalism, social justice, both, and neither. *Antipode* 39(3): 479–99.

McAfee, K. and E. Shapiro. 2010. Payments for ecosystem services in Mexico: Nature, neoliberalism, social movements, and the state. *Annals of the Association of American Geographers* 100(3): 579–99.

McCormack, F. 2011. Levels of indigeneity: The Maori and neoliberalism. *Journal of the Royal Anthropological Institute* 17(2): 281–300.

McCormack, F. 2012. The reconstitution of property relations in New Zealand fisheries. *Anthropological Quarterly* 85(1): 171–201.

McCormack, F. 2013. Commodities and gifts in New Zealand and Hawaiian fisheries. In F. McCormack and K. Barclay (eds) *Engagement with Capitalism: Cases from Oceania*. UK: Emerald Group Publishing, pp. 53–82.

McCormack, F. 2015. Mauss, interestedness and disinterestedness: Hawaiian and Mäori fisheries. *Anthropological Forum* 25(4): 384–404.

McGuire, J. 2014. Virtual fish stink, too. In E. Paul Durrenberger and Gisli Pálsson (eds) *Gambling Debt: Iceland's Rise and Fall in the Global Economy*. Boulder, CO: University Press of Colorado, pp. 121–36.

Nautilus Consultants. 2007. *An Assessment on the Gaeltacht Islands of Ireland: Sustaining Island Traditions*. Available at: http://www.corkcoco.ie/co/pdf/390026846.pdf (accessed 27 April 2016).

Parla, A. 2009. Remembering across the border: Postsocialist nostalgia among Turkish immigrants from Bulgaria. *American Ethnologist* 36(4): 750–67.

Peebles, G. 2010. The anthropology of credit and debt. *Annual Review of Anthropology* 39(1): 225–40.

Pinkerton, E. 2014. Groundtruthing individual transferable quota. In E.P. Durrenberger and G. Pálsson (eds) *Gambling Debt: Iceland's Rise and Fall in the Global Economy*. Boulder, CO: University Press of Colorado, pp. 109–20.

Roitman, J. 2005. *Fiscal Disobedience: An Anthropology of Economic Regulation in Central Africa*. Princeton, NJ: Princeton University Press.

Runolfsson, B. and R. Arnason. 1999. Evolution and performance of the Icelandic ITQ system. Available at: https://notendur.hi.is/bthru/iceitq1.html (accessed 27 April 2016).

Sassen, S. 2014. *Expulsions: Brutality and Complexity in the Global Economy*. Cambridge, MA: The Belknap Press of Harvard University Press.

Scott, A. 1955. The fishery: The objectives of sole ownership. *Journal of Political Economics* 63(2): 124–42.

Strathern, M. 1992. Qualified value: The perspective of gift exchange. In C. Humphrey and S. Hugh-Jones (eds) *Barter, Exchange and Value: An Anthropological Approach*. Cambridge: Cambridge University Press, pp. 169–91.

Stringer, C. and G. Simmons. 2014. Stepping through the looking glass: Researching slavery in New Zealand's fishing industry. *Journal of Management Inquiry* 24(3): 253–63.

Todorova, M. and Z. Gille (eds). 2010. *Post-communist Nostalgia*. New York: Berghahn.

Verdery, K. 2003. The vanishing hectare: Property and value in postsocialist Transylvania. Ithaca, NY: Cornell University Press.

Warming, J. 1911. Om grundrente af fiskegrunde (on rent of fishing grounds). *Nationalbkonomisk Tidsskrift* 49: 499–505.

Yandle, T. 2008. Rock lobster management in New Zealand: The development of devolved governance. FAO fisheries technical paper 504. Rome: FAO, pp. 291–306.

9

Distributions of Wealth, Distributions of Waste

Abject Capital and Accumulation by Disposal

David Boarder Giles

> If there's technology and machinery on the planet that can make a television set for every man, woman, and child ... and you don't have a television because you don't have the money, the money is a way of inventing scarcity. (Peter Coyote 2008)

Introduction

In the wake of the global financial crisis, as many tumbled down the socio-economic ladder and a handful of oligarchs scaled it to new heights, the twin ironies of surplus and scarcity have commanded renewed public attention. Among the themes animated by this concern, one, long hiding in plain sight, has been rediscovered by a range of documentaries, books, blogs, government reports and lurid exposes: we throw away a lot of valuable things. Some of the most poignant such coverage has focused on is food waste. In the USA, for example, half of the food produced is thrown away uneaten (Gustavsson et al. 2011) and, in turn, half of that again before it has spoiled (Kantor et al. 1997). Of that abandoned share of wealth, commercial waste has often made the best copy, as businesses turn a profit by throwing food away while so many go hungry. The coverage is admirable, but often anaemic, proposing easy algebraic solutions to the non-linear calculus of economic value. It inevitably highlights heroic examples of philanthropic food recovery, but rarely pays attention to the cultural logics that create the waste in the first place, or that determine what happens to it afterwards

– what Gille calls 'waste regimes' (Gille 2007). While the distribution of wealth has become a legitimate subject for popular debate again, the *distribution of waste* is left largely unexamined.

This chapter explores distributions of waste in Seattle, where I conducted ethnographic research over five years, both with communities of Dumpster divers and with an anarchist soup kitchen called Food Not Bombs (FNB). Such meal providers recover a great deal of wasted food. Indeed, in this fashion, across the USA and other industrialised nations, food banks, soup kitchens and other organs of the emergency food system constitute something like an aftermarket shadow economy, recirculating the food industry's abandoned surpluses to people largely abandoned by the market (Giles 2013).

Such shadow economies, I argue, reflect a nascent movement within post-Fordist capital accumulation. Where mid-century Fordism represented an era of overproduction, mass consumption, and rapid product obsolescence – a kind of accumulation by disposal – it also created a great deal of still useful waste. However, as Karl Polanyi (2001 [1944]) would have it, market societies are necessarily in flux as they struggle to reconcile the market's contradictions. And as the Fordist economic pattern has given way to a range of post-Fordist adaptations, extensions and transformations over the last four decades or so, one incipient strategy to overcome these contradictions has been the recovery of some of these wasted surpluses for capital accumulation, albeit in ways that do not disrupt the primary markets that abandoned them – a sort of accumulation by recapture. Below I explore some of the implications of this trend. I pay particular attention to the disposal and recovery of food, which, because it is so fundamental to life, expresses most poignantly the relationship between value, capital accumulation and survival in the post-Fordist era.

The Means of Overproduction

The history of capitalism is a history of waste. Capital is cut of a cloth of surpluses, equally born of the twin projects of creating value and detritus. The long arc of its voracious increase can be nothing but a trail of spent resources, obsolete goods and congealed, exhausted labour, used up in the constant turnover of old wealth for new.

For the creation of value – capitalist or otherwise – follows a logic of distinction (Bourdieu 1984). It elevates certain people, places or things at the expense of others. There are, as Graeber suggests (2001), three distinct but related ways in which social theorists have discussed value: in terms of (1) cultural conceptions of the good or ideal; (2) economic exchangeability, and desirability; or (3) denotation and the signifier's semiotic value. These different modes of evaluation are interdependent, and often fungible, as, for example, when 'cultural capital' is monetised (Bourdieu 1986), or when we read economic value as a semiotic or 'social hieroglyphic' (Marx 2000 [1865]: 475). In every sense, where there is a value, it is defined in contradistinction to either an *opposed* value, negatively defined (de Saussure 1966; Lévi-Strauss 1966; Graeber 2001), or to the sheer *absence* of value – the 'ex-commodity', for example, which is unexchangeable either through its sacredness or through abjection, and therefore quite literally 'priceless' (Kopytoff 1986). Such abjection plays a vital role, as we will see, in accumulation by disposal.

These distinctions imply a remainder that is either *unvalued* or *devalued*. Structuralists and semioticians, for example, recognised the 'cooked' in contradistinction to the 'raw' and the 'rotten' (Lévi-Strauss 1966), 'dirt' or 'danger' as 'matter out of place' with respect to a given cultural system's categories (Douglas 1984), and so on. Similarly, theorists of values as ideals, following Dumont, argue that value inevitably comprises a hierarchy (Dumont 1980; Iteanu 2013). And lest our thinking dwell too abstractly on such structures and ideals, George Bataille (1991) reminds us that they always leave a tangible residue, an 'accursed share' of wasted material wealth. Waste, therefore, may be understood as both the debased pole of value and its material substrate.

A growing literature of Discard Studies has therefore approached the question of value from behind, so to speak, through the question of waste. Taken together, this literature is as untidy and heterogeneous as its subject matter (for an overview, see Giles 2013; Evans 2013). For my purposes, therefore, it is necessary here just to pull on a few characteristically loose threads. Key among these is the role of spatial and material waste in establishing a cultural order. Following the pioneering work of Mary Douglas, for example, Roland Munro points out that to 'dispose' of a thing inevitably entails both an act of material *disposal* and one of cultural *disposition* – of ordering objects and subjects with respect to each other (Munro 2013). A second, related thread concerns the visceral affects addressed to such disposed objects. Similarly, taking her cues from Douglas, Julia Kristeva describes the abhorrence and refusal of such disavowed objects as 'abjection'. Abject and abjection, she wrote, are 'the primers of my culture' (1982: 2). Both threads highlight the larger affective, semiotic and spatial structures founded on acts of distinction and material disposal. The non-deterministic play of such systems and signifiers across our material-phenomenological habitat, then, suggests a two-fold meaning for the word 'waste'; not only 'material detritus', but also 'thriftlessly wasted', and hence harbouring unredeemed use-value.

And, in both senses, the capitalist mode of production proceeds apace. With rare exceptions (e.g. Thompson 1979; O'Brien 2013) theorists have skirted the role of waste in capitalism. However, like the other sources of value described above, the commodity-fetish is produced not only materially, but also discursively, and with it, an inevitable remainder. Indeed, the semiotic quality of exchange-value is central to the generation of waste – and vice versa. Capitalist value, for Marx, was a Rosetta Stone that encoded not only concrete acts of production but the entirety of capitalist social relations (both discursive and material). In a precisely parallel manner, waste represents an abject fetish, bearing the stamp of producer, retailer, distributor, advertiser, consumer and so on. To paraphrase Marx: could waste itself speak, it would say, 'My "uselessness" may be a thing that concerns men. It is no part of me as an object.'[1]

Consider, for example, the mountain of unspoiled grocery surpluses in many industrialised countries' waste streams. To wit, US producers, distributors and retailers annually discard at least[2] 2.4 million tonnes (5.4 billion pounds) of unspoiled food before it ever reaches a point of sale (Kantor et al. 1997). Similarly, UK retailers annually discard 1.6 million tonnes of food (Ventour 2008). Although it is not clear what proportion of that waste would have been edible, it seems likely that it is reckoned useless not according to any inherent property of the food itself, but rather by social relations and rhythms of commercial exchange.

In such a fashion, capitalist production makes waste its business in the two-fold sense of the word that I described above. Not only does the production and circulation of commodities entail a great deal of material detritus – from potato peel to carpet remnants – but the production and circulation of new value, embodied in those commodities, continually obsolesces the old – amounting to a constant turnover of otherwise useful goods from the shelves. Marx pays particular attention to the latter consequence. Indeed, although he rarely uses the term 'waste', it is at the core of his critique of capitalism: *overproduction* was, he wrote in the *Grundrisse*, the 'fundamental contradiction of developed capitalism' (2000 [1941]: 399). Marx recognised that the myriad relations of production that amount to capitalism were not a zero-sum game. They yielded untenable, contradictory pressures and limits, chief among which was the pressure to produce and realise as much value as possible while compensating its labourers – also its chief customers – as little as possible. He writes:

> [T]he periods in which capitalist production exerts all its forces regularly turn out to be periods of over-production, because production potentials can never be utilised to such an extent that more value may not only be produced but also realised; but the sale of commodities, the realisation of commodity-capital and thus of surplus-value, is limited, not by the consumer requirements of society in general, but by the consumer requirements of a society in which the vast majority are always poor and must always remain poor. (Marx 2000 [1893]: 225)

Here, then, the fundamental tension in capitalism is a question of surplus. From one perspective, a surplus population keeps wages low. From another, surplus production yields more goods than consumers can afford. Writing at the height of nineteenth-century capitalism's heady industrial expansion, Marx believed such overproduction was both so fundamental and so fatal to capitalism that it would ultimately fall, yielding to a newer, more just economic system. As we will see, he was only half right. The way in which capitalist enterprises reckoned with their overproduction – and, indeed, found a way to profit from it – was fundamental to the successful reorganisation of capitalism in the twentieth century, and may yet prove fundamental to its reorganisation in the twenty-first.

Disposable Capitalism

Had he lived into the twentieth century, Marx might have enjoyed a bit of *Schadenfreude*. By some accounts (e.g. Sparke 2013), the Great Depression itself was a crisis not simply of over-speculation but of oversupply – capitalism's unparalleled productive potential was echoed in the optimistic speculation of its ledgers, but not in demand for its wares, as Marx had warned. And it heralded transformations which, in many ways, did spell the end of capitalism as Marx had known it: not only the century's socialist revolutions, but also the rise of Keynesianism, the welfare state and demand-side economics in capitalist countries represented attempts to resolve, in various ways, capitalism's fundamental contradictions (Sparke 2013). By 1953, Paul Mazur, a Wall Street investment firm partner, was able to distil the spirit of both demand-side economics and, perhaps unwittingly, Marxist critique:

> The giant of mass production can only be maintained at the peak of its strength when its voracious appetite can be fully and continuously satisfied ... it is absolutely necessary that the products that roll from the assembly lines of mass production be consumed at an equally rapid rate. (quoted in Packard 2011: 36–37)

To this end, Marx had said, capitalism was 'permanently revolutionary, tearing down all obstacles that impede the development of productive forces, the expansion of needs' (2000 [1941]: 398). With perhaps less rhetorical flair, Karl Polanyi amended this somewhat, positing an ongoing 'double movement' inherent in market societies by which (like a rubber band placed under tension and released) they are reorganised first as capital tears down obstacles and creates markets, and second as the constraints of ecology, social reproduction and sheer human survival assert themselves. While Polanyi represented this cycle's second movement as a resistance to market logic, it was nonetheless a resistance in which he acknowledged the business classes sometimes participated, if they knew what was good for them. If, for Marx, capitalism would eventually prove its own biggest obstacle, the logic of Polanyi's double movement implied that capital would surely tear that down too. And to that end, faced with dwindling demand, capitalism rebuilt itself in the compromises between business, organised labour and state intervention reflected in mid-twentieth-century Fordism, Keynesianism and demand-side economics.

These compromises shored up demand, expanding the ranks of the middle class in many industrialised nations. Nonetheless, they did little to address the pressures that led to overproduction in the first place. Although the new consumers learned eagerly to incorporate the goods of industrial Fordism into new visions of (largely bourgeois, white, patriarchal) domesticity, they could not do it fast enough. By mid century, consumer demand dwindled as many markets became saturated and a majority of middle-class families had acquired all the new commodities they could fit into the household. One American manufacturer argued to the public, without a hint of irony, that 'Every family needs a second home' (quoted in Packard 2011: 43).

Ingeniously, in this context, manufacturers reinvented the contradiction of overproduction as its own solution. Waste-making became an explicit fix, anticipating by some years other post-Fordist strategies like the 'time-space compression' of globalisation (Harvey 2007) that maximise the return of surplus value by minimising the turnover time between investment, production, circulation, and consumption. Late-Fordist manufacturers remarked with brutal candour in the 1950s and 1960s on the value of accelerated *obsolescence* and *disposability* in producing consumer demand and renewing economic growth. As one marketing consultant argued: 'our enormously productive economy ... demands that we make consumption our way of life ... We need things consumed, burned up, worn out, replaced, and discarded at an ever increasing rate' (quoted in Packard 2011: 37–38). Through aesthetic and technical innovation, planned obsolescence and the production of new consumer subjectivities, then, many industries invested in remaking consumption to serve accelerated capital accumulation. The legacy of this strategy is a consumer culture of waste and disposal. This culture partly accounts, for example, for a 50 per cent increase in US consumers' per capita food waste between 1974 and 2003 (Hall et al., 2009: 1–2). Through such transformations in consumption, then, waste-making became an increasingly prominent feature of Fordist capitalism, and ultimately a keystone of the post-Fordist economy.

Abject Capital: Throwing Away One's Cake and Having it Too

This waste-making has partly consisted of a consumer shift towards products with a built-in practical obsolescence, from plastic cups to disposable nappies. But equally it has involved the perceived (even enforced) obsolescence of items that continue to have use-value. And while consumers have a direct hand in this waste, much of it happens before it ever reaches a point of sale. As one experienced Dumpster-diver wrote, 'chances are, if they sell it in front, they throw it away out back' (CrimethInc. 2004: 220). This point raises an interesting question within the context of this volume on the anthropologies of value: some of the contributors emphasise the counter-capitalist meaning-making of individual economic agents as they de-commodify objects – culturally abnegating their exchange-value in deference to other forms of value; a remarkable thing that one discovers when looking at processes of waste-making is that, for its own reasons, capitalism itself sometimes does the same thing.

Such discarded surpluses are the result of a distinctive, paradoxical logic in the process of contemporary capital accumulation (Giles 2013). Food, electronics, clothing, and a cornucopia of other commodities are evicted from the shelves in remarkable quantities to make way for newer or more highly valued commodity capital to circulate. To diminish this circulation time, and thereby to accelerate the rate of return on investments, goods are produced and circulated in superfluous quantities, often to be abandoned a short time later. These wasted surpluses, therefore, represent a kind of lapsed commodity capital, one which may never see a direct return on the investment made in its constituent labour and raw materials.

Naturally, different commodities are abandoned for different reasons. In my own research, for example, I found that produce was often abandoned due to minor cosmetic blemishes. Artisanal bread fetched a high enough premium when fresh out of the oven, that it was profitable to clear it off the shelves a mere day or two later in favour of fresher loaves. Fruit juice or milk near, but not beyond, its sell-by date was often discarded simply because it would not sell as readily as goods with a longer shelf-life stamp. And so on. As long as the premium which consumers are willing to pay for these goods is high enough, it remains profitable to overstock them, as the profit of a potential sale often outweighs the overhead cost of potential waste and disposal. Tristram Stuart illustrates this logic with the example of a UK sushi outlet:

> The retail price of any item is two to three times the cost price, which means that it is better to waste two of each product than lose even just one sale ... The size of profit margins and the low cost of food waste disposal influences the amount of waste retailers create as an 'affordable' by-product. (2009: 17)

In addition, Stuart identifies both poor prediction by food workers and the 'impression of infinite abundance' conveyed by full shelves as key contributors to overstocking (2009: 27–28).

What these examples fail to convey individually, however, and what Stuart's analysis only hints at, is that food waste represents more than a simple quantitative development in relations of production, consumption and circulation time. These abandoned surpluses amount to a *manufactured scarcity* – one inherent in the logic of commodity exchange itself. To wit, the commodity form functions as a threshold to legibility and exchangeability, one whose economic and semiotic value reflects a tacit social contract between sellers and buyers that some things will be saleable and others not – a determination that, in day-to-day commerce, rests largely with sellers. Sellers, of course, inevitably claim to be responding to consumer demand – the appeal of the 'impression infinite abundance' described above, for example; Stuart cites evidence that this demand is more flexible than supermarkets claim (Stuart 2009: 27).

Consider, for example, the difference between a dozen eggs on the shelf and eleven perfectly good eggs in the Dumpster (a common find for many Dumpster divers). Quantitatively, the difference is a cracked egg in the carton. Qualitatively, the difference is between a legible, standardised exchange-value and 'matter out of place'. In this way, the abandonment of almost-dozens of eggs in the Dumpster bears a loose family resemblance to the practice of dumping milk to keep dairy prices high, or the US government's slaughter of hogs during the Great Depression to keep pork bellies profitable. However, unlike spilt milk or slaughtered hogs, disposed of by fiat, the cultural and spatial dispositions of eleven uncracked eggs rest more squarely on the social contract between buyer and seller. While they are still useful, their exchange-value is understood to be annulled – particularly once they cross the threshold of a Dumpster.

Indeed, the logic of market exchange relies upon the effective enclaving of such surpluses. Precisely because they still have use-value, they cannot be recirculated in spheres of market exchange without undermining the price structure. As such, they occupy the position of a kind of shadow commodity. They leave a trace on the market precisely through their absence. This shadow commodification resembles the ambiguous status of commodities that have quantitatively depreciated beyond the point of exchangeability, but that retain latent value which affords them the possibility of recapitalisation at a later date – antiques, for example, that make the passage back from unwanted trinket to rare collectible (Thompson 1979). Unlike this submerged value, though, the demand-side value of useful surpluses submerged in the Dumpster – say, bananas – is less at issue than the supply-side determinations of businesses. In any case, however, as it stands, this ambiguous, abandoned capital with its annulled exchange-value is an indispensable element of the structure of many commodity markets.

Elsewhere, I have used the term *abject capital* to describe this ambivalent state, both valuable and valueless, within and without the market (Giles 2013, 2014). 'Abject', in its etymology, means literally 'thrown away'.[3] However Julia Kristeva's more elaborate definition for the term, cited above, is appropriate too. For Kristeva, abjection is the experience of those lacunae in systems of signification and subjectivity 'where meaning collapses' (1982: 1), where tidy categorisations fail, and where matter is therefore irredeemably, disturbingly out of place – from the corpse to the abhorrent skin on a glass of unhomogenised milk. This is precisely the case for those shadow commodities described above. I found this ambiguity expressed acutely by produce workers and other food retailers, for example, who in practice were often, by turns, efficient to the point of callousness about clearing edible food from the shelves and deeply uncomfortable with throwing it away. While its value or valuelessness was often all too readily apparent within specific regimes of value – an 'affordable byproduct' according to the bottom line, and eminently edible according to a rumbling stomach – the usual fungibility between exchange-value, use-value and demand broke down in troubling ways.

The resultant artificial scarcity represents a definitive aspect of the logic of capital accumulation, but distinctly so in the throwaway culture of the post-Fordist era. Abject capital, and the manufactured scarcity which it makes possible, represents one of the key strategies by which capitalism has resolved its contradictions, and continued to make a strength of its fundamental weakness, overproduction.

Wasted Futures: Mechanisms of Abject Recapture

Such manufactured scarcity is, of course, not a permanent solution to the contradictions of capitalism. To begin with, it takes a great deal of socio-cultural labour to maintain. Just as the commodity's definitive feature, its exchange-value, must be continually reified through the cultural work of encoding, enclaving and evaluation, or through the establishment of 'commodity contexts' where its exchangeability is its most salient feature (Tsing 2013; Appadurai 1986; see also essays by Angosto-Ferrández, Barnett-Naghshineh, Horan and Presterudstuen in this volume), the persistent use-value of an ex-commodity must be encoded and enclaved to keep its exchangeability muted. Elsewhere I have described this work as the *labour of refusal* (Giles 2015). This is work which actively refuses recirculation to abject capital, isolating it from the commodity contexts in which it might be recapitalised or otherwise recovered. This might be as simple as putting it in the Dumpster, a deterrent to most would-be consumers – or locking the Dumpster and chasing off would-be Dumpster divers. But it also includes a range of labours and circuits that seclude or transport this abject capital without disrupting the norms of market circulation that characterised its former social life – from converting it to biofuels to donating it to a soup kitchen (more on these examples below).

The proliferation of such post-commodity contexts makes it possible, however, for capital to throw away its cake and consume it too. While it often serves the purposes of profit-making perfectly well to clear goods from the shelves and send them straight to the dump, nonetheless the value of this abject capital remains unredeemed. Within these enclaved contexts, then, it is possible to put abject capital back to work without it ceasing to function as abject capital.

As I described at the outset, recent years have seen a renewed concern with food waste in industrialised Anglophone countries – increasingly mindful, perhaps, of both the stark inequalities of neoliberal capitalism and the anthropocene era's growing ecological crises. These are, of course, precisely the kind of ecological and social limits that drive Polanyi's double movement. Much of this attention, however, simply decries the outrage of wasted resources and food insecurity, and calls for businesses to donate more to emergency meal programmes. They share this conservative critique, in a way, with a growing number of food retailers, who they have largely celebrated for their efforts to put surplus food back to work – without putting it back on the shelves. (Recall that, for Polanyi, often the business classes themselves find it advantageous to participate in the double movement.) Sainsbury's in the UK, for example, has successfully diverted all of its waste from landfills, instead donating some of its surplus food to charity and processing the rest of its organic waste into biofuels or electricity (Feldman 2014). As Martin O'Brien points out, this is an increasingly common move for food retailers:

> Whereas early twentieth century concern about waste centred heavily on the loss and recuperation of physical commodities ... early twenty-first century policy is dominated by the loss and recuperation of energy: effectively, the energy problem is slowly supplanting the commodities problem as the official value of waste's recuperation. (2013: 197)

These strategies are examples of what I'll call *mechanisms of abject recapture* – means to repurpose, recirculate, and ultimately even *recapitalise* the disposed surpluses without reintroducing them into their original markets. As such, they continue to function as abject capital, even while still being put to work for capital accumulation.

Philanthropic donations are, for example, cheaper for retailers than paying to have the waste hauled away, and so buoy up the bottom line *without the waste becoming recommoditised*. Bio-energy promises a yet more direct kind of recapitalisation of the ex-commodity. Although it represents a transformation of both use-value and exchange-value – barely recognisable in the usual terms of economic investment and return – it nonetheless reflects the harvesting of caloric energy cultivated by agricultural labour, and processed and transported by industrial labour. Thus, in some fundamental sense, the value recouped as bio-energy is still a sort of surplus value in the classic Marxist sense.

What I want to argue here is that, in strategies like these, we can identify a nascent development in the logic of capital – one founded partly on the cultural logic of disposal, but distinct from it. It remains to be seen whether these moves represent a passing thought or a prescient adaptation of the basic blueprint of capitalism.

Consider in this light the latest venture by Doug Rauch, former president of the upmarket USA grocery chain Trader Joe's. His new retail outlet, The Daily Table, aims to sell ugly and expired produce and hot, nutritious meals drawing upon the surplus produce, meat and dairy of grocery stores, in precisely the same fashion as emergency meal programs have done for years. 'It's the idea about how to bring affordable nutrition to the underserved in our cities', he says: 'It basically tries to utilize this 40 percent of this food that is wasted' (sic. quoted in Simon 2013). The key difference between emergency food pantries and The Daily Table is that he will sell the food at a price to compete with fast food. More importantly, he identifies the target market as 'underserved' and 'inner-cities' – his first store will open in Roxbury, a low-income suburb of Boston. He explicitly points out that Trader Joe's has no stores in such areas, so he won't be competing with his suppliers. This is particularly significant. By my definition, mechanisms of abject recapture function as such only and precisely insofar as they do not disrupt the primary social relations of production, distribution and consumption wherein the commodity acquires its value. In practice, of course, the horizons of these commodity contexts are not always clearly or sharply delimited. They often rest on culturally conditioned assumptions about relationships between geography, class, race, and identity. This new enterprise in junked food, then, is explicitly able to recapture the surplus value in Trader Joe's wasted goods without upsetting Trader Joe's custom thanks to both geographic and social distances that are as prohibitive as any Dumpster for the chain's largely white, upper middle-class customer base.

This strategy, of course, is not unlike that of other discount retailers like the Grocery Outlet, which purchase and resell overstocked goods in secondary commodity contexts in ways that do not compete directly with those primary markets for which the goods were originally destined. Such discount retailers have long allowed manufacturers and distributors to recoup some value from their initial investment in production, thus partially resolving, or at least deferring, the quandary of overproduction. Mechanisms of abject recapture represent an extension of this logic beyond the end of a commodity's social life as such, into the ambiguous real of abject capital.

The two examples above – bio-energy and recaptured fast food – are framed, both by news coverage and by the protagonists themselves, in progressive terms: as reduction in carbon footprint, and a humanitarian intervention in urban food deserts, respectively. But they address these quandaries in ways that extend rather than challenge the logic of capital accumulation. Mechanisms of abject recapture do not extend this logic, however, simply by padding specific commercial endeavours' bottom lines. They must also remake the forms of social reproduction upon which capital depends. And, as I will argue in the next section, emergency meal projects offer a telling window into precisely these sea changes in the landscape of capitalist societies.

Waste Redistribution

Like the other post-Fordist fixes, from just-in-time production to the feminisation of labour, mechanisms of recapture are significant not simply because they permit a greater return on investments. Rather, they have had a hand in remaking the qualitative landscape of market societies and redistributing their waste. This effect is not unlike the wealth redistribution that David Harvey (2007) argues is the primary function of neoliberal reforms. Harvey's argument is worth elaborating briefly here: neoliberal reforms have not been terribly effective at generating new wealth or value, he suggests – overall global economic growth in the neoliberal era has tended to be rather unimpressive; nonetheless, these years have been terribly profitable for the upper echelons of bourgeois society, as the share of income and material wealth has been largely redistributed upwards from working classes, or expropriated through privatisation and 'primitive accumulation'.

In a parallel fashion, the mechanisms of abject recapture I describe redistribute both commodity surpluses and surplus populations in time and space. Where the middle decades of the twentieth century saw Fordist mass consumption of ever more disposable commodities, the production of these surpluses continues unabated while the spending power of consuming classes has transformed in significant ways. Ever more people find themselves falling from one echelon of the economy to another – a pattern whose ultimate expression is the stunning and steady growth of homelessness and hunger over the last thirty years in many neoliberal, post-Fordist societies, most acutely in the USA. This neo-lumpenproletariat finds itself excluded from public circulation in much the same manner as abject capital.

In this, then, we may begin to imagine the larger consequences of abject recapture. While the examples I have given above are both illustrative and portentous, they remain marginal for the moment – it remains to be seen whether energy reclamation or surplus fast food will come to remake the landscape of twenty-first-century capitalism in the way that disposability and abject capital has constituted the post-Fordist present. As the growth of grocery surpluses continues to be matched by the growth of homelessness and hunger, however, the rise of emergency meal programmes may help us detect some of the larger qualitative shifts already at hand.

Emergency food projects are not directly responsive to any single business's bottom line, of course. Ostensibly, they are humanitarian projects. Their recent history in the USA, however, is the history of growing disparities between stark poverty and consumer excess. In other words, we might just as easily give a supply-side account of their genesis, as their emergence corresponds to the growth of commercial and federal food surpluses in need of pathways for abject recirculation (Poppendieck 1998, 2010; Dickinson 2014). 'Herein lies the particular genius of emergency food', writes Janet Poppendieck: 'much of the food distributed by the emergency food system is food that would otherwise go to waste ... and many corporate donations to the emergency food system would otherwise end up in the landfill' (1998: 42). Indeed, some of the earliest, longest-standing free meal programmes in the USA have not been administered by a department of health, but rather by the United States Department of Agriculture (USDA), which in the wake of the Depression bought up enormous surpluses of produce and livestock to keep the prices up and the farmers afloat. Some of these surpluses, as I have mentioned, were destroyed outright. Others were channelled into school lunches and other early federal welfare programmes, and continue to be channelled into the national network of food banks and soup kitchens (Poppendieck 2010; Dickinson 2014).

The genesis of the food bank has an etiology similarly rooted in waste. The first 'food bank' so named was inspired in 1967 by the overflowing grocery surpluses donated to one Midwestern soup kitchen (Saint Mary's

Food Bank Alliance n.d.). The term 'bank' emphasised the unequal distribution of surpluses which could be deposited by some, and withdrawn by others. The innovation was not unique, of course. The Black Panther Party founded their free breakfast programmes the same year, and radical street theatre group the San Francisco Diggers held their free feed-ins the following year, all inspired by donated grocery surpluses (Dickinson 2014; Dolgin and Franco 2007). It is no accident that these innovations came in the late 1960s, on the brink of the post-Fordist era, which, as I have already suggested, saw per capita food waste grow almost exponentially for the following three decades. But the real growth of food banks came in the 1980s (Poppendieck 1998; Dickinson 2014), as a result of several factors: the ongoing surplus of USDA agricultural commodities; the proliferation of flows of abject capital (in Seattle, for example, food grew steadily for several decades as a component of the commercial waste stream, stabilising at roughly 30 per cent);[4] and the twin legacies of Ronald Reagan's USA – the atrophy of federal welfare programmes and the shocking growth of income inequality, poverty and homelessness. Far from simply feeding people, then, these projects capitalise on growing quantities of unspoiled food devalorised and donated by the food industry. Moreover, they buffer the disparities in wealth and consumption practices which create this waste.

In this context, anthropologist Maggie Dickinson has called emergency food programmes 'non-profit contractors' who manage federal and commercial food surpluses (2014: 107). Dickinson focuses on federal surpluses, which she calls 'the backbone' of emergency food programmes. But donated commercial surpluses are equally significant. In my own research, for example, formal food recovery agencies like Food Lifeline, the Meals Partnership Coalition or the University District Food Bank collected donations on a daily basis from grocers and markets across the city. In my own work with FNB, our efforts ran parallel to a plethora of other such organisations. When seeking new donors, we frequently found grocers and markets were already being visited by several food recovery projects. Occasionally, we would arrive within hours of each other. It is telling that there was almost always enough food for all of us.

Emergency meal programmes, therefore, are complex mechanisms of recapture. While the donation is worth a tax write off and is cheaper than paying a waste disposal company, their bigger contribution to the bottom line is indirect. They recapture surpluses and channel them into shadow economies that, much like the Dumpster, are segregated from the markets and publics by which commodity exchange is accomplished (Giles

2013). We might imagine them, then, both as part of a progressive double movement to redress the profound food insecurity of the neoliberal era and, more conservatively, as an outsourced 'third tier' of the atrophied welfare state, buffering the structural unemployment or surplus population on which capital accumulation rests (Dickinson 2014: 118).

In so doing, they discipline their clients in accordance with the demands of those larger markets and publics from which abject capital is excluded. Here, it is important to remember that mechanisms of abject recapture function precisely to the extent that geography, class, race and identity circumscribe the social horizons of a market. The most glaring example from my own ethnographic work in Seattle saw all but one meal programme prohibited from operating outdoors – in other words, excluded from public visibility. The remaining outdoor programme, Operation Sack Lunch, is permitted to operate under the freeway, a stiff uphill walk from most of the shelters and downtown foot traffic. Such policies, I would argue, are deeply implicated in the refusal of recirculation to wasted surpluses. While such policies often devolve the labour of refusal onto the police, meal providers themselves are often obliged or persuaded to take on the work as well. In Seattle's case, for example, Operation Sack Lunch and its larger umbrella group, the Meals Partnership Coalition, actively advocate for the outdoor meal site and attempt to persuade rogue soup kitchens like FNB to join the fold. As such, these programmes actively participate in the racial and economic segregation of the city's downtown public spaces. Like many forms of segregation, this is a segregation that not only reflects the interests of downtown businesses, but forms the foundation of that exclusive public sphere within which market exchange and bourgeois consumption are thinkable and practicable.

Seattle is not unique in this respect. In an increasing number of cities around the world, from London to Las Vegas, free outdoor meals have been criminalised (Giles 2013; National Coalition for the Homeless 2014). I would argue we have to understand this as the twin project of disciplining homeless and working-class bodies and attenuating the aftermarket circulation of food surpluses. In other words, as part of a logic of abject recapture.

Conclusion

The twin proliferation of emergency food programmes and outdoor feeding prohibitions is troubling in its own right. But it casts a longer shadow. As a complex apparatus of abject recapture, they suggest one of the virtual, incipient futures for the capitalism of the twenty-first century. What I have argued above is that waste represents one of the fundamental contradictions of capitalism, embedded in the production and expropriation of surplus value. Capital has already reinvented (or deferred) this contradiction at least once, and in the process made profitable even more waste through the accelerated obsolescence of virtually everything it makes, from microprocessors to razor blades to fruit and vegetables. In the present era of financial and ecological crisis, then, it is increasingly clear to even some of the most cynical free market enthusiasts that this waste will not disappear behind a miraculous technical fix. If the waste has become both sociologically and environmentally unsustainable, capital must experiment with new ways to make its weakness its strength. In particular, I have argued that where scarcity – and hence exchange-value – has been invented through the premature abandonment of useful goods – a process I have framed within the concept of *abject capital* – one such way in which capitalist society may reinvent itself is to reshuffle its surpluses in time and space, recapturing the surplus value in its wares without re-commoditising it. The evolution of emergency food and feeding prohibitions, then, points to the way in which such a redistribution of surpluses – surplus food and surplus people – has already taken place under our noses, and to the more troubling dimensions this strategy could take on.

This tendency is, of course, only one possible component of the ongoing 'double movement' through which we are perhaps living. In stark, optimistic contrast to these mechanisms of abject recapture, many have imagined fundamentally counter-capitalist 'circular' or 'degrowth' economies, for example. Indeed, many of the Dumpster divers and FNB collaborators with whom I have worked imagine their efforts as a prefigurative stepping stone towards such economies, albeit one still subsidiary to capitalism itself. The future, then, depends on experimentation and struggle. Whether the mechanisms of abject recapture I have described above represent a passing structural adjustment in the logic of capital, or a fundamental adaptation to reconcile the creation and enclosure of surplus with the twin crises of poverty and ecological devastation, their implications are worth sniffing out.

Notes

1. In the first volume of *Capital*, Marx wrote:

> Could commodities themselves speak, they would say: 'Our use-value may be a thing that interests men. It is no part of us as objects. What, however, does

belong to us as objects is our value. Our natural intercourse as commodities proves it. In the eyes of each other, we are nothing but exchange values.' (2000 [1865]: 480)

2. More recent research suggests that this number may now be much higher, as overall food loss has continued to grow, although no recent research quantifies *unspoiled* food discarded (see Buzby et al. 2014).
3. The word is derived from *abiecere* – '*ab*' meaning 'off' or 'away' and '*iacere*' meaning 'to throw' or 'cast'.
4. In 1996, 2000, 2004, 2008 and 2012, food represented 22.2 per cent, 25.0 per cent, 29.9 per cent, 31.6 per cent and 29.8 per cent of commercial waste in Seattle, respectively (Cascadia Consulting Group, Inc., with Seattle Public Utilities Staff 2002, 2008, 2013; Cascadia Consulting Group, Inc. et al. 1997, 2005).

References

Appadurai, A. 1986. Commodities and the politics of value. In *The Social Life of Things: Commodities in Cultural Perspective*. New York: Cambridge University Press.

Bataille, G. 1991 [1949]. *The Accursed Share: An Essay on General Economy*, vol. I. New York: Zone Books.

Bourdieu, P. 1984. *Distinction: A Social Critique of the Judgment of Taste*, trans. R. Nice. Cambridge, MA: Harvard University Press.

—— 1986. The forms of capital. In J.G. Richardson (ed.) *Handbook of Theory and Research for the Sociology of Education*. New York: Greenwood, pp. 241–58.

Buzby, J.C., H.F. Wells and J. Hyman. 2014. *The Estimated Amount, Value, and Calories of Postharvest Food Losses at the Retail and Consumer Levels in the United States*. EIB-121. Washington, DC: U.S. Department of Agriculture, Economic Research Service.

Cascadia Consulting Group, Inc., in cooperation with Seattle Public Utilities Staff. 2002. *2000 Commercial & Self-haul Waste Streams, Composition Study, Final Report*, October. Seattle: Seattle Public Utilities.

—— 2008. *2008 Commercial & Self-haul Waste Streams, Composition Study, Final Report*, July. Seattle: Seattle Public Utilities.

—— 2013. *2012 Commercial & Self-haul Waste Streams, Composition Study, Final Report*. Seattle: Seattle Public Utilities.

Cascadia Consulting Group, Inc., Sky Valley Associates, E. Ashley Steel, and Hopkins Environmental, in cooperation with Seattle Public Utilities Staff. 1997. *1996 Commercial & Self-Haul Waste Streams, Composition Study, Final Report*, September. Seattle: Seattle Public Utilities.

Cascadia Consulting Group, Inc. and Sky Valley Associates, in cooperation with Seattle Public Utilities Staff. 2005. *2004 Commercial & Self-haul Waste Streams, Composition Study, Final Report*, September 2005. Seattle: Seattle Public Utilities.

Coyote, P. 2008. Book reading at Book Passage, Corte Madera, California, 10 December. Archived by Fora.tv. Available at: http://fora.tv/2008/12/10/Peter_Coyote_Emmett_Grogan_and_the_Diggers (accessed 10 March 2012).

CrimethInc. Ex-Workers' Collective (collectively authored). 2004. *Recipes for Disaster: An Anarchist Cookbook*. Salem: CrimethInc. Ex-Workers' Collective.

de Saussure, F. 1966. *Course in General Linguistics*, 3rd edn, edited by C. Bally and A. Sechehaye in collaboration with A. Reidlonger, trans. W. Bakins. New York: McGraw-Hill.

Dickinson, M. 2014. *Consuming Poverty: The Unexpected Politics of Food Aid in an Era of Austerity*. PhD dissertation, Department of Anthropology, City University of New York.

Dolgin, G. and V. Franco, dirs. 2007. *Summer of Love*. 60 mins. San Francisco: American Experience in Association with the Public Broadcasting Service.

Douglas, M. 1984. *Purity and Danger: An Analysis of the Concepts of Pollution and Taboo*. London: Ark.

Dumont, L. 1980. On value. *Proceedings of the British Academy* 66: 207–41.

Evans, D. 2013. *Food Waste: Home Consumption, Material Culture, and Everyday Life*. London: Bloomsbury.

Feldman, J. 2014. UK Supermarket to Use Food Waste to Power Itself. *Huffington Post*, 24 July.

Giles, D.B. 2013. *'A Mass Conspiracy to Feed People': Globalizing Cities, World-class Waste, and the Biopolitics of Food Not Bombs*. PhD dissertation, Department of Anthropology, University of Washington, Seattle.

—— 2014. The anatomy of a dumpster: Abject capital and the looking glass of value. *Social Text* 118: 93–114.

—— 2015. The work of waste-making: Biopolitical labour and the myth of the global city. In J.P. Marshall and L.H. Connor (eds) *Environmental Change and the World's Futures: Ecologies, Ontologies, Mythologies*.

Gille, Z. 2007. *From the Cult of Waste to the Trash Heap of History: The Politics of Waste in Socialist and Post-socialist Hungary*. Bloomington: University of Indiana Press.

Graeber, D. 2001. *Toward an Anthropological Theory of Value: The False Coin of Our Own Dreams*. New York: Palgrave.

Gustavsson, J., C. Cederberg, U. Sonesson, R. van Otterdijk and A. Meybeck. 2011. *Global Food Losses and Food Waste: Extent, Causes, and Prevention*. Rome: Food and Agriculture Organization of the United Nations.

Hall, K.D., J. Guo, M. Dore and C.C. Chow. 2009. The progressive increase of food waste in America and its environmental impact. *PLoS ONE* 4(11): e7940.

Harvey, D. 2007. Neoliberalism as creative destruction. *ANNALS of the American Academy of Political and Social Science* 610: 21.

Iteanu, A. 2013. The two conceptions of value. *HAU: Journal of Ethnographic Theory* 3(1): 155–71.
Kantor, L.S., K. Lipton, A. Manchester and V. Oliveira. 1997. Estimating and addressing America's food losses. *Food Review* 20(1): 2–13.
Kopytoff, I. 1986. The cultural biography of things: Commoditization as process. In A. Appadurai (ed.) *The Social Life of Things: Commodities in Cultural Perspective*. New York: Cambridge University Press.
Kristeva, J. 1982. *Powers of Horror: An Essay on Abjection*. New York: Columbia University Press.
Lévi-Strauss, C. 1966. The culinary triangle, trans. P. Brooks. *Partisan Review* 33: 586–95.
Marx, K. 2000 [1865]. *Capital*, vol. I. In D. MacLellan (ed.) *Karl Marx: Selected Writings*. Oxford: Oxford University Press, pp. 452–525.
—— 2000 [1893]. *Capital*, vol. II, edited by F. Engels. Available at: http://www.marxists.org/archive/marx/works/1885-c2/ch00.htm (accessed 10 May 2015).
—— 2000 [1941]. *Grundrisse*. In D. MacLellan (ed.) *Karl Marx: Selected Writings*. Oxford: Oxford University Press, pp. 380–422.
Munro, R. 2013. The disposal of place: Facing modernity in the kitchen-diner. In D. Evans, H. Campbell and A. Murcott (eds) *Waste Matters: New Perspectives on Food and Society*. Malden, MA: Wiley-Blackwell, pp. 212–31.
National Coalition for the Homeless. 2014. *Share No More: The Criminalization of Efforts to Feed People in Need*. A Report for the National Coalition for the Homeless, October, edited by M. Stoops. Washington, DC: National Coalition for the Homeless.
O'Brien, M. 2013. A 'lasting transformation' of capitalist surplus: From food stocks to feedstocks. In D. Evans, H. Campbell and A. Murcott (eds) *Waste Matters: New Perspectives on Food and Society*. Malden, MA: Wiley-Blackwell, pp. 192–211.
Packard, V. 2011 [1960]. *The Waste Makers*. Brooklyn: Ig Publishing.
Polanyi, K. 2001 [1944]. *The Great Transformation: The Political and Economic Origins of Our Time*. Boston, MA: Beacon Press.
Poppendiek, J. 1998. *Sweet Charity: Emergency Food and the End of Entitlement*. New York: Penguin.
—— 2010. *Free for All: Fixing School Food in America*. Berkeley: University of California Press.
Saint Mary's Food Bank Alliance. n.d. About us. Available at: http://www.firstfoodbank.org/history.html (accessed 10 January 2012).
Simon, S. 2013. Trader Joe's ex-president to turn expired food into cheap meals. *The Salt*, National Public Radio, 21 September. Available at: http://www.npr.org/blogs/thesalt/2013/09/21/222082247/trader-joes-ex-president-to-turn-expired-food-into-cheap-meals (accessed 10 May 2015).
Sparke, M. 2013. *Introducing Globalization: Ties, Tensions, and Uneven Integration*. Malden, MA: Wiley-Blackwell.

Stuart, T. 2009. *Waste: Uncovering the Global Food Scandal.* Harmondsworth: Penguin Books.

Thompson, M. 1979. *Rubbish Theory: The Creation and Destruction of Value*. Oxford: Oxford University Press.

Tsing, A.L. 2013. Sorting out commodities: How capitalist value is made through gifts. *HAU: Journal of Ethnographic Theory* 13(1): 21–43.

Ventour, L. 2008 *Food Waste Report: The Food We Waste*. Banbury: WRAP: Material Change for a Better Environment.

10

'The University is Kind of an Impossible Place'

Universities Towards and Against Capitalism

Fern Thompsett

Introduction

Over recent years, the world has been rocked by a series of demonstrations with the university at their epicentre. In 2009, students occupied University of California campus buildings across the state, protesting against the government's plan to hike tuition fees by a third. When Quebec's state government made a similar announcement in 2012, the response was overwhelming, with just under one-tenth of university students going on strike – many calling for the abolition of tuition fees altogether – and hundreds of thousands of supporters taking to the streets. Meanwhile in Chile, student activists sustained a three-year campaign with such tenacity, even in the face of violent repression, that their demand for free university education eventually muscled its way onto the state agenda. More recently, marches and occupations have swept across the Netherlands, the UK, Canada and Australia, often mobilising not only the student body, but teaching and administration staff as well. The mounting frequency of these sorts of events suggests that far from subsiding, storm-clouds over the university are only continuing to gather.

While the focus of each demonstration is locally specific, their common denominator is a resounding opposition to the ways in which capitalist regimes have come to inhabit and transform universities – a phenomenon Silvia Federici (2009) describes as the global 'enclosure of knowledge'. As such, we can read these landscapes in two ways. The first tells us that universities are in crisis. The second weaves together these many crisis points to reveal a more complex background: the university has become a key crucible in which struggles within and against the global machinations of capitalism play out. A central figure on this scene is the notion of value. Whereas the dictates of the capitalist market frame university education as a commodity defined by its exchange-value, dissenters attempt to reorient learning *away from* capitalist, profit-seeking ends and towards others, such as strengthening social fabric, sharing otherwise marginalised bodies of knowledge, or simply reframing learning as a valid end in and of itself.

Efforts to wrest university education from the throes of capitalist restructuring and the discursive dominance of market rationality take place on many grounds. While movements targeting state policies and established universities are vital, they constitute only part of the landscape. Other, less known, but equally important parts of the story play out in the margins, around the shadowy edges of campuses and cityscapes, after-hours and underground. Enter here the 'free universities' – autonomous but loosely networked projects that radically re-imagine what study could be, starting from their own terms.

This is a realm in which I am directly implicated, not only through my work as an anthropologist, but politically, as an organiser and activist. In late 2012, I co-founded the Brisbane Free University (BFU), which, as of this writing, is still in operation. BFU seeks to challenge the enclosure of knowledge by bringing academic research and theory-based discussions off campuses and into the streets, for free. We recognise, however – as have countless other critical scholars and activists (for example, Federici 2009; Haiven 2014) – that the rising paywall around universities is not an isolated phenomenon, but symptomatic of, and intertwined with, broader capitalist processes of enclosure and commodification. As such, at the core of BFU's experiment is an attempt to build and sustain a microcosm outside of the cash economy altogether. In concrete terms, this means that no money changes hands between organisers, speakers, equipment providers or any funding bodies, and only once have we (as organisers) paid to hire a venue.

Translating this particular principle into action has been fraught with tensions and compromises, and my curiosity about how others might navigate these complexities compelled me to explore similar projects through an anthropological lens. This chapter draws primarily from the research I gathered thereafter – namely, participant-observation I conducted at 15 free university projects across Canada, the USA and Mexico, as well as semi-structured interviews with around 45 organisers of, and participants in, those projects – in which I include my own experiences and perspectives as an organiser and supporter of the movement more broadly.[1]

Two main threads wove throughout the conversations I had with free university organisers. The first was their mission to fray the fabric of capitalism on multiple fronts – both within and beyond the university and its enclosure of knowledge. The second was their 'prefigurative' or 'alter-political' praxis, which, rather than aiming to overthrow the existing order (which would be an 'oppositional' or 'anti-political' strategy), sets about cultivating alternative realities in its cracks and interstices – or, to use a familiar adage, building the new world in the shell of the old (Hage 2012: 292). The grounds upon which these two threads converge constitute the political terrain of free universities, where we are invited to imagine not just a better university but a better world.

Attempts to bring this world into being, however, throw up their own problematic binds. Organisers often find the actualisation of their ideals frustrated by thorny on-the-ground realities, as they face constraints that cannot be fully disentangled from capitalist systems. Their operational framework instead occupies a complex liminal landscape simultaneously inside and outside of capitalism, bound by tensions between resistance and complicity, idealism and compromise, emancipation and exploitation. Paradoxically, while these movements seek to unsettle the totalising potential of capitalism, such constraints at times appear to reconfirm its hegemony.

Even so, I suggest that these landscapes can be read in other ways. Just as organisers might find it impossible to raise pure non-capitalist microcosms out of the capitalist world around them, their projects equally demonstrate that capitalism's stronghold is never impenetrable or absolute (see Gibson-Graham 1996, 2006). Furthermore, even if their work might be stymied on material grounds – and in this chapter, I focus on space and labour – we must not underestimate free universities' potential to instigate change in the immaterial realm.

To elaborate on this latter point, scholar-activist Max Haiven (2014) argues that if capitalism appears hegemonic, it is largely due to the reshaping of our imaginations through a dialectical process that unfolds with the transformation of social values. Capitalist systems reproduce themselves by 'recalibrating most spheres of life to look like the capitalist marketplace, injecting values of competition, accumulation, hierarchy, coercive power, exploitative labour and imagined differences' (2014: 22). These values impact how we imagine our place in the world, which in turn affects how we categorise, attribute meaning to, and rank our relationships with things and others – and so the cycle continues. Free universities can provide a counterpoint to these potentially totalising feedback loops by staking out space beyond capitalist paradigms in which non-capitalist ways of relating to the world might take root and grow. Their means of doing so are many, but include developing alternative modes of study, reinstating commons of space and labour (however ephemerally), and ultimately cultivating diverse subjectivities that can collectively imagine worlds beyond capitalism.

Situating the Value of Values

In his 1892 play *Lady Windermere's Fan*, Oscar Wilde had one of his characters describe a cynic as 'a man who knows the price of everything and the value of nothing'. This quip could just as much be said in reference to today's *homo economicus* living in a world dominated by the 'hyper-inclusive logic of neoliberalism' (Coté et al., 2007: 317). Within this framework, goods and labour are converted into commodity forms, which trump their use-value not only in the market sphere, but how we relate to them in our everyday lives, as 'market rationality' takes hold across all realms of existence (Turner 2008: 50). Universities are no exception, and have been transfigured in multiple ways, such as through the redefinition of education primarily in market terms.

The neoliberal paradigm is premised on the notion that market rationality is natural – that is, that human nature is inherently individualistic and acquisitive, predisposed to act according to a 'minimal output/maximum gain' formula (Graeber 2001: 6–7). Anthropologists have been able to counter these blanket assumptions by showing the vast diversity of actually existing social and economic arrangements against and beyond such reductive rubrics – in fact, anthropology has furnished myriad anti-capitalist movements with proof that capitalism, inequality and the drive for 'endless growth' are not inevitable, but historically and culturally contingent (Martin 2012: 128; Mauss 1979: 32, cited in Valeri 2013: 263; Robinson and Tormey 2012: 144). Against market rationality's tendency to subsume goods and labour under a universalising commodity framework, anthropologists have argued that people can (and still do) reconfigure meaning around these things according to more flexible and inclusive forms of social consciousness (Turner 2008: 50). Free universities make useful case studies to demonstrate how dominant capitalist logics can be refused, resisted and re-imagined from within, even when they cannot be overwritten entirely. In doing so, they reveal a double diversity – not only do value frameworks differ tremendously across time and space, but a single site can, especially through struggle, come to comprise what Graeber calls overlapping 'universes of value', which remain open to change through internal flux, interaction and mutual co-constitution (2013: 231).

The notion of value requires a degree of further unpacking. As Graeber notes, 'value' in its singular form lays out a comparative rubric for commodified goods and labour within a monetised system of exchange, as under capitalism (2013: 224). He contrasts this to the plural: 'values', which describes the far messier realm of that which cannot be commodified or exchanged but remains inalienable ('family values', for instance). A key differentiating factor is money, which makes it possible to equivocate between exchangeable goods, whereas 'the value of "values" ... lies precisely in their lack of equivalence ... They cannot and should not be converted into money' (Graeber 2013: 224). To reinvoke Wilde's cynic, however, market rationality sees the first category encroaching upon the second, as social values are increasingly subordinated to 'the supreme value of money' (Haiven 2014: 43).

Karl Polanyi described this phenomenon as the rise of 'market society', emphasising that such transformations do not simply unfold in the economic sphere, but depend equally upon interconnected social, cultural and psychological shifts, often imposed by force (2001 [1944]). Key to this process is the disruptive, if not violent, translation of social relations to land and labour into a commodity framework, to be mediated by money where once they were seen as inalienable parts of the fabric of human existence. Polanyi observed, however, that as the free market disembeds itself from societies and gains power to shape myriad aspects of human existence in its image (whereas once it had been shaped *by* society through the reverse power dynamic), resistances spontaneously emerge, often at the grassroots level, to protect the primacy of the social over market forces in a process he called the 'double movement'. Reframing this in Graeber's terms would describe the reclamation of social 'values' outside of a market-derived 'value' framework as part of a broader movement to re-imagine human sociality beyond the capitalist paradigm – often, as we will see in this chapter, with a particular focus on redefining relationships to space and labour *without* money.

We can bring these theories to bear in the university context to see that we are not witnessing a struggle *within* either category of 'value' or 'values' but *between* them. When we refer to the 'value' of university education, it might be possible to imagine that we are discussing how best to regulate market prices to secure, for example, equitable access and affordability. However, contestation around universities concerns far more than the capitalist number games that determine tuition fees, student debt, staff wages and so forth. In fact, to give these aspects too much weight would not only miss the bigger picture, but obliquely reinforce neoliberalism's totalising assumptions about the inevitability of market rationality and the 'maximising' drive that allegedly defines human nature. Importantly, there is a radical thrust within these struggles that would not be content to simply level the playing field upon which commodified versions of knowledge and labour can be more equitably distributed. Instead, in ways that reflect Polanyi's 'double movement', many seek to abandon the game altogether, provoking us to consider education a social good, rather than a marketable good – something that should not be reduced to a commodity, priced and exchanged.

Free universities attempt to lift education out of a reductive 'value' rubric and reposition it within a framework of non-capitalist 'values' by providing open access to spaces of learning, all the while emphasising that such learning need not be oriented towards productivity in the capitalist sense, or the labour market. However, their mission extends beyond redefining education. The 'free' in 'free universities' deliberately invokes a double meaning, referring to being 'free of charge' and 'emancipatory', in some sense. While the former removes money from the equation, making it harder to reduce education to a commodity, the latter engages anti-capitalist praxes within the messier realm of 'values' more broadly. Echoing Polanyi, free university organisers recognise that capitalism's impacts are not only economic, but profoundly social, cultural and psychological as well. Universities are key here, increasingly perceived as institutions through which, to quote Max Haiven, 'capitalist values are stitched into the fabric of society'.[2] As such, free universities go beyond unshackling knowledge from the cash economy, and attempt to fundamentally reconfigure human sociality against and beyond capitalism.

Contextualising the Capitalist University

Struggles around the university represent valuable examples of 'double movements' towards and against capitalism. Importantly, universities do not merely *reflect* global shifts towards capitalism – they also *drive* them by commodifying knowledge, and moulding students' subjectivities through processes of 'social reproduction' to internalise capitalist proclivities (Althusser 1971; Bourdieu and Passeron 1977; Haiven 2014: 135). As such, this section positions the university as an institution from which capitalist paradigms take root and expand, and one that has equally catalysed resistances to capitalism more broadly.

It would not make sense to refer to 'the university' as a singular, internally cohesive institution, hermetically sealed from the rest of society. Rather, universities exist as diverse and complex networks of sites, structures and interest groups that blur the boundaries between their internal and external worlds. Moreover, they have always been defined by contestation and conflicting possibilities, shaped and reclaimed by students, staff and others in myriad ways, ranging from strikes and union actions, to more 'everyday' acts, such as the use of radical pedagogy (Coté et al. 2007: 320). Although universities' histories are too vast and complex to be addressed in adequate detail here, it is useful to outline some key moments of transformation from the last century, in order to contextualise today's struggles. In line with the scope of my fieldwork, I focus this section on North America and countries with linked or analogous histories, including Australia and the UK.

Today's universities are vexed institutions, beset by rifts between the ideals with which they are habitually associated and the actual experiences of staff and students (Hil 2012, 2015). While they are commonly upheld as sites of democratic citizenship, critical thought and holistic self-development, critics argue that these principles are fundamentally imperilled by the encroachment of capitalist regimes (Haiven 2014: 140). Though this is certainly cause for alarm, it is also worth pausing to question whether the university has ever truly embodied such ideals. A closer reading of its history reveals a trajectory so punctuated by paradox that 'the university', as Alex Khasnabish surmised, 'is kind of an impossible place'.[3]

Once highly elitist, universities across the global North were opened up to people from diverse socioeconomic backgrounds following the Second World War, largely due to boosts in state funding (George 2012: 190). Many other access barriers were removed over subsequent decades via the struggles of feminists, people of colour, indigenous activists and other marginalised groups (Newson 2012: 43). These shifts were both symptomatic and generative of a widespread transformation in how university education was commonly perceived. Having formerly served to reinforce class divisions and colonial dominance, it was recast as a social good that could propagate critical intellectualism and socio-political awareness through equal opportunity. Universities came to be seen as bastions of civic virtues, charged with the democratisation of knowledge and power (Jeppsen and Nazar 2012: 94; Haiven 2014: 144). If universities did approach such a utopian moment, it was in the early 1960s, when mainstream society was permeated with a strong sense that university education should be universally available. State-funded universities with nominal tuition fees proliferated across Western nations, and campuses became hubs for critical civic engagement and political activism (Brophy and Tucker-Abramson 2012: 22–23).

To allow Alex Khasnabish to expand his previous statement, however, the paradox here is that 'just as the doors of the university were thrown open to more people … it was recognised that the university served a really vital function in the reproduction of capitalist labour relations'.[4] Many critics argue that the university has never truly embodied the ideals it appeared to front, but has always been in the service of power, its history simply tracing a shifting allegiance from church to nation-state to capital (Readings 1996). Canadian scholar-activist Stephen Collis argues that, by the 1960s, universities across the global North were already bolstering capitalist regimes by, on the one hand, directing research towards new saleable products and, on the other, marketing university education as key to the upward mobility of a growing consumer middle class.[5] In the USA, this complicity was also manifest in universities' role in the military-industrial complex, which engendered, as many student activists argued, a crackdown on critical thinking and creativity more broadly (Meza-Wilson 2012: 34–35).

The university's capitulation to capitalist interests deepened from the 1970s onwards as austerity regimes swept across the global North, bringing rollbacks of state funding and rising tuition fees in their wake. Now we have arrived at a moment characterised by the 'enclosure of knowledge', as universities are restructured to resemble private 'user-pays' corporations driven primarily by efficiency measures and the profit motive (Federici 2009: 458). Indeed, many of the university's (former) ideals have been so thoroughly eclipsed by market rationality that 'in a global sense [it] has ceased to be a university – its primary purpose is no longer education, but circulation', namely of capital (Whitener and Nemser 2012: 165).

For many, these changes have cast education in a profoundly different light. Instead of a social good to be widely disseminated, university education – or perhaps more accurately, the university degree – circulates as a commodity, contributing foremost to the generation of 'human capital' (Coté et al. 2007: 319). Critical thinking bows out in favour of more utilitarian end points of employability and entrepreneurialism, and civic virtues such as democratic engagement and social justice are overshadowed by capitalist cornerstones like competition and profit-driven productivity. University accreditation acts to furnish certain participants in the labour market with advantages over others, thereby deepening, rather than dismantling, socioeconomic inequalities (Federici 2009: 455). This is coupled with rising tuition fees, which, as Max Haiven argues, is instrumental in the university's devolution into a 'debt factory, precisely orchestrated in order to make [students] more compliant workers once they graduate'.[6] University education orients students towards the labour market by repackaging learning as an investment for financial gain, while reinforcing the profit motive on a different level through the disciplinary mechanism of debt (Williams 2009).

Problematic shifts echo throughout the ranks of university labour, especially for teachers and researchers. Many find their work subjected to market-centred metrics that subsume creativity under profitability. The catchcry driving Danish universities' reforms, for example, is 'from idea to invoice' (Shore and Wright 2004: 100). This flags an analogous shift in how university-generated knowledge is framed – less as a social good, and more as a commodity to be sold to corporations (as research 'output') or students (as units for accreditation), all the while boosting universities' brand power (Magee 2012: 171; Polster 2012: 122). Critics identify risks on several fronts. First, quality and rigour may be jeopardised by the speed at which research must be generated in order to be commercially competitive (Wright and Rabo 2010: 2, cited in Vostal and Robertson 2012: 156). Second, academic integrity and critical inquiry are stymied by the profit motive, which circumscribes research focuses within commercial viability (Jeppsen and Nazar 2012: 95–96). Third, many object to the sorts of bodies financially tied to universities, such as mining corporations with histories of human rights abuses and environmental destruction, fossil fuel industries, or developers of technology with questionable health impacts, such as nanotechnology (Brophy and Tucker-Abramson 2012; Lyons 2014).[7]

It would be misleading to suggest that this snapshot of universities' current state holds true across the board. In reality, universities are changing in diverse ways – some in concert with, and others in counterpoint to, the shifts I have outlined above. Furthermore, internal resistances are multitudinous and fruitful on many fronts, meaning that just as capitalist structures proliferate in universities, so too, as Polanyi would predict, do non-capitalist ones. Nonetheless, critics consistently describe universities' reorientation towards market rationality on a global scale, particularly through processes of commodification, enclosure and social reproduction. Civic aims like social justice and critical enquiry are stifled under these conditions, but continue to haunt universities with immense symbolic power. The growing abyss between these ideals and the capitalist regime that undermines them represented a great source of frustration and motivation for many free university activists with whom I spoke.

The Emergence of Free Universities

It is no coincidence that free universities emerged during the 1960s. The first so-named 'free university' transpired as part of the Free Speech Movement at University of California Berkeley, led by the activist group Students for a Democratic Society (SDS). Seeing the university as 'the only mainstream institution that is open to participation by individuals of nearly any viewpoint' and therefore an obvious starting point for socio-political change, student activists were frustrated that this potential was so stymied by bureaucratic control and corporate (including military-industrial) interests (Hayden 2005). As one amongst many strategies to reclaim their campus, SDS organised their own free university classes, ranging from 'Revolutionary Organizing, Terrorism and Sabotage' to 'Zen Basketball'. More broadly, the project formed around these precepts: 'Anyone can learn, Anyone can teach, Informal structure, Credentials as meaningless, The community as learning environment, Linking knowledge and action, Process over content, Low cost and/or free education, Responsiveness to the community's characteristics, and Education for social change' (Draves 1980: 121, cited in Meza-Wilson 2012: 34–35).

Today's free universities continue along similar political lines to those drawn by SDS. Importantly, although many emerge from an oppositional movement *against* the university, their goal is not necessarily to replace or abandon it. In fact, many organisers were equally involved in struggles within conventional universities. For all its shortcomings, they maintained that aspects of the university – even if only in the idea of the university, rather than the actual institution – were worth saving, such as rigorous research, the pursuit of knowledge and critical inquiry. Free universities attempt to proliferate spaces outside of the capitalist paradigm in which these sorts of ideals might be preserved and realised, or in which a radically alter-university might be imagined anew.

Furthermore, organisers acknowledged that practices of collective study have been integral to diverse political mobilisations, not all of which have been directly concerned with the university (Harney and Moten 2013). Inspirations ranged from the *Escuela Moderna* of 1900s Spain to the Freedom Schools of the civil rights movement, the teach-ins of the Vietnam War era, and more recent anarchist and anti-authoritarian movements including Occupy. While the university might constitute one landmark within their political purview, free university organisers extend the potentialities of study far more broadly, and into more radically creative (and prefigurative) realms.

To offer too specific a definition of today's free universities would obscure one of their most important attributes: their deliberate evasion of any rigidly calcified agenda, identity or long-term vision. Each emerges organically from its own set of contextual specificities, and maintains enough flexibility to embody and respond to shifting local conditions. Projects go by a variety of names, but in broad terms, here I use 'free university' to refer to projects of collective study that: are open to anyone and free to attend, avoid state affiliation, gather in physical (offline) spaces, and implicitly or explicitly include a goal of emancipation. They are generally organised using non-hierarchical praxes, and often favour flat-structured pedagogies, although the latter is decided on a case-by-case basis and varies across the board. Classes – or as a co-founder of the Free Skool Santa Cruz quipped, 'post-apocalyptic revolutionary logistic training'[8] – are offered by diverse participants including organisers and others, and span the full horizon of what it is possible to teach and learn, ranging from Marxist feminism to bee-keeping, self-defence, bike mechanics, immigration law, Japanese cinema, and everything in between.

Free universities position collective study within anti-capitalist praxes on a variety of grounds. First, they challenge the commodification and enclosure of knowledge by removing access fees. This is coupled with a mode of studying that sees resources, labour and decision-making shared communally, which counters universities' replication of capitalist labour relations based on hierarchy and enclosed separation. Second, they unsettle the social reproduction of capitalist subjectivities by foregrounding 'radical' content. Free universities' curricula include a whole gamut of anti-capitalist theories such as feminist Marxism and Situationist histories alongside practical skill shares such as DIY bike maintenance or backyard food production, all intended to provide participants with tools and knowledge to distance themselves from the commodity market. Free universities thus seek to re-embed study in social justice struggles by on the one hand aligning their content with non-capitalist praxes, and on the other, directly embodying these praxes in their manner of organising classes.

At times, however, organisers were divided over the role that learning should play in anti-capitalist projects such as theirs. For some, learning should orient people towards particular forms of social or political action beyond the realm of study itself, whereas others expressed frustration at radical activists' tendency to translate everything into immediate, concrete political consequences. Instead, they defended the importance of simply appreciating study for its own sake – furthermore, that this reframing could itself embody a powerful move beyond the rigidly ends-oriented logic upon which market rationality depends.

Scholar-activists have articulated these positions by drawing a semantic distinction between study and education (Bousquet et al. 2009). Under this rubric, education involves a pre-determined object-orientation that puts learning at the service of a particular agenda, be it preparation for the labour market, or any political ideology, even that of anti-capitalism. Many (though not all) free university organisers are careful to distinguish their projects, or parts thereof, from education in this sense. As New York-based organiser Joe Kay told me, 'education always hangs out with its drinking buddy, ideology. We're not that goal-oriented. We're not educating people; we're providing the possibility for a conversation.'[9] For Joe, it was important that sessions remained open to the 'flow' of the group, rather than guiding participants towards any specific end point. Study can be understood as endless in both senses of the word, and is to the Marxian notion of species-being what education is to the accumulation of exploitable labour-power, or 'human capital' (Bousquet et al. 2009: 160). By abandoning the very sense of a predefined objective, it embodies a move not directly *against* but *beyond* capitalist logic, which speaks to the prefigurative aspect of free universities. As David Brazil, an organiser of the Bay Area Public School, explained: 'In the ideal world, we would be studying these things for their own sake, so we're acting as though we're already in that world.'[10]

This aspect of free universities should not be misconstrued as inherently anti-capitalist or invulnerable to cooptation, however. Autonomous Marxists, for example, contend that our era is characterised by high-technology capitalism that cultivates and exploits the 'general intellect' as a form of human capital itself. 'Study', therefore, does not represent a pure space outside of market rationality, but activists recognise that in order to constitute an anti-capitalist praxis, it must be constantly and consciously reclaimed (Coté et al. 2007).

Space

Free universities challenge not only the ideological enclosure of knowledge, but the spatial enclosure of lands. Just as Marx identified the enclosure of traditional commons, including land, as key to the rise of capitalism, contemporary scholars argue that proprietorship of space, and the power dynamics that determine its use, remain core to capitalist dominance, especially in urban contexts (Harvey 1990, 2012). In a world that sees spaces overwhelmingly commodified, the possibility of an urban commons seems increasingly out of reach.

In this context, it is important to clarify what is meant by a spatial commons, in contrast to public space. While public spaces might appear freely accessible, they remain under the administration of the state, which regulates access and use, often in analogous ways to private proprietors. Furthermore, since many states in the global North increasingly operate as profit-seeking bodies themselves, public spaces are often implicated in broader capitalist frameworks of exchange, rent and profit. The commons, by contrast, emerges as a third category that extends beyond the public/private duality by retaining the inalienable qualities of collective control and irreducibility to an exchange-value (Harvey 2012: 73). This should not, however, lead us to imagine that spatial commons are immune to capitalist appropriation in other ways. Scholars and activists are wary of the potential for urban commons to carry cultural capital and obliquely contribute to commercial exploitation or gentrification (Harvey 2012: 74–75). Nonetheless, we see the idea of spatial commons echoing throughout anti-capitalist praxes as a means to challenge the capitalist stronghold.

If only as a landmark of utopian imagination, the commons thus continues to stake out its place within communities of activists and organisers. As Stephen Collis, who was involved with the Vancouver Institute for Social Research and Occupy Vancouver, noted:

> the commons is virtually non-existent. But I've found, historically, at the moment of its disappearance like that, we return to it, we notice that erasure ... What we really seem to be craving is that kind of common space in which we can be a community, a public together.[11]

The desire for communal, open space related to the desire for communal, open modes of learning in ways that were linked, on the one hand, politically – to dismantle the intertwined enclosures of space and knowledge – and on the other, pragmatically – as Sara Larsen, an organiser of the Bay Area Public School, told me: 'one of the big things was just having a place to collectively *be* in public'.[12]

Herein, free universities run up against a thorny constraint, in that there is a vast difference between being able to use certain spaces as ephemeral commons, and engendering any kind of lasting structural change. Classes tend to take place in public parks and libraries, donated halls and galleries, private living rooms, parking lots or buildings after-hours. Some use commercial spaces that offer relatively open access, such as cafes and bars. For several organisers, including David Brazil, this perpetual motion approach offered its own political sense: 'there's a certain … Deleuzian sort of rhizomaticity of just being in different places and taking almost a free and resourceful mentality'. But ultimately, organisers are forced to acknowledge that none of these options exist outside of the capitalist stronghold. As Brazil elaborated:

> If you're having classes at somebody's house, you're depending on the fact that they paid rent. It's a total system. There's no way out of that system. Except I guess if you're meeting somewhere like a public park, but I think as Occupy demonstrated, there's limits to the ability to meet in a public park.[13]

Here, organisers are faced with compromises – they can piggy-back on the state or private rent-payers, or simply abandon a level of idealism and pay rent themselves.

Although this might read like a dead-end within a capitalist spatial hegemony, organisers were not always so easily discouraged. Stephen Collis, for example, offered his perspective thus:

> the pessimist looks at the totality, the seeming totality of capital, and says, 'Oh my god, where? What can we do? There isn't a space outside it to inhabit. So how can we possibly resist it?' … Then the more optimistic side, I think, looks at that and *does* really notice the cracks and fissures, however small and infrequent they can be, and sees, well, there's something that can be built and worked on there.[14]

Other organisers reiterated his position, explaining that their projects are not aiming to overthrow state and capitalist control of urban space absolutely, but to open interstitial alternatives, however fleeting, in which to collectively imagine what a non-capitalist urban commons could mean. In this way, they are bringing the spectre of the commons one step closer to a tangible reality, by drawing it into the realm of the radical imagination and reconfiguring subjectivities around it. Spaces that might otherwise only be considered valuable in market terms become a sort of political palimpsest, overwritten with non-capitalist praxes as a way to scaffold an alter-politics emerging between political imaginaries and material realities.

Labour

Free university organisers face similar tensions in their attempts to re-situate labour outside the capitalist paradigm. Marx famously pointed out that capitalism is the only economic system that commodifies human labour and assigns it a price. Since money establishes itself as the universal mediator of commodity exchanges, capitalist subjects come to read the social significance of their actions primarily in the medium of money (Graeber 2001: 66–67). As Max Haiven explained, 'money is capitalism's form of self-representation and it's a key form of discipline. It is the way in which all labour, even labour that we enter into out of joy or love or solidarity, becomes conscripted into the system.'[15] Analogously to the enclosure of space, human activity can thus become totally subsumed under equivocations to market value. In attempting to remove labour from a capitalist paradigm, however, organisers find themselves struggling to balance their ideals against pragmatic sustainability.

For some organisers, avoiding the cash economy was at the inalienable core of their project. Several justified this in pragmatic terms – that distancing labour from the monetary realm could enhance projects' long-term resilience, as organisers found ways to sustain projects independently of the approval of external funders (Thorne 2011: 110). Dan Adleman, a co-founder of the Vancouver Institute for Social Research (VISR), explained that operating on the basis of what he called 'sweat equity'[16] – wherein labour is treated as a non-monetarised commons to which people contribute in kind – served to protect critical thinking by maintaining political autonomy from universities and other funding bodies. But for many, remaining cash-free was an important symbolic act, contradicting otherwise taken-for-granted assumptions about the ubiquity of the profit motive with evidence that people can and do organise without 'even a modicum of greed or preoccupation with money changing hands'.[17]

This realm of non-capitalist praxis is infused with its own tensions. Cash-free projects like these bank on the enthusiasm of a vast pool of labour – organisers, facilitators, speakers, artists, publicists, etc. – who are able to offer time and energy without remuneration. By and large, however, these participants remain dependent upon the capitalist economy in other ways. Many found themselves living double lives – simultaneously within and against capitalism – and burning out under the added burden of unpaid work. Ultimately, organisers recognise that 'freeness comes with privilege, and the possibility of exploitation as well, and so it's not as pure as it sounds'.[18] While a few projects are able to sustain themselves on an entirely cash-free basis, many others have collapsed from cumulative exhaustion, or cycle through participants who burn out, retreat and re-engage.

Some activists drew links between this form of work and reproductive labour, which, despite its crucial contribution to maintaining capitalist society, cannot be commodified or designated an exchange-value, and therefore exists categorically outside the wage-labour system (Turner 2008: 46). Marxist feminist scholars have long contested the unwaged nature of reproductive labour as out-and-out exploitation under capitalism (Federici 2004). Harvey argues, however, that similarly exploitative forms of labour are just as present in anti-capitalist projects like workers' cooperatives and autonomous zones as in capitalist enterprises – the difference being that in the former, the absence of hierarchical systems of authority leads to the collective *self-exploitation* of workers (Harvey 2012: 122). Harvey contends that so long as they remain embedded in capitalist structures on other levels, these sorts of non-capitalist microcosms cannot present viable alternatives and, in fact, risk replicating many of the harmful aspects of capitalist systems that they seek to resist. Stephen Collis forwarded a more nuanced perspective than this, arguing that we can draw from these sorts of spaces 'just a little bit outside of capitalism', which, despite being 'roped up, and hooked up, and being pumped by capitalism all the time to get that free energy', nonetheless 'offer the potentiality of other kinds of organising, and other kinds of alternate capacity building so we can resist'.[19] Herein lies a central bind: how can free university organisers negotiate the tensions between prefiguring a form of labour emancipated from the market, while risking self-exploitation and burn-out?

Given the central role that money plays in positioning labour inside or outside of the commodity framework, it is unsurprising that many discussions returned to this topic. David Brazil, from the Bay Area Public School, explained the crux of these tensions thus:

> Articulating with money at all is really hard when you're critical of money, when you're a radical ... In the life of our school, it's ... the tension between something you could shorthand as the purity of vision and the desire to compromise for the sake of making certain kinds of things actually happen. So I'm perfectly clear about no money and the wage relation and so on. Nevertheless, here we are in this actual world; how do we deal with that tension?[20]

Isaiah Berlin coined the term 'tragic choice' to refer to similar predicaments, whereby making difficult compromises between ends that are fundamentally at odds with one another is ultimately an 'inescapable part of the human condition' (1998: 239, cited in Robbins 2013: 100). This would certainly seem to describe the position occupied by anti-capitalist, prefigurative projects like free universities. Torn between their discomfort with cash, born of radical idealism, and complex risks around self-exploitation that seem an inevitable consequence of its removal, many have accepted simply dealing with money, in the absence of the full anti-capitalist structural overhaul that may never eventuate. Max Haiven concluded that the best hope for these sorts of projects is to

> figure out ... positive and thoughtful and proactive ways of working with money, as if we were dealing with a hazardous substance. Because that's what it is – it's corrosive, it's poisonous, it's toxic – but there's lots of things like that that you still use.[21]

Many free university organisers resolved to provide payment or honoraria for certain forms of labour, while maintaining free access to their spaces and classes. In these cases, funding was secured through a variety of means – by fundraising, applying for government grants, or obtaining long-term sponsorship, sometimes from universities. As one New York-based organiser put it, this was a compromise bound by the recognition that 'it is above our pay grade to call for the extrication of the machinations of capital'[22] from projects like free universities, which are already stretched thin by running in the shadows of capitalism. For others, it was a strategic way to siphon funds from a flawed system, and redirect them towards 'something radical'.[23]

Conclusion

As prefigurative projects that remain embedded within a broader world, free universities cannot fully escape the clutches of capitalist structures. Not only were their attempts to establish cash-free commons of space and labour compromised by more complex material realities, but there was also a widespread recognition that even these moves, along with the focus on learning for its own sake, risk obliquely contributing to the capitalist logics of profiteering or exploitation. As Dan Adleman commented, 'isn't that the vitality, the self-revolutionising dynamism of capitalism, that it can re-assimilate and metabolise anything?'[24]

In failing to draw non-capitalist archipelagos out of a world heavily defined by market rationality, free universities are by no means unique. Graeber (2001: 88) notes that while radical movements might imagine alternatives to market-centric value frameworks as neatly bounded, fully functional totalities, bringing these into being is complicated and inevitably intersects with frameworks that might be quite contradictory. Free university organisers are often forced to toe a more nuanced line, acknowledging that these tensions cannot be resolved in 'any absolutely hygienic fashion [but] in a problematic fashion'.[25]

Ultimately, it would be a mistake to conclude that if free universities' praxis falls short of non-capitalist purity, they are politically irrelevant. Their hybridised operation of capitalist and non-capitalist systems does not simply indicate resistance *or* complicity, but the ever-present potential for both. In short, they demonstrate that non-capitalism is never 'pure', but neither is capitalism absolutely hegemonic (see Gibson-Graham 1996). Furthermore, the material realm does not constitute the only, or even necessarily the most important, grounds for resistance. Proliferating radical imaginaries beyond capitalism is key to unsettling the stronghold of market rationality, and the collective formation of non-capitalist social values is critical to this end (Haiven 2014: 68). By presenting possibilities for valuing learning, space and labour outside of market rationality – even if these ideals can only be partially translated into material reality – free universities can show that, in the words of Stephen Collis, 'capitalism is nearly total, but it's not total. I don't think anything *can* be … And that seems to be something we can draw upon … that we *never* stop resisting as human beings.'[26] It may be beyond free university organisers to overwrite capitalism entirely, even within ephemeral alter-political microcosms, but their projects stand as testament to the endless human capacity for resistance and creativity in the face of capitalism's otherwise potentially totalising paradigm, and this, in itself, is surely something of great significance.

Notes

1. Here I am indebted to Jeffrey Juris's (2007) theorisation of a 'militant ethnography', which allows me to make sense of my political embeddedness in the movement without compromising the validity of my research. Juris has formulated a useful methodological approach through which anthropologists can 'write themselves into' their ethnographies not only as observers, but as active participants in political alignment with the subject of their study.
2. From interview, Halifax, Canada, 5 June 2014. Max Haiven is a scholar-activist who holds a teaching position within a conventional university, and simultaneously organises radical popular education sessions within the Halifax community. Along with Alex Khasnabish, he also developed a project called 'The Radical Imagination', which gathered interviews from activists around Halifax on the subjects of sustainability, burn-out, relationships to money and labour, etc. My interview with Max Haiven spanned his own work, as well as the material he gathered over the course of conducting the Radical Imagination project.
3. From interview, Halifax, Canada, 5 June 2014. Alex Khasnabish is an anthropologist employed by a conventional university who also organises and engages in popular education within the community more broadly. He collaborated with Max Haiven on the Radical Imagination project.
4. From interview, Halifax, Canada, 5 June 2014.
5. From interview, Vancouver, Canada, 7 March 2014. Stephen Collis is a professor of literature at a Vancouver-based university and has also been involved in the Vancouver Institute for Social Research, a free university project. Furthermore, he was an activist as part of Occupy Vancouver for a number of months. My interview with Stephen spanned the breadth of these three topics.
6. From interview, Halifax, Canada, 5 June 2014.
7. Examples of these financial alliances are multitudinous, but include Simon Fraser University's partnership with Goldcorp, a gold mining corporation (Brophy and Tucker-Abramson 2012), and various research centres within the University of Queensland receiving funding from mining and biotechnology corporations including Rio Tinto, Santos and Dow Chemical (Lyons 2014).
8. From interview with Wes Modes, Santa Cruz, USA, 27 January 2014. The Free Skool Santa Cruz has ceased operation in the time since this interview was conducted, but ran for approximately 10 years in the Santa Cruz community with a changing body of organisers. Wes was one of the founders of the Free Skool Santa Cruz, but had stepped back from an organiser role just before

I conducted this interview, largely due to a lack of time and energy for the project.

9. From interview, New York City, USA, 28 May 2014. Joe Kay is one of the organisers of the Bruce High Quality Foundation University, which is a free university project that specifically offers sessions on fine art practice and theory. The project has been running for several years, and remains in operation as of this writing.
10. From interview, Oakland, USA, 30 January 2014. The Bay Area Public School operates as part of the loosely networked Public School projects, which exist in several different countries, and several different cities in the USA. However, each project is very different to the other, and their networked links are predominantly to do with sharing a website. David Brazil was one of the co-founders of the Bay Area Public School, which has been running for several years, and remains in operation as of this writing. David is still an active organiser of the project.
11. From interview, Vancouver, Canada, 7 March 2014.
12. From interview, Oakland, USA, 25 January 2014. Sara Larsen is one of the co-founders of the Bay Area Public School, and remains an active organiser as of this writing.
13. From interview, Oakland, USA, 30 January 2014. In this comment, David was referring to the eviction of the Occupy Oakland encampment, which he witnessed first-hand.
14. From interview, Vancouver, Canada, 7 March 2014.
15. From interview, Halifax, Canada, 5 June 2014.
16. From interview, Vancouver, Canada, 5 March 2014. The Vancouver Institute for Social Research is a free university project that specifically focuses on critical theory sessions. Dan Adleman is a co-founder of the project, with Am Johal, and remains an active organiser as of this writing.
17. Dan Adleman, from interview, Vancouver, Canada, 5 March 2014.
18. Ibid.
19. From interview, Vancouver, Canada, 7 March 2014.
20. From interview, Oakland, USA, 30 January 2014.
21. From interview, Halifax, Canada, 5 June 2014.
22. Joe Kay, from interview, New York, USA, 28 May 2014.
23. Organiser of the Purple Thistle Centre, from interview, Vancouver, 8 March 2014. The Purple Thistle Centre is an anarchist project for youth that has a permanent rented space in downtown Vancouver. Here the organiser was referring to the fact that the project runs on government grant money, for which the organising group reapplies annually.
24. From interview, Vancouver, Canada, 5 March 2014.
25. Ibid.
26. From interview, Vancouver, Canada, 7 March 2014.

References

Althusser, L. 1971. Ideology and ideological state apparatuses. In L. Althusser (ed.) *Lenin and Philosophy and other Essays*. London: New Left Books.

Bourdieu, P. and J.C. Passeron. 1977. *Reproduction in Education, Society, and Culture*. London: Sage.

Bousquet, M., S. Harney and F. Moten. 2009. On study: A *Polygraph* roundtable discussion with Marc Bousquet, Stefano Harney, and Fred Moten. *Polygraph* 21: 159–75.

Brophy, E. and M. Tucker-Abramson. 2012. Struggling universities: Simon Fraser University and the crisis of Canadian public education. *TOPIA: Canadian Journal of Cultural Studies* 28: 21–39.

Coté, M., R. Day and G. de Peuter. 2007. Utopian pedagogy: Creating radical alternatives in the neoliberal age. *Review of Education, Pedagogy, and Cultural Studies* 29: 317–36.

Federici, S. 2004. *Caliban and the Witch*. Brooklyn: Autonomedia.

—— 2009. Education and the enclosure of knowledge in the global university. *ACME: An International E-Journal for Critical Geographies* 8(3): 454–61.

George, E. 2012. The university system: Alienation or emancipation? *TOPIA: Canadian Journal of Cultural Studies* 28: 188–98.

Gibson-Graham, J.K. 1996. Queer(y)ing capitalist organization. *Organization: Social Organization of Knowledge* 3(4): 541–45.

—— 2006. *A Postcapitalist Politics*. Minneapolis: University of Minnesota Press.

Graeber, D. 2001. *Toward an Anthropological Theory of Value: The False Coin of Our Own Dreams*. New York: Palgrave.

—— 2013. It is value that brings universes into being. *HAU: Journal of Ethnographic Theory* 2(2): 219–43.

Hage, G. 2012. Critical anthropological thought and the radical political imaginary today. *Critique of Anthropology* 32(3): 285–308.

Haiven, M. 2014. *Crises of Imagination, Crises of Power: Capitalism, Creativity and the Commons*. London: Zed Books.

Harney, S. and F. Moten. 2013. *The Undercommons: Fugitive Planning and Black Study*. New York: Autonomedia.

Harvey, D. 1990. Between space and time: Reflections on the geographical imagination. *Annals of the Association of American Geographers* 80(3): 418–34.

—— 2012. *Rebel Cities: From the Right to the City to the Urban Revolution*. London: Verso.

Hayden, T. 2005. *The Port Huron Statement: The Visionary Call of the 1960s Revolution*. New York: Thunder's Mouth Press.

Hil, R. 2012. *Whackademia: An Insider's Account of the Troubled University*. New South Wales: NewSouth Books.

—— 2015. *Selling Students Short: Why You Won't Get the University Education You Deserve*. Crows Nest, NSW: Allen & Unwin.

Jeppsen, S. and H. Nazar. 2012. Beyond academic freedom: Canadian neoliberal universities in the global context. *TOPIA: Canadian Journal of Cultural Studies* 28: 87–113.

Juris, J.S. 2007. Practicing militant ethnography with the movement for global resistance in Barcelona. In S. Shukaitis and D. Graeber (eds) *Constituent Imagination: Militant Investigations/Collective Theorization*. Oakland, CA: AK Press.

Lyons, K. 2014. 'Partner or perish'? The convergence of public and private interests poses new questions for controversial university research. *Chain Reaction* 121: 32–34.

Magee, P. 2012. The scholarly affair is self-love. *TOPIA: Canadian Journal of Cultural Studies* 28: 171–79.

Martin, K. 2012. The 'potlatch of destruction': Gifting against the state. *Critique of Anthropology* 32(2): 125–42.

Meza-Wilson, A. 2012. Educational projects for decolonization: Anti-authoritarian allyship and resistance education in the Americas. Master's thesis, University of British Columbia.

Newson, J. 2012. Academic feminism's entanglements with university corporatization. *TOPIA: Canadian Journal of Cultural Studies* 28: 41–63.

Polanyi, K. 2001 [1944]. *The Great Transformation: The Political and Economic Origins of Our Times*. Boston, MA: Beacon Press.

Polster, C. 2012. Reconfiguring the academic dance: A critique of faculty's responses to administrative practices in Canadian universities. *TOPIA: Canadian Journal of Cultural Studies* 28: 115–41.

Readings, B. 1996. *The University in Ruins*. Cambridge, MA: Harvard University Press.

Robbins, J. 2013. Monism, pluralism, and the structure of value relations: A Dumontian contribution to the contemporary study of value. *HAU: Journal of Ethnographic Theory* 3(1): 99–115.

Robinson, A. and S. Tormey. 2012. Beyond the state: Anthropology and 'actually-existing-anarchism'. *Critique of Anthropology* 32(2): 143–57.

Shore, C. and S. Wright. 2004. Whose accountability? Governmentality and the auditing of universities. *Parallax* 10(2): 100–16.

Thorne, N. 2011. An experiment in liberation fuelled by love: Hamilton FreeSkool, prefigurative politics and anthropological practice. Master's thesis, York University, Canada.

Turner, T. 2008. Marxian value theory: An anthropological perspective. *Anthropological Theory* 8(1): 43–56.

Valeri, V. 2013. Marcel Mauss and the new anthropology. *HAU: Journal of Ethnographic Theory* 3(1): 262–86.

Vostal, F. and S. Robertson. 2012. Knowledge mediators and lubricating channels: On the temporal politics of remissioning the university. *TOPIA: Canadian Journal of Cultural Studies* 28: 143–64

Warner, M. 2015. Learning my lesson: Marina Warner on the disfiguring of higher education. *London Review of Books* 37(6): 8–14.
Whitener, B. and D. Nemser. 2012. Circulation and the new university. *TOPIA: Canadian Journal of Cultural Studies* 28: 165–68.
Williams, J. 2009. The pedagogy of debt. In the Edu-Factory Collective (eds) *Toward a Global Autonomous University*. New York: Autonomedia.

Notes on Contributors

Luis Fernando Angosto-Ferrández is a lecturer in anthropology and Latin American studies at the University of Sydney, and an associate member of the Center for Intercultural and Indigenous Research (CIIR – Grant: CONICYT/FONDAP/ 15110006). His recent publications include *Venezuela Reframed: Bolivarianism, Indigenous Peoples and Socialisms of the 21st Century* (Zed, 2015) and *Democracy, Revolution and Geopolitics in Latin America: Venezuela and the International Politics of Discontent* (Routledge, 2014).

Olivia Barnett-Naghshineh is a PhD candidate in social anthropology with a focus on agricultural economies, gender politics and the global political economy of food. She carried out ethnographic fieldwork in Papua New Guinea and has worked with organisations in the UK and Togo that focus on food sovereignty and adaptation to climate change. While researching the ways in which people integrate monetary systems of exchange with local cultural practices, she has a parallel interest in alternative economic paradigms including human economy.

John Cox has been working in the Pacific region for twenty years as a development practitioner and consultant anthropologist. His PhD on fast money schemes in Papua New Guinea won the 2012 Australian Anthropological Society Prize for Best PhD Thesis. He is finalising a monograph on this topic for publication with Indiana University Press. He is currently a visiting lecturer with the School of Culture, History and Languages at the Australian National University.

David Boarder Giles is a lecturer in anthropology at Deakin University. He writes about cultural economies of waste, homelessness and the politics of public space in global cities. He has done extensive ethnographic fieldwork in Seattle and several other cities in the United States and Australasia with Dumpster divers, grassroots activists, homeless residents and chapters of Food Not Bombs – a globalised movement of grassroots soup kitchens.

Marina Gold is a social anthropologist with an area expertise on Cuba. She is a researcher at Bergen University, affiliated to an ERC Project entitled 'Egalitarianism: Forms, Processes, Comparisons' headed by Professor Bruce Kapferer, where she explores human rights discourse and the refugee crisis in Europe. She also works with an NGO on a project to identify Latin American migrants with Chagas disease in Switzerland. She currently holds a guest researcher position at the University of Zurich.

Jane Horan received her PhD in social anthropology from the University of Auckland in 2012. Her thesis looked at the interactions of value, values and valuables in the Cook Islands ceremonial economy in New Zealand, the Cook Islands and Australia. She currently has a research associate position in the Property Department at the University of Auckland Business School to look at the escalation of value and price in the Auckland Housing Market from an economic anthropology perspective.

Fiona McCormack is a senior lecturer at the University of Waikato. Her research interests include fisheries, indigeneity, property, environmental and economic anthropology. She conducts research in Aotearoa and Hawaii and, more recently, Ireland and Iceland. Her forthcoming book, *Private Oceans: The Enclosure and Marketisation of the Seas* (Pluto Press), engages with these research themes and sites.

Geir Henning Presterudstuen is a lecturer in anthropology at Western Sydney University. He has conducted long-term fieldwork in Fiji since 2009 and his main research interests, on which he has published widely, include the intersections between social categories such as gender, ethnicity, class and sexuality in the context of the modern market economy. He is the co-editor of *Monster Anthropology in Australasia and Beyond* (Palgrave Macmillan 2014).

Fern Thompsett is now working toward her PhD at McGill University, Canada. In 2012, she co-founded the Brisbane Free University and Radio Reversal, a research-based community radio programme on 4ZZZ fm Brisbane, both of which she ranks among her most important educational experiences to date.

Moira White is Curator, Humanities, at the Otago Museum, Dunedin, New Zealand. She has published on a wide variety of aspects of the museum's history, donors and collection – from Melanesian material culture to New Zealand studio jewellery.

Index